IN ENEMY HANDS

This absorbing and authoritative book takes us back to a terrible moment in the history of the modern world, a time when South Africa still counted internationally as one of the virtuous nations in that most titanic struggle against fascist tyranny, the Second World War. Then, tens of thousands of the country's inhabitants volunteered to fight overseas in the Allied cause. For some, the brutal war which engulfed them brought neither victory nor glory, but the early shock of surrender and the lingering ordeal of becoming the captives of their Italian and German enemies.

In *In Enemy Hands*, her pioneering account of the fate of South African prisoners of war, Karen Horn reclaims a raw, fascinating and moving history which has been all but forgotten. These gripping pages capture their everyday experience, their consciousness, and the ways in which they coped with camp life – a world stalked by fear, hope, despair, opportunism, resilience, human fallibility, and rocky moral values.

Drawing on vivid oral reminiscences as well as documentary sources, *In Enemy Hands* is impressively lucid, deeply humane, and packed with shrewd insights. Dr Horn's major study is a superb achievement in bringing a trapped and chafing part of South Africa's Second World War generation out of the shadows.

Professor Bill Nasson, Stellenbosch, 2015

*Dedicated to the memory of my parents,
Fred and Estelle Horn,
and to the love of my life, André Olivier.*

IN ENEMY HANDS

South Africa's POWs in World War II

KAREN HORN

Jonathan Ball Publishers
JOHANNESBURG & CAPE TOWN

All rights reserved.
No part of this publication may be reproduced or transmitted,
in any form or by any means, without prior permission
from the publisher or copyright holder.

© Karen Horn, 2015

Originally published in South Africa in 2015 by
JONATHAN BALL PUBLISHERS (PTY) LTD
A division of Media24 Limited
P O Box 33977
Jeppestown
2043

ISBN 978-1-86842-651-5
EBOOK 978-1-86842-652-2

Permission has been granted by the following:
Echoing Green Press for the quotations from the copyrighted memoirs, *For the Adventure of It*
by Cyril Crompton, and *On the Run in Wartime Italy* by Peter Johnson, which are published
in *Luck's Favours: Two South African Second World War Memoirs*

David Brokensha for the quotations from his autobiography *Brokie's Way: An Anthropologist's
Story: Love and Work in Three Continents*

Flesch Publications for quotations from Ike Rosmarin's memoir *Inside Story*

Eleanor Muller on behalf of David & Hilary Shearing for quotations from *From Jo'burg to
Dresden: A World War II Diary by EB Dickinson*

Twitter: http://www.twitter.com/JonathanBallPub
Facebook: http://www.facebook.com/pages/Jonathan-Ball-Publishers/298034457992
Blog: http://jonathanball.bookslive.co.za/
Cover design by Michiel Botha
Front cover and top back cover images: Reproduced with kind permission
from David Brokensha
Bottom back cover image: Reproduced with kind permission from Anthony Mortlock
Design and typesetting by Triple M Design, Johannesburg
Printed and bound by Paarl Media, Paarl
Set in 10.75/15pt Stempel Garamond MT Pro

CONTENTS

ABBREVIATIONS vi
PREFACE vii
ACKNOWLEDGEMENTS viii

1 For Dr Smuts, not for Dr Hertzog 1
2 Every Man for Himself 20
3 Trek Oxen in August 69
4 Wire Happy 113
5 Uneasy Inertia 151
6 The Art of Being a POW 184
7 Anxious Annies 231

NOTES 260
GLOSSARY 286
SELECTED SOURCES 288
INDEX 297

ABBREVIATIONS

BFC	British Free Corps
ICRC (or IRCC)	International Committee of the Red Cross
MI9	British Military Intelligence
MOTHS	Memorable Order of Tin Hats
NCO	Non-commissioned officer
OKW	Oberkommando der Wehrmacht (High Command of the German Armed Forces)
POW	Prisoner of war
POWRA	British Prisoner-of-War Relatives Association
POWRFA	South African Prisoner-of-War Relatives and Friends Association
PWIB	Prisoner-of-war Information Bureaux
RAF	Royal Air Force
RDLI	Royal Durban Light Infantry
SAP	South African Police
Sgt	Sergeant
SS	*Schutzstaffeln*
UDF	Union Defence Force

PREFACE

When we read about war, we are more often than not spellbound by the heroic acts of the men in the firing line, their bravery, endurance and all too often, their sacrifices. We speculate and wonder about the heart-wrenching, or heartless, decisions and military tactics of the generals and politicians who put these young men at risk.

Today, books on World War II are plentiful, yet for some reason, there seem to be remarkably few publications on South Africa's role in this war, which had such an influence on how we live today. There is even less written about those who participated on the margins of the war, especially those who were physically removed from the battlefields through capture by enemy forces. South Africa's prisoners of war during World War II, their experiences and recollections, were almost forgotten.

In 2010 I tracked down a number of former POWs, all of whom expressed surprise at being asked to share their experiences of almost 70 years earlier. Together with written memoirs and archival documents, their interviews revealed rich narratives of hardship, endurance, humour, longing and self-discovery. Instead of fighting, these men adapted to another war, one which was fought on the inside of many prison camps. It was a war against hunger and deprivation, at times against ever-encroaching despondency and low morale amongst their companions in captivity.

Considering their experiences, I found it astonishing that almost all of them claimed not to be heroes of any kind. Almost all of the former POWs stated this 'fact' at the beginning of each interview. When one considers that they returned home in 1945 to a country which soon afterwards tried its utmost to promote national amnesia with regard to its participation in the war and that the official war history project was unceremoniously stopped, it is perhaps understandable that these men found it unusual that someone would be interested in their stories many years later.

However, as one of the former POWs put it, they 'saw history from the inside', and we would do well to take note of what they saw. Seeing the war from the enemy's point of view and seeing what it did to its citizens changed how all of them viewed the world. If anyone can teach us anything about the futility of war, it is these men who looked the enemy in the eye every day. This book is about these heroes, the POWs who came back home and who carried on with life.

Acknowledgements

This book would not have been possible had it not been for the former POWs David Brokensha, Stanley Smollan, Fred Geldenhuis, Wessel Oosthuizen, Michael de Lisle, Bill Hindshaw, Clive Luyt, Bernard Schwikkard, Mathys Beukes, Fred van Alphen Stahl, Dick Dickinson and George Tewkesbury who gave their time and patiently answered my many questions. All of the direct quotes by these men in this book were taken from personal interviews that I conducted between 2010 and 2012 in Cape Town, Fish Hoek, Mossel Bay, Hartenbos, Bloemfontein, Johannesburg and Pretoria.

Thank you also to the families and friends of former POWs in making available veterans' memoirs and photographs, especially Ilse Geldenhuis, Cheryl Reeves, Elizabeth Mugglestone, David Saks, Enid Bates, Marcia Beckley, Donald Gill, Taffy and David Shearing and Anthony Mortlock.

Karen Horn
STELLENBOSCH, 2015

CHAPTER ONE

FOR DR SMUTS, NOT FOR DR HERTZOG

We were playing bridge with some New Zealanders, and this New Zealander told us beforehand how they skin rabbits [...] There was hardly any food left in camp at all, but we were still playing bridge and in came a cat, walking from I don't know where, [...] and I think Percy said to the New Zealander, 'how do you skin a rabbit mate?' And he picked up the cat [...] we cleared the table of cards [...] and it was in the pot cooking in about ten minutes. And they asked for contributions, you know, somebody had a potato, somebody had a turnip, somebody had a piece of *mangel wurzel*, somebody had a piece of bread, and this was all cooked up and dished out. It was a remarkably good stew.

The men who feasted on the cat stew together with the story-teller, Fred van Alphen Stahl, were all Allied prisoners of war in Stalag VIIIB near Lamsdorf, one of the largest prison camps in German-occupied territory during World War II.[1] During the early months of 1945, desperate deeds were ever more common as it became apparent that the Germans were about to be overpowered by the Allied forces. Millions of refugees, prisoners of war and fighting forces found themselves fighting more for survival than for victory.

Among the Allied captives were thousands of South Africans who had volunteered their services to the Union Defence Force (UDF) a few years earlier. Each man's decision to join up was based on a unique set of circumstances, resulting in an army made up of an assortment of cultures, languages and political beliefs. However wide their differences, the UDF volunteers all had one thing in common. None of them had ever contemplated spending most of the war in a prison camp.

Bernard Schwikkard was one of these men, and although Schwikkard is a German surname, he was ready to join the Transvaal Scottish Regiment to fight alongside the Allies when the war started. After the war, Bernard was still the only member of his family who spoke German – and not because of the ancestral connection, but because of the long time he had spent in Germany as a POW. Bernard volunteered along with his brothers, and his sisters volunteered for the nursing corps.

For Fred Geldenhuis, the decision was made long before the war actually started. His reason for volunteering his services was not so much to join the UDF as to get away from home. His stepmother had made it very clear that he was not wanted, and so in 1937, when he was 16, he joined the Special Service Battalion. The day before Fred left home, his father gave him a Valet razor, and he shaved for the first time. Fred started his career in the battalion as a bugle player, but from day one he considered himself an army man who 'took to soldiering like a duck to water'. Fifteen months later Fred was promoted to corporal, but thanks to his skill on the parade ground and in making a favourable impression during inspections, he was promoted to sergeant a month later. This promotion led to him being the lead bugler at the ceremony of the laying of the foundation stone at the Voortrekker Monument in 1938.

Fred took great pride in his accomplishments, especially when he thought about how miserable he had often felt while he was dependent on his stepmother and her family. By the time he celebrated his eighteenth birthday, he reckoned it was time for a career change, and he joined the South African Police as a trumpeter. The work of the SAP appealed to his adventurous spirit because their 'mobile units with mule carts used to patrol for about 3 weeks at a time in the rugged country of the Transkei'. The SAP also offered higher pay than the Permanent Force. His meteoric rise up the ranks meant that by the time he was

Fred Geldenhuis.
COURTESY ILSE GELDENHUIS

The letter in which Fred Geldenhuis's father gave permission for his son to join the ranks of the South African Police Force.
COURTESY ILSE GELDENHUIS

19, he was lance sergeant drill instructor in the SAP Training Depot. When the Union declared war, Fred volunteered and took the oath with many others in the SAP, although he remembered how one man whom he hero-worshipped resigned and apparently joined the right-wing Ossewabrandwag.²

In the Free State, Wessel Oosthuizen faced his own problems. He and his three brothers had been trying to make a living on their farm, Koppieskroon, but Wessel realised that he would have to find another form of income because, as he put it, they were going to 'stagnate' on the farm. He unsuccessfully tried to find work on the railways and in the post office and in the end he was forced to join the SAP, but 'he didn't like it one bit'. When the war started, Wessel was not eager to volunteer. He remembered very well how his older brother used to tell stories of how the family was transported in cattle trucks to British concentration camps during the South African War. His mother survived the camps, but his grandmother died there. Wessel clearly did not view Germans as 'the real enemy', but apparently he was told by a recruitment officer that he had already shown, by joining the SAP, that he was loyal to the state and therefore had to wear the red tabs – contemptuously referred to as *'rooi luisies'*, or red lice, by Afrikaner nationalists – donned by all volunteers who took the oath to fight anywhere in Africa.³

Although Fred and Wessel were both Afrikaans-speaking, they obviously felt differently about the Union's decision to support Britain. From their recollections, however, it would seem that the UDF was desperate for volunteers and may perhaps have tried a bit too hard to convince some to join its ranks. During an interview in 2010, Fred stressed that although, in his experience, some men signed the oath voluntarily, others had taken the oath against their will.⁴ The issue of strong-arming volunteers in the SAP was investigated by the National Party government in 1950. According to the Police Commissioner of the time, there were no written instructions on the taking of the oath with regard to the SAP. He explained that those SAP members between the ages of 21 and 24 were called to the Police College in June 1940 where some took the oath while others did not. Wessel Oosthuizen was only 19 in 1940. The Commissioner declared that those who did not take the oath were not pressured into doing so and were used as guards in Pretoria and later sent back to their different areas where they performed normal police duties.5

In Durban, the life of the Brokensha family was considerably more comfortable than that of many others struggling with the economic depression that had been prevalent since the late 1920s. David, the youngest of the three Brokensha brothers, described his childhood as happy and 'full of satisfyingly rich memories'. Four of his uncles served in World War I, but his own father was rejected for medical reasons. In 1937, his eldest brother, Guy, joined the Fleet Air Arm in Britain. Two years later, when the Union declared war on Germany, David was so inspired by Guy's adventures that he too wanted to become a pilot. Both he and Paul, the second brother, volunteered – but they ended up as dispatch riders, not pilots. Many years later, David recalled that their motivation for going to war was based more on romantic ideas of war than on reality. For them, to miss out on the action was simply unimaginable: as he said, 'There was a war on and I didn't want to miss it, you know it was sort of this boy's adventure story.' This enthusiasm was not necessarily matched by other English-speaking South Africans at the end of the 1930s: as David remembers, shortly after he and Paul volunteered, their father mentioned having told a friend at the elite Durban Club that he was worried because all three of his sons had joined up, and that the other man had confessed to being worried because not one of his three sons had.

Durban at that time was 'very provincial' and David admitted in his memoirs that the first time he came into contact with black South Africans and Afrikaners was when he joined the Army. It was especially his friendship with Piet Pieterse that led him to new insights:

> [Piet] was completely different. He was a year older, I was 17, he was about 18; he'd spent some years at a reformatory; we kidded them that they hadn't worn shoes till they joined the army, which may have been true, he was from you know, an *arme blanke* background and yet he and I, he was my buddy, I mean ...

Thereafter, he seemed to reserve his scorn for those who had been too slack to do their duty. Many years after his decision to join the UDF, David still held the same opinion of those who stayed at home, saying 'even now I rather look down on those who didn't [volunteer]'.

The Air Force played a part in Dick Dickinson's decision to volunteer. At the time, Dickinson was a student at the University of the Witwatersrand and when a classmate and good friend of his was shot down in East Africa, it convinced him to enlist. Dick grew up in the Eastern Cape town of Queenstown and attended Queen's College, whose buildings remind one of a miniature Oxford or Cambridge. His father was a Gilbert and Sullivan singer and as a result Dick became a lover of opera, so much so that he spent his £5 blazer money on opera tickets. His father, apparently sympathetic to his dilemma, immediately sent another £5.

In 1940, while still busy with his Honours year in Botany and Geology at Wits, 'the war had begun to pull' at Dick, and when his application to attend a drilling course in Johannesburg was unsuccessful, he 'turned up anyway'. A week later his subterfuge was discovered, but he and a friend had decided by that time that they would join the 2nd Transvaal Scottish Regiment.[6] Dick firmly believed that he and his fellow volunteers were not anti-Germany so much as anti-Hitler and pro-British.

With a similar attitude, Michael de Lisle volunteered because he 'had a pretty fair idea of right and wrong and we'd been recognising over the years that Hitler was a threat to peace' – so he joined up out of principle, feeling that it was his duty to 'try and protect freedom'. Michael grew up in Cape Town and was one of three children. His father passed away when he was twelve and he described his childhood as 'poor', but his mother gave her children a 'good education and love and good background and provided us with music and love of the mountain'. Although Michael had a deep sense of duty and responsibility towards his mother, he nevertheless volunteered after studying for only six months at the University of Cape Town. According to Michael, the university offered students credit for the full academic year if they volunteered.

The 2nd Anti-Aircraft Regiment's 'rousing send-off' from Cape Town on 17 June 1940. They marched from the Castle along Darling and Adderley streets to the train station where they set off on their journey to the Potchefstroom training base. COURTESY ENID BATES

It was during the first few weeks of training with the 2nd Anti-Aircraft Regiment that Michael and Fred van Alphen Stahl met, and they have remained friends ever since. Fred grew up in Malmesbury, a town which has been traditionally more Afrikaans than English. By the time the war started, he had noticed that the 'war-friendly community in Malmesbury ... they were rather small'. He remembered how the '*herstigters*' and the '*verkramptes*' taunted those who had taken the service oath and wore red tabs on their uniforms. Despite this, he was influenced by Smuts's views of a united white South Africa, viewing himself simply as a South African rather than an Afrikaner.

Fred Stahl's reason for taking the oath and joining the 2nd Anti-Aircraft Regiment in Cape Town was slightly less ideological than his views on South Africanism, and he also did not have a very specific sense of duty towards Britain, because he did not feel that he was 'fighting for the king and country and glory; it was just something that was going on, so let's go'.

Howard Bates, a surveyor in Cape Town, had been a member of the Cape Field Artillery since 1936. He remembered that it was not until the war gained momentum in Europe that his entire office decided to volunteer their services. Like Fred and Michael, Howard became a member of the 2nd Anti-Aircraft Regiment, and on 17 June 1940, his section marched, amid 'a rousing send-off', from the Castle along Darling and Adderley streets towards the station where they set off on their journey to the training camp in Potchefstroom.[7]

Also from the Cape Province, Mathys Beukes felt that language was irrelevant, and described his parents as 'English-Afrikaans'. By 1938, when Europe was already well on its way to war, Mathys had already started on his career path in the magistrate's office in Winburg. When Smuts's circular asking for volunteers reached him, he immediately declared his willingness. Initially, he was held back as his services were seen as essential, and it was only in 1940 that he was eventually able to join his friends in the Regiment President Steyn in Bloemfontein. Things did not go smoothly for Mathys, however, and he developed a severe illness, thought to be meningitis, soon after joining up. While recuperating, he heard that his regiment was on embarkation leave and set off to join it in Durban. As Mathys boarded the ship, he was spotted by the Admiral who asked what he was doing, as he was classified medically unfit for service. When the Admiral ordered him to see him in his cabin the next morning, Mathys knew that he would be told to go home. However, he also knew that the ship would be setting sail at 10h00, so he made sure that he was a little late for his appointment, leaving the Admiral with no option but to take him along.

Another UCT student and articled clerk when the war started was Clive Luyt, who recalled not being much moved by what he called the 'rather dead war' or the first-phase 'phoney war' when Britain and France took up a defensive attitude while building up their military capacity against Hitler's forces.[8] It was Germany's invasion of Belgium which motivated Clive and his friends, all of whom were busy with examinations at the time, to volunteer: 'We went and had a couple of beers after writing our exam and we said, "Look, what are we doing about the war?" and we said, "Well, we'd better go and join up", so after a couple of beers we joined up.'

In more than one case, peer pressure played a role in the young men's decisions to volunteer. Stanley Smollan admitted that he volunteered because all his friends were doing the same, although he added that 'we just thought we had to do it, so it was a voluntary thing and we joined in May 1940, the Transvaal Scottish, where I was a private soldier, not a conscript, a volunteer'. Being young and easily influenced also played a part, and this aspect was especially exploited by the recruitment campaigns, as Stan admitted that they were 'easily roused by flag waving [but] then we came down to the real reality, that we were soldiers under strict discipline and committed, because we'd volunteered'. He also felt that he had been influenced during his school days at Parktown Boys' High School in Johannesburg where the local regiments were already training recruits through the school cadets.

Bill Hindshaw's childhood days were in stark contrast to Stan's. Bill's father, a construction worker in Durban, was retrenched when the tentacles of the depression reached the firm he was working for. Both of Bill's sisters were working as secretaries at the time, but Bill was forced to leave school to supplement the family income. Sunbeam offered him a job handling the orders for their shoe polish, and he did this for a year and a half at £5 per month. When his father was offered a position with his old employer, the family moved to Johannesburg, and Bill managed to secure an apprenticeship as a bricklayer.

When the war started, Bill had already been inducted into army life because he had been a reservist in the Active Citizen Force since the age of 16. He found the decision to volunteer easy as he 'wasn't married and girlfriends were no hindrance, you see. So I enjoyed the army, I really enjoyed myself in the army, the peace time army and then war came and I was on.' Bill's enjoyment of all things military may have been a consequence of the fact that he was 'brought up on the shooting range'. He was a proud member of the Rand Light Infantry, a regiment that he considered to be 'the premium regiment of shooting in South Africa'.

Divisions and disagreements

No doubt many of these young men boarded their troop ships with mixed feelings, whether fear of the unknown, or thoughts of heroic deeds to be performed while 'doing their bit'. Some climbed on board reluctantly, holding onto their pay books, hoping to support their families with the relatively meagre income provided by the UDF to the enlisted men. Whatever their reason for volunteering, they were all in for a rude shock – it was not death or glory that awaited them, but captivity. By the end of the war a total of 334 324 men and women had served with the UDF. Of these 16 430 were captured or reported as missing. This number included all of the men mentioned above.[9]

The astonishment among the men as they were rounded up by victorious and gloating German soldiers in the Libyan Desert was equal among all the Allied soldiers. With or without rank, South Africans, New Zealanders, Australians, Indians and British soldiers all stood incredulous as they watched the German Afrika Korps gain the upper hand with ease. For all of these unfortunate men, captivity would bring hardship that could only be dealt with if they managed to adjust physically and – perhaps more importantly – mentally. For the South Africans, however, the country's complex past made the mind-shift slightly more complicated. Divisive politics had been a prominent and long-standing facet of life that split families, language groups and different races from each other. News of the internal struggles of the country even reached the ears of the enemy, as one German soldier jibed that the South African captives were obviously 'for Dr Smuts, not for Dr Hertzog'.[10]

The rivalry between the supporters of Jan Smuts and those backing JBM Hertzog had been brewing for some time. Through the United Party, these two men governed the country and represented substantial sections of the white South African population. While the Afrikaans- and English-speaking inhabitants took opposing political views, they were nevertheless the only enfranchised sections of the population; the black inhabitants were for the most part ignored when it came to deciding about the war. Smuts's South African Party and Hertzog's National Party had joined forces in 1934, but hardly five years later, the onset of

World War II caused the long-fermenting differences between these groups to spill over. The political debacle resulted in Hertzog's dramatic resignation as Prime Minister and in Smuts leading the country into the third and last war of his lifetime.[11]

The bitterness between the two white language groups had a long history. It was especially during the South African War (1899–1902) that resentment among many Afrikaners towards the British reached a peak. In Germany, public support leaned towards the Boer cause, and although the German government did not want to sour relations with Britain, the British public formed the view that the Germans were not well-disposed towards their colonial interests.[12] Coincidentally, it was during this conflict at the start of the century that one of the key players of World War II experienced a hint of what many young Union Defence Force soldiers would go through between 1939 and 1945.

On 15 November 1899, Winston Churchill became a prisoner of the Boer forces when the armoured train he was travelling in was captured on its way to Ladysmith.[13] When writing *My Early Life,* he described the experience of being a prisoner of war as 'the least unfortunate kind of prisoner to be, but it is nevertheless a melancholy state [...] Hours crawl like paralytic centipedes. Nothing amuses you.'[14] At the time of Churchill's captivity, Smuts had already made his debut into South African politics and filled the position of state attorney for the Transvaal government. As a war general Smuts was committed to the cause of uniting the Boer republics and he was determined that Britain would not control the southern tip of Africa.[15] The friendship that later developed between these two men was to play a defining role in the Union of South Africa's participation in both the World Wars.

At the turn of the century, however, the South African War divided the region's Afrikaners into three groups. The *Bittereinders* were those strong-minded, some would say obstinate, individuals who believed that by fighting to the bitter end, they could teach the British Empire a lesson. Sadly their efforts came to an end as their food and ammunition dwindled and their wives and daughters starved in the British concentration camps. In some cases the men were so convinced of their cause that they continued to fight until they were left with nothing but animal skin for clothing and emaciated mules to carry them from one futile skirmish to the next. Basic foodstuffs became scarce and while in many cases the men came up with substitutes, the lack of essentials such as salt caused their teeth to break like dry twigs.[16] When at last they were forced to surrender in 1902, they found the mandatory oath of allegiance to the British Crown a final insult and flatly refused. Remaining loyal to the defeated Boer Republics, they had no choice but to leave the land they had been fighting for, settling as far away as Angola, Argentina and North America.[17] The *Bittereinders* were clearly not the negotiating type.

The Joiners, all 5 500 of them, were far more open to traverse the treacherous trails of treason.[18] At different points during the war, each of them came to the realisation that the British could not be defeated. However, these men did not only lay down their weapons, they joined the ranks of the enemy. By putting their knowledge of the terrain to good use, they helped British forces by informing them of Boer commando movements. They were also adept at helping to destroy Boer farms and moving the occupants to the hated concentration camps. Although the Joiners were at the opposite extreme when compared to the *Bittereinders*, their betrayal of the Boer cause was often motivated by the economic hardships they had been suffering in the years before the war.[19]

At the time of the war, both the *Bittereinders* and the Joiners probably had reason to refer to the third group, the *Hensoppers,* as cowards. This was the group who, like the Joiners, realised that the war against Britain was futile. Rather than joining the Boer guerrilla fighters or spying for the British, they took the passive option. By taking an oath of neutrality, the *Hensoppers* hoped to distance themselves from the conflict, but many found themselves in concentration camps along with the families of *Bittereinders*. Defining this group is problematic. The concentration camps held older men who were deemed unfit to fight, yet the *Bittereinders*, for instance, applied a stern interpretation of the word 'unfit' that was different from that of the *Joiners* or the *Hensoppers*. For Boers in prisoner-of-war camps taking the oath of neutrality was also a way of returning to their families, although their families were most often to be found in concentration camps.[20]

Regardless of the efforts of the *Bittereinders*, the British were relentlessly seeking victory. Their determination to gain control over the Boer Republics – and the mineral riches found within them – began to pay off. By 1900 both the Orange Free State and the South African Republic had been annexed. However, it was not only the stubborn among the Boers who would not accept peace. Lord Alfred Milner, High Commissioner for South Africa and Governor of the Cape Colony, would have preferred to place the country in the hands of the English-speaking (but not necessarily British) loyalists whose ranks were made up by the Cape loyalists and the so-called *Uitlanders* in the Transvaal colony. It is here that the first hints of mutual agreement are to be seen between Smuts and Churchill. Both men wanted the war to end, and both recognised that the Boers should play the leading role in the post-war relationship with Britain. Following emotional and energy-sapping debates among the Boer leaders, it was finally agreed, to Milner's disappointment, that the signing of a peace treaty was the only option. On 31 May 1902 the South African War finally ended.[21]

Perhaps it was when the Boer leaders realised that the divisions among their people were the thing that would ultimately lead to their defeat that they finally agreed on signing the peace treaty with the British. It was most likely also this realisation, spurring the Afrikaners on to unite and to mend their divisions after the war, that created in them a strong and determined desire to regain their independence. It was the divisions among them that led to their subjection under the British, and it would only be through unity that they would gain true liberation. But the emphasis on unity by and among Afrikaners was elusive. The great divisive factor in the years following the South African War was the British Empire. Some Afrikaners believed that being part of the Empire could only benefit South Africa. Others, however, were adamant that complete independence was the only option and that true freedom would never be a reality as long as Britain had any say in the country. Before the war started, the predominant split in the country was between the English- and Afrikaans-speaking communities. Now, after four years of fighting, the split remained, but a further division was evident, that between those loyal to the Crown and those loyal to a wholly independent country.

As soon as the war ended, the great Anglicisation of the Afrikaners began in an effort to create a proper British colony from the remnants of the two Boer Republics. A priority was to jump-start the production of gold and to get the economy going again. While Lord Milner encouraged immigrants to settle, the Afrikaners continued to rebuild their devastated farms. Smuts and his fellow Boer leader, General Louis Botha, were eager to unite the English and Afrikaans speakers and through Het Volk, the first Afrikaner political party, they carefully managed expectations on language and education. By 1907 Het Volk came to power and with the help of Chinese labour and new technology, the mines flourished. While many Afrikaners probably still preferred farm life, they were now moving in greater numbers to the cities as the economy adapted to changing circumstances.[22]

Self-government granted to the Transvaal and Free State in 1906 and 1907 provided a dim flicker of hope of independence to the Afrikaners in whose memories the hardships of war were still fresh. But it seems imperialism was infectious: by the time World War I started in 1914, Jan Smuts and Louis Botha both believed that South Africa's future would be brighter as a British Dominion within the folds of the largest Empire of the world. For many Afrikaners who still clung to the ideals of independence, the Union's acceptance of Britain's request to invade German South-West Africa was the last straw.[23] *Bittereinder* generals devised ambitious plans of overthrowing the government and raising Republican flags. The first shot of the rebellion was unplanned and intended for a different target, however. It came from a policeman at a road block who thought he was firing at a criminal gang, but the bullet from his gun ricocheted off the road and killed Koos de la Rey, a general of the Boer War and, at that moment, a hesitant rebel.[24]

World War I, like the South African War which ended 12 years earlier, divided the Union, but the lines of division were redrawn in this conflict. While the rebels saw no alternative but to take up arms against the government, many English- and Afrikaans-speaking South Africans believed that to fight for Britain was to ensure the survival of the Empire, and therefore also of the Union. Feelings of loyalty towards the British Empire also extended to black communities who declared their unwavering support to the Prime Minister.[25] Those men who found themselves in the trenches and the battlefields of the war developed a sense of camaraderie. Survival was after all more important than class or race. By contrast, those on the home front, far away from world events, became preoccupied with an idealised past, yearning to claim the opportunities of independence lost in 1902.[26]

From 1924 to 1939 JBM Hertzog was Prime Minister, and for a short while the Union tried to rid itself of the burden of the British Empire. However, Smuts, waiting for an opportunity to reclaim his leadership, lost as a result of his fierce handling of the 1922 miners' strike, still believed that the country would prosper under the British Imperial flag.[27] In 1934, Smuts compared the Union's situation with that of Scotland's 'grand compromise' with England. In 1603 the kingdoms of Scotland and England had united as James VI became James I of England. A century later, the Scottish and English parliaments joined forces in the Act of Union of 1707. As a result of this 'compromise' Scotland's economy gained strength, but many patriotic Scots remained doubtful about joining hands with England, which had been sending troops across the Scottish borders for at least 1 000 years.[28] Using Scotland as an example, and because he believed that South Africa's loyalties lay with Britain, Smuts emphasised cooperation between the two countries during a speech in St Andrews saying that 'in the long run only the spirit of international comradeship can solve the problems of freedom and of peace'.[29] Being an idealist and a philosopher, Smuts was obviously focusing only on the positive aspects of Scotland's union with England.

The independently minded Afrikaners had other ideas. As Europe moved towards war, the tentacles of Nazism reached the Union and found fertile ground in Afrikaner nationalists who were still hoping to achieve their dream of independence outside of the British Empire. Their determination manifested itself in the formation of the Afrikaner Broederbond and later with the building of the Voortrekker Monument. On the eve of the war, Nazi ideology became most apparent in the establishment of the Ossewabrandwag and its auxiliary *Stormjaers*. Although this group was modelled on Hitler's storm troopers, its main aim was to oppose the Union's war effort, whereas its German counterpart actively promoted conflict. These sentiments did not abate during the war, and led to the National Party coming to power in 1948.[30]

The 1938 centennial celebrations of the Great Trek served to re-awaken patriotism in many of those Afrikaners whose loyalties had been buried by the realities of poor white poverty and depression during the 1930s. Adolf Hitler's rise to leadership and awareness of his beliefs and ideas served as inspiration to staunch Nationalists throughout the pre-war years. During the same year that Hitler became Germany's Führer, Oswald Pirow, Minister of Defence, had concluded a lucrative trade agreement with the Nazi government. As a result of this deal, Germany became the principal buyer of South African wool and a major exporter of manufactured goods to the Union.[31] Pirow was also determined to affirm the Union's independence by establishing South African Airways with a fleet of German-made Junkers. This was of great concern to the British, not only because of the close relations between the Union's Defence Minister and the Nazi government, but also because until that time British Imperial Airways had held the upper hand with air transport across Africa.[32] With the outbreak of war in 1939 the Nationalists, and especially the Ossewabrandwag, gained new impetus with which to oppose Smuts's plans.

Hitler had made his ideas on *Lebensraum* and the *Untermensch* very clear, and when Germany invaded Poland the Allied powers were obliged to act, as they had earlier promised to guarantee Poland's sovereignty.[33] On 3 September 1939 Britain declared war on Germany, and now the Union was forced to make up its mind once and for all on the issue of neutrality or participation. Hertzog's loyalties still lay with an independent Union and he stuck to his position of neutrality in the war. The Nationalists believed that Hitler ultimately had honourable intentions, despite the fact that he had been invading one European country after another.

Smuts, on the other hand, was immovable about South Africa's duty as a Dominion and insisted that the country support Britain. Unlike

1914, the differences in opinion did not lead to a rebellion, but a vote in Parliament put a stop to any ideals of neutrality for the time being. Amid wild rumours of invasions and accusations of treachery, the matter went before the House on the night of 4 September. The outcome was in favour of war, if only by 13 votes, but enough to bring about Hertzog's resignation.[34]

'A large number of our own people are dupes'[35]

If it is true that Hitler laughed when he heard about South Africa's declaration of war on Germany, it would seem he had enough reason to do so. The Union Defence Force was appallingly ill-equipped. The Permanent Force had 5 385 men, 353 of whom were officers.[36] The Active Citizen Force was a bit better off, with about 122 000 in its ranks, although many of these men had no military training. There were about 10 million black South African men in the military age group, but none of them was considered by the authorities to play a part, at least not in the early stages of the war.[37] To put these figures in perspective, the number of Polish dead during the first weeks of Hitler's successful invasion in September 1939 amounted to about 66 300.[38] By the time the Union had made up its mind to assist Britain, Poland's losses were already more than 12 times South Africa's total available force.

Equally abysmal were the supply and availability of military equipment, ammunition, aircraft and naval vessels. For instance, the Army only had two tanks, two armoured cars and two armoured trains, all of which were obsolete. Smuts's eagerness to assist the Allied cause is mildly ironic when one considers the unpreparedness of the Union to actually do so, yet he wasted no time in getting the UDF prepared and armed. The agreement between Britain and the Smuts government to use the Union as a training base for the Air Force resulted in the Joint Air Training Scheme of 1940, which propelled the South African Air Force ahead and also brought about development of infrastructure in the Union.[39]

Added to this dismal state of affairs in 1939 was the pro-Nazi hangover that the new Smuts government had to deal with following

Hertzog's resignation. Smuts's relief at winning the vote in parliament to support Britain must have been immense, since men like Oswald Pirow were now prevented from further influencing the government with pro-Nazi ideas. Apparently, according to Smuts's reckoning, Pirow had managed to transform Hertzog from a conservative Afrikaner into a Nazi. When Hertzog resigned, Pirow was replaced, but by this time he had managed to spread the Nazi net fairly widely across the Union.[40]

The exploits of the pro-Nazi section of the population were not limited to the opening months of the war, as the deeds of Robey Leibbrandt, Olympic boxer and Nazi spy, showed in 1941. His mission was to assassinate Smuts and overthrow the government. With the help of the *Stormjaers*, Robey came very close to achieving his aim, but was betrayed by the leader of the Ossewabrandwag, who felt that the boxer was gaining too much popularity among conservative Afrikaners through his anti-war activities. Robey's arrest helped the authorities to clear the SAP of those members who were plotting against the government's war effort. In all about 400 police men were arrested, some for manufacturing explosives in their homes to be used in sabotage operations.[41]

The pro-Nazi element caused Smuts and his supporters great headaches, and when the South African Chief of the General Staff, General Sir Pierre van Ryneveld, referred to 'dupes' among the South African population, he well may have had the influence of Pirow in mind. Yet it was exactly because of these 'dupes' that the Smuts government had to be sensitive in the way it recruited men to increase the meagre ranks of the permanent force. In an effort to avoid another rebellion, Smuts relied on volunteers and did not impose conscription.

In February 1940 those who volunteered took a service oath in which they pledged to fight anywhere in Africa. By January 1943 the oath was changed, and now volunteers were promising to fight wherever they were needed. Many who had been part of the UDF or of the SAP before March 1940 refused to take the oath and were utilised on the home front.[42] Others who were eager to volunteer in 1939, mostly for financial reasons, had second thoughts when they realised they would be required to fight outside of the Union's borders.[43]

During the recruitment drives, Smuts's aim was to convince both Afrikaans- and English-speaking men to volunteer. By promoting the idea of service to the country as that of fighting a war, rather than fighting for or against a specific cause, the military authorities were relatively successful in boosting the ranks of the UDF. Leaving out a specific cause and focusing solely on the idea of war, political ideas did not affect those who were swept up by military displays and rousing speeches. The prime minister pursued this martial line by attracting the attention of Afrikaners through reminders to them of the 'high adventure' of venerated South African War heroes, and then luring the attention of younger men with impressive displays of weaponry. Still, many Afrikaners chose to join the ranks of the Ossewabrandwag to show their disdain for Smuts's allegiance with their British enemy of less than 40 years earlier.[44] Other Afrikaners joined the UDF reluctantly, motivated by financial needs and not because they felt in any way duty bound to do so. In the end, the UDF was more or less equally divided between Afrikaans- and English-speaking South Africans.[45]

CHAPTER TWO

EVERY MAN FOR HIMSELF

On 8 September 1940 the *Llangibby Castle* arrived at Mombasa harbour in the British colony of Kenya. The Ack-Ack men of the 2nd South African Anti-Aircraft Brigade were on board, among them Clive Luyt, Fred van Alphen Stahl and Michael de Lisle. Most of the men had been disappointed by the training they received at the Zonderwater camp and at Simon's Town, which had involved 'a great deal of instruction and drill, but very little actual firing'.[1] That experience was matched by that of Bernard Schwikkard and his two older brothers, who arrived on the troopship *Westernland* three months later. Their six weeks' training in Barberton and Komatipoort had entailed mostly bayonet practice, which Bernard regarded as 'completely obsolete'.[2]

Also on the *Westernland* were Cyril Crompton and his friend George Norris. They were originally part of the Bluff Battery in Durban, but following months of boredom and a few unpleasant incidents with '*hardegat*' Afrikaner Permanent Force men, they decided to join the Royal Durban Light Infantry (RDLI). Deserting from the Bluff, they swam across the harbour into town and were, apparently, accepted into the RDLI without question because they said they wanted to see action. No sooner had they reached the Zonderwater training camp near Cullinan, east of Pretoria, however, than they were arrested for deserting in the face of the enemy and sent back to Durban for a court martial. According to Cyril, 'common sense had prevailed' and the charges against them were dropped. They were transferred to the 1st South African Anti-Aircraft Regiment, 3rd Battery. Following a month's training in Cape Town which, happily for these two, coincided with a wine show and 'passed in a flash' they boarded the *Westernland* on their way to Mombasa.[3]

At the start of the war, Italy was the smallest of the industrial nations in Europe. The country was extremely poor and also the least ready for conflict, in a political or military sense. Benito Mussolini, the fascist *Il Duce*, seemed to be continually vacillating between different viewpoints. During the early years of Hitler's reign, Mussolini was not in favour of Austria becoming part of the greater German Reich, and neither did he agree with the anti-Semitic ideology of the Nazis.[4]

The civil war in Spain changed everything. It provided the two dictators with a common enemy – Marxism. Both Hitler and Mussolini supported the rebels against the leftist Spanish government, and by 1937 their newfound friendship had led to an agreement between Italy and Germany.[5] Hitler pledged that Germany would not interfere with Italy's colonial ambitions in the Mediterranean and in return, Mussolini would stop meddling in Hitler's plans to bring Austria under German control.[6] Mussolini was eager to expand his empire in Africa as this would provide raw materials for the war machine.[7] The possession of colonies would of course also increase Italy's prestige in Europe, where the so-called 'Scramble for Africa' had been making and breaking economies and egos alike for decades. With Hitler putting threatening pressure on the Austrian chancellor to accept the *Anschluss*, Mussolini's government left the Austrians at the mercy of the Nazis.[8]

Mussolini did not realise that by leaving the Austrians in the lurch, he had taken sides with the Nazis and for the first year of the war he tried to maintain Italy's neutrality. However, with Hitler breathing down his neck, Mussolini finally declared war on the Allies in June 1940, blaming Churchill for depriving him of 'a small place in the African sun'.[9] The Italian colonies of Eritrea, Abyssinia and Somaliland in East Africa, as well as the North African colony of Libya, were all located next to British colonies. Britain was determined to protect its own colonial interests in Africa and control of the Mediterranean was crucial, so it had no intention of allowing a fascist dictator to run riot in this important theatre of war. Sadly for Mussolini, the ordinary Italians seemed to have considerably less motivation to go to war; they had no energy for anything but the daily fight against poverty.[10]

The Italian forces in East Africa were inadequately trained, badly equipped and disorderly. Michael de Lisle remembered that they showed no interest whatsoever in attacking Mombasa.[11] Letters he wrote to his mother during this time reveal that – unlike the troops in the European theatre – the UDF men had not yet been exposed to the full force of warfare. He described the 'wonderful scenery', camping 'under a snow peak glittering white under the full moon' and the men taking 'turns to enjoy a meal in bed'. The closest Michael came to describing a war-like incident was of the

> tragic news of a young Air Force officer who had made a forced landing outside our lines and was shot by a friendly Native irregular after almost finishing his long march to this place. I had the privilege of doing two hours' guard over his body from midnight. It may be meet and right to die for the fatherland but this is a terrible waste that a valuable life should be thrown away like this.[12]

Certainly for Bernard and Cyril, Abyssinia and Italian Somaliland held no great danger either. Cyril recalled that there was not much for the anti-aircraft gunners to do, as the Italians did not pose a threat from the air. The closest he got to seeing any action in East Africa was when one of the anti-aircraft batteries 'shot down a Caproni fighter at a place called Afmadu, but that's about all'.[13] Bernard's regiment was involved in 'two minor skirmishes, the capture of Hobok and Fort Mega', but despite this, he still regarded mosquitoes and lions as their biggest enemies.[14]

Looking back on his total war experience, Clive regarded his time in East Africa as completely inconsequential. He summed up the entire campaign in one sentence: 'We chased the Italians out of East Africa; that was no problem.' There is no doubt that the South Africans were

Except for getting stuck in the mud, East Africa did not present great difficulties to the Union Forces. COURTESY ENID BATES

very successful in this early phase of the war, and they certainly showed that they were adept at mobile bush warfare. Unfortunately though, their 100 per cent success rate in this theatre of war and against this specific enemy led the UDF men to believe that they were unbeatable. Many South Africans who fought in East Africa took a dim view of the Italians – as one of them said, they were 'scruffy little devils' who were 'primitive' and not a worthy enemy. In the deserts of Libya, however, the South Africans were in for a surprise.[15]

The Royal Natal Carbineers, the Duke of Edinburgh's Own Rifles, and the 1st Battalion Transvaal Scottish, all part of the 1st South African Infantry Division, were sent to Libya to take part in Operation Crusader, which started on 17 November 1941. The aim of the operation was to relieve the harbour town of Tobruk where Australian forces were besieged. They were also to recapture Cyrenaica. To achieve these aims, the UDF men were to face General Erwin Rommel's formidable Afrika Korps. Once in the wastelands of North Africa, it was not long before the South Africans realised that their previous battle experience in East Africa was more or less meaningless and that the Germans posed a tenacious challenge.[16] For Bernard Schwikkard and

Howard Bates and his mates making the most of their Cairo leave, February 1942. COURTESY ENID BATES

Visiting the Jewish Club in Cairo, Stanley Smollan and friends. COURTESY STANLEY SMOLLAN

Cyril Crompton this shock came at the Battle of Sidi Rezegh, the first of South Africa's major setbacks.

Sidi Rezegh

The landscape in the Libyan Desert was vastly different from the bush in East Africa. It was bare, windy, dry and dusty. During the day the extreme heat was made worse by the sirocco winds and sandstorms. Added to these conditions were the squadrons of flies that plagued the UDF men, preventing them from eating and sleeping properly.

Even before they arrived in Libya, Cyril and what he called his 'pretty lawless crowd' came face to face with a new type of lawlessness. In Cairo, as ever on the lookout for merriment, they bought what they thought was whisky from the local Egyptians, only to realise they had been hoodwinked when they tasted cold tea. As a result 'a lot of *donnering* took place'. The carefree days came to an end when the regiment was moved to Mersa Matruh to supply anti-aircraft protection. There, according to Cyril, they 'experienced for the first time the war they were meant to be fighting'.[17] Bernard, also at Mersa Matruh at the time, remembered being addressed by the Commander in Chief Middle East, Sir Claude Auchinleck, before they were to 'take the offensive' in relieving the Australians at Tobruk. As they were the Transvaal Scottish, a piper piped them into battle. Bernard was not impressed, and recalled that 'although the enemy was nowhere in sight, we had to fix our bayonets to our rifles ready to charge the enemy [...] we formed the spearhead of the attack but were out targeted by the Germans who had superior long-distance bazookas and machineguns'.[18]

The use of outdated tactics was only one of the problems facing the Allied forces in the desert. They were plagued by fuel supply problems, inadequate and outdated equipment and the disruptions of constant changes in battle plans. Like most other battles in North Africa, the use of tanks and airpower was especially important at the Battle of Sidi Rezegh. However, it would certainly seem as if the commanders of the recently formed Eighth Army were struggling to find their feet. The rank and file took note of this apparent ineptness: a jaundiced soldier noted in his diary that one such commander, Norrie, had 'been compelled to leave the break-out troops of the Tobruk garrison to their own devices ... [and] Cunningham[19] ... had lost his nerve'.[20]

Bernard had little time to reflect on their old-fashioned weapons, because on 23 November 1941 'all hell broke loose'. The Germans attacked with heavy artillery and mortar fire, while Bernard was stuck with a so-called sticky bomb that had no detonator:

> The [detonators] were only to be handed to us when it became obvious that the German tanks were going to arrive. The detonators were in the safe custody of a Sgt Major Hansen. The idea was that we had to wait until the [German] tanks passed over the top of us before we smashed the glass sticky bomb against the bottom of the tank and blow it up. Of course no one drew attention to the fact that we would be blown up with the tank. Fortunately for us, when the tanks eventually arrived, Sgt Major Hansen was nowhere to be found.[21]

A Bofors gun at the ready near Bardia. COURTESY ENID BATES

Cyril was not far away from the Transvaal Scottish where Bernard was frantically trying to avoid the issue of the detonators. Although Cyril's regiment were able to set up their Bofors anti-aircraft guns, they had no rifles or side arms for use in close-up battle. For Cyril the battle moved 'tremendously fast. More German tanks and armoured cars came into view and came straight at us. The horrendous noise of the different kinds of munitions screaming past and flying in all directions was awesome [and] most devastating was the heavy artillery barrage that descended upon us.' The brutal reality of war became piercingly clear when in the midst of the battle Cyril saw an old friend who had been separated from his regiment. As they jokingly shouted warnings and sarcastic comments about the battle at each other, his friend was hit and 'fell dead into the sand'. Cyril was one of only four men from his gun crew to come out of the battle alive. In a desperate effort to avoid capture they climbed into a truck, but in the confusion of battle they drove straight into German lines and were 'made to lie face down. And thus we were taken prisoner.'[22]

Bernard had no intention of being captured. When he heard the order to retreat, he decided it was now a matter of 'every man for himself'. Sadly it was too late: the Germans were already overrunning their positions. Realising that he had no option but to surrender, he then saw his brother 'obstinately refusing to surrender and shouted an appeal to him to surrender for my sake rather than to act foolishly'. For Bernard and for his brother, becoming prisoners of war was a 'shattering experience' that never crossed their minds until that moment.[23]

The casualty list at the end of the battle revealed the extent of UDF losses. Of the 5th South African Infantry Brigade 224 were killed and 379 wounded, while 3 000 were captured from the total force active at Sidi Rezegh.[24] Captured along with Cyril and Bernard were Newman Robinson of the 10th South African Field Ambulance[25] and Herbert (Aussie) Hammond[26] of the 1st Brigade Signal Corps.[27]

For Newman Robinson, each German soldier he encountered during the battle was a study in determination. Newman saw armoured motorcyclists moving towards him, and 'each man wore a grim, set expression as though his eyes were fixed on a vision of the Fuehrer beckoning him on to victory from somewhere above the skyline'.[28] To some degree this is reminiscent of the clichéd image held by many Allied soldiers of their German enemies, but it also shows something of the awe with which the inexperienced UDF soldiers viewed the tactical superiority and discipline of the Afrika Korps. For Newman the battle was horrific, and when his harmless Ambulance Unit inadvertently blocked the path of oncoming German tanks, which seemed as if they 'roared like rush hour traffic over the Eastern horizon', his mind refused to accept what was happening to him, and he found himself

> in very much the same way as a man sometimes stands outside himself in a nightmare, and looks on with helpless horror at what is happening to him. I see myself standing alongside my truck in blank amazement, with a plate of porridge in one hand and a mug of coffee in the other, wondering what on earth had gone wrong, and feeling mildly resentful that it should have done so at breakfast time.[29]

Newman's surprise at being captured was aggravated by the fact that he believed the 10th Field Ambulance had been assured of ample British tank protection, and when tanks started roaring past him he at first assumed that they must have been British. When he noticed the black crosses on the side of the tanks, the unmistakable insignia of the Afrika Korps, he 'felt like a victim of a practical joke'. He surrendered to a German soldier whose appearance was so detestable that he found it hard to believe that his captor could in fact be German. As he was led to where the other POWs had been assembled he was convinced that they would be lined up and shot. Luckily for them, the Germans seemed more interested in their nationality and one soldier, 'bigger, cleaner, more truculent looking [and with] a bigger gun,' came closer to the group and started a conversation about their political affiliations towards Smuts or towards Hertzog.[30]

The reality of defeat and of becoming a prisoner bluntly confronted Aussie in the afternoon of 23 November, when German tanks surrounded his unit and then moved in to seize the men who were trapped inside the circle. In the path of the tanks lay the bodies of the dead and the injured. The 'piercing screams of men trapped beneath the giant wheels' came with the knowledge that they had finally lost the battle. 'A sick feeling stirred in my stomach and hovered about my throat,' he wrote. Aussie's first stop as a POW was a South African first aid post where he and other uninjured men were put to work laying out the bodies of those less fortunate.[31]

After the war, the South African military authorities collected statements from soldiers who had been taken prisoner at Sidi Rezegh and these reveal similar opinions regarding risky or misguided tactics, poor defensive cover and battlefield chaos. A medical officer with the 5th South African Brigade who described fighting with inadequate tank and artillery support stated that his brigade had been devastated by a Panzer division which 'drove right through Brigade Headquarters'.[32] It is very possible that this medical officer was in the same Ambulance Unit as Newman Robinson, who also described how German tanks drove through their camp. A letter written by Lieutenant-Colonel BP Purchase, another medical officer, described events at Sidi Rezegh as 'terrific' – in the sense of 'causing terror' – and that 'our fellows were shot down like dogs while attending to the wounded'.[33]

The UDF men at Sidi Rezegh did not surrender easily, and many tried to escape the relentless German advance. In one case, a non-combatant auxiliary soldier simply referred to as Johannes decided to take matters into his own hands. Johannes worked in the 5th Brigade field kitchen, and according to the Brigade diary, its 'Non-European' auxiliary troops had been issued with captured Italian rifles and ammunition for self-protection. As German tanks approached the trenches around the field kitchen, Johannes used his rifle to shoot a German soldier emerging from a tank. The man dropped to the ground and the tank then withdrew from the area around the field kitchen. Johannes and Ambrose, another kitchen worker, found a truck and escaped, rejoining the Brigade after the battle.[34] A note accompanying the document in which their exploits were recorded states that the extract concerning Johannes was cut from the official Brigade diary on the instructions of Major General Brink, probably because the issuing of weapons to auxiliary troops was not allowed and the 5th Brigade had actually acted against this official policy. By shooting the German soldier, Johannes had shown that black volunteers were able to do more than their assigned auxiliary tasks like driving, cooking, and cleaning, exposing the impotence of months of debates on the issue between Smuts's supporters, Afrikaner nationalists and even the African National Congress, which had been trying to formulate a response to the government's unwillingness to arm black volunteers.[35]

The writer Uys Krige, a war correspondent at the time, was also captured at Sidi Rezegh. The event made such an impact on him that he came to regard the experience of that day as the most important in his life.[36] In a prose work entitled *Totensonntag*, he described how, while taking cover in a slit trench during the heavy bombing, the mad thought of plucking the bombs out of the sky as if they were poppies entered his mind.[37]

Although Krige was not a soldier, he experienced much the same treatment as most other POWs who were captured in North Africa. Unfortunately for him, he had lost his rank card during the battle, and the corresponding loss of privileges pushed him down from captain into the common pool of POWs. His status was later restored in Italy, but this rough early experience gave him a unique perspective on the POW life of the rank and file

With the great loss of life and the many captured, it is difficult to determine if the offensive at Sidi Rezegh was successful. The eventual victory came almost by chance and at very high cost. According to some historians, higher command failed during tank battles as infantry were deployed before the tank battle was determined.[38] Following the battle, Acting Lieutenant General Sir Charles Willoughby Moke Norrie[39] went so far as to give the credit to the South African 5th Brigade in his report, stating that their sacrifice resulted in the turning point of the battle, giving the Allies the upper hand in North Africa at that time. In the Allied balance sheet, the loss of the 5th Brigade was also considered insignificant in view of the fact that the Afrika Korps had lost half of its tanks.[40]

For those captured at Sidi Rezegh it did seem as if the Allies' use of inferior tactics resulted in many losses, notably the number of prisoners taken. Indeed, most men experienced a sense of resentment or helplessness, believing that they were seen as dispensable by their commanders, who appeared not to realise the precariousness of their situation regarding equipment and tactics.[41]

Tobruk

'I wonder if the true stories of this campaign will ever be told; the absolute jumble up and disorder of things'.[42] Dick Dickinson wrote these words in his diary shortly after the siege of Tobruk came to an end in November 1941. He was referring to the confusion during the battles and the rumours about Eighth Army bravery versus German cruelty and Italian incompetence that spread like wildfire among the men after each battle. During the early months of 1942, Dick's mood became increasingly pessimistic and in May he noted the persistent rumour that the morale of the UDF soldiers was the lowest among the men in the Eighth Army.[43]

The Eighth Army consisted of British, South Africans, Indians, Australians and New Zealanders. The Army was commanded by

Lieutenant-General Neil M Ritchie, who in turn reported to Sir Claude Auchinleck.⁴⁴ 'The Auk' was an uncompromising man who had little sympathy for weakness in those under his command. In April 1942 he wrote to the War Office with a proposal to reinstate the death penalty for desertion because he believed the men of the Eighth Army lacked motivation to fight.⁴⁵ On the other hand, Auchinleck was also known as a commander whose concern for fighting men caused him to approach each battle with great care. This made for a heavy burden of responsibility, but it was one he was reluctant to assign to anyone else.⁴⁶

Some of the UDF men in the Western Desert at that time had arrived from East Africa, but others, like the 2nd SA Division, left South Africa on the *Mauritania*, the *Isle de France* and the *Nova Amsterdam* troopships and went directly to Egypt. They arrived in the Western Desert in October 1941 under the command of Major-General IP de Villiers and had no battle experience whatsoever. Adapting to military life in those harsh conditions was also a greater shock to these men than to those who were almost eased into it through East Africa. For one thing, food and water rations were strictly controlled and the men started to appreciate every single meal. A volunteer in the Middellandse Regiment, Jack Mortlock, recalled in his memoirs that his regiment was 'duly welcomed by intense heat and swarms of hungry flies. Some unit or other had organized a field kitchen and were serving bully beef stew well-seasoned with dead flies! We were too hungry to be finicky about the flies and only picked out those that we saw.'⁴⁷ The regiment arrived in Suez but was sent directly to Amariya, near Alexandria, for training in desert navigation.

David Brokensha and his brother Paul found themselves closer to the Libyan border in Mersa Matruh. David believed that as dispatch drivers, they were 'hardly an essential part of the plan for victory' and as such he did not find life in the desert especially stressful. By the time their unit moved to the outskirts of Tobruk, he had come to appreciate the thrill of long stretches of tarred road and fast motorcycles. It was on one of his solitary expeditions on a BMW bike that he noticed another biker coming towards him at great speed. As the two joy riders approached each other both of them realised that they were

Left: In Egypt, 'far enough away from headquarters, not to be bothered by stray officers', Jack Mortlock, 2nd right. COURTESY ANTHONY MORTLOCK Right: Jack Mortlock's brother Harry, somewhere in North Africa. COURTESY ANTHONY MORTLOCK

Jack Mortlock outside his 'desert home', November 1941. COURTESY ANTHONY MORTLOCK

from opposite sides of the enemy line and they both 'turned abruptly around, giving each other a friendly wave, and raced back to [their] respective bases'. This was David's first encounter with the formidable German enemy; most of his time in the Western Desert was characterised by visits to Alexandria, relaxed swims in the sea and even playing games like *jukskei*.[48]

In January 1942 some of the UDF men gained battle experience during the Battle of Benghazi, and most of them were in some way

Dispatch rider in the North African desert – David Brokensha. COURTESY DAVID BROKENSHA

or another involved with what became known among troops as the Benghazi Handicap and the Gazala Gallop, apt phrases for describing the to-and-fro nature of the North African battles.⁴⁹ In most cases, however, UDF men were ordered to dig defences in the unfavourable 50-kilometre bottleneck between the Mediterranean and the Qattara Depression at El Alamein.⁵⁰ The lack of what they saw as active participation in the war caused many soldiers to become very critical of their commanders. As early as October 1941, Dick wrote in his diary that 'the feeling within the detachment just now isn't altogether A1 – there's frequent bickering and quarrels. Don't really know why, except that we're bored.' In April 1942, Dick and a friend represented a number of men who complained to their company commander, whose leadership style they believed negatively affected camaraderie among the men.⁵¹ Whatever their feelings towards each other or their commanders, when Rommel launched his attack on Tobruk, very few of the men were ready for what awaited them.

Dickinson's 'jumble up and disorder' of earlier battles are words too feeble to describe the battle around Tobruk in June 1942 – it was utter chaos. For everyone involved at Tobruk, the frenzied and confused nature of the battle is what stands out most. Many of the men were not even aware of the full extent of the actions on the battlefield, as these were spread out over a very wide area. The experiences of the rank and file were certainly dwarfed by larger factors beyond their control. Auchinleck wanted brigades to operate independently from divisions in an effort to ensure greater mobility; Ritchie believed otherwise. He had created a system of defensive boxes along a line that ran from Gazala to Bir Hakeim, a stretch of 80 kilometres that became known as the Gazala line. This line was protected by fixed infantry brigades linked by minefields.

The defences around Tobruk were not the only aspect on which these two men disagreed. At first Auchinleck believed that Tobruk should be abandoned by the 8th Army if circumstances demanded it and if Rommel was in a position to 'invest it effectively'.[52] Later he changed his mind and expressed his belief that a garrison should remain within Tobruk while a mobile force on the outskirts would be 'capable of preventing the fortress being permanently besieged'.[53] Although Ritchie did not share this view, he never voiced his opinions to Auchinleck. While Auchinleck instructed Ritchie to hold Tobruk, Ritchie ordered the Gazala garrisons to the frontier of the Tobruk defences because he regarded withdrawal to the Egyptian border as the only option left for the 8th Army. This left an isolated South African garrison under command of Major-General Klopper in Tobruk.[54] By this time the depleted troops in the immediate vicinity of Tobruk could not withstand an attack and the scene was set for defeat.

Had it not been for the disagreements, misunderstandings and lack of openness between these two commanders, military events may have developed differently. Things would certainly have been a lot easier for Klopper. He was in command of Tobruk for one month before he surrendered to Rommel, causing criticism and recriminations against him and against the UDF forces.[55]

The defences around Tobruk were deficient, and the foot soldiers were well aware of this fact. For instance, Michael de Lisle remembered that the 'minefields had not been maintained and defensive positions had filled with sand'.[56] AJ Cremer, attached to the 2nd SA Division and a member of the Divisional Headquarters, also noted in his memoirs the bad state of the minefields and that the mines themselves were so old that they were completely ineffective. He records that both Klopper and De Villiers continually asked for new mines but were told there were no supplies. New mines were being stored in Tobruk but the generals could not use them as they were reportedly reserved for the Royal Engineers. When Tobruk fell, these mines were appropriated by the Germans.[57]

Ritchie's faith in the Gazala line was misguided, not only because it was weak, but also because the two defensive boxes towards the south of the line were too far apart to effectively repel the Afrika Korps' advance.[58] When Rommel attacked, he easily smashed the defences and bypassed the Gazala line. For a short time, those in Tobruk thought that Rommel would continue to move further east towards Egypt. This would mean that the town would be besieged for a second time, something which Ritchie was prepared to allow. In London, *The Times* reported on 20 June 1942 that 'pressure on Tobruk at present is slight, as Rommel has thrust his main forces east towards Egypt from El Adem'.[59] However, Rommel's intention was to attack Tobruk from the eastern side at first light the next morning,[60] using the full force of Stuka dive bombers and Mark III and IV tanks, as well as the superior German anti-tank and anti-aircraft guns. These armaments, combined with highly effective tactics, ensured an advantageous position for German victory.[61]

The unexpected move put the South Africans at a huge disadvantage as they had their backs towards the Afrika Korps. Adding to the confusion were strange incidents such as the one reported after the war by Captain DG Fannin. According to him, a package containing Rommel's plan of attack had been dropped by an aircraft immediately following the cut-off of Tobruk, but this information had not been acted upon. As bizarre events such as these are difficult to verify, they are for the most part categorised as rumours resulting from the fog of war.[62]

Even before Rommel's attack on 21 June and before Klopper finally decided to surrender, there was confusion about the actual situation. On 20 June the 1st South African Police Battalion were ordered to hand in their equipment, but an hour later the same equipment was reissued to them. Then, during the evening of the same day, they were told to move towards the coast as the Navy would be coming to their rescue. However, there were no clear orders and without proper directions some men started to destroy their rifles while others simply walked away into the desert. Gert van Zyl, a member of the 1st SAP, described the troops as 'sheep without a shepherd'.[63]

According to Fannin, in the late afternoon of 20 June, the order of 'every man for himself' was given, but his statement reveals that after this order, sporadic attempts were still being made to contact regiments and to give orders, such as one to send out a 'tank-hunting' force during the night. Fannin went on foot to inform Brigadier Johnson of the order, but found him 'quite unperturbed … the HQ was having tea'.[64] Their problems were compounded during the night when Klopper and members of the High Command discussed the situation. As a result of disagreements in the group a tentative decision was reached to continue fighting but to permit commanding officers to surrender if they thought it necessary.[65]

In this highly volatile atmosphere, the accuracy or consistency of many of these statements is also doubtful, as many of them do not correspond with other known positions. For instance, Klopper's account of the events of 20 and 21 June contradicts other statements made after the war. According to Klopper, he 'stressed to General Gott that he felt very uneasy at the prospect of being invested [in Tobruk] and understood from him that the higher command would make every effort to prevent this'.[66] In contrast, a 1946 interview with Colonel Richards paraphrased Klopper's earlier remark that if the Australians could hold Tobruk, then so could the South Africans. It was as a result of this difference in opinion that Richards offered to be relieved of his command as he believed Klopper did not value or trust his view of the situation.[67] Another inconsistency in perception concerned ammunition supply which, according to Klopper, was 'the fatal factor' in his decision to surrender.[68] Many former POWs supported this view – for instance, Fred Geldenhuis said that they had no weapons whatsoever, and that not a single shot was fired where he was when the Germans came through.

Yet, in contrast with the widely held opinion that there was a shortage of ammunition at Tobruk, Captain Fannin stated in an interview in 1946 that 'there was plenty of amn in Tobruk, the only serious shortage was in shells for the medium arty'.[69] This view was supported by Major Wessels, who, in another 1946 interview, stated that the ammunition supply was adequate.[70] The matter of the perceived shortage of ammunition may to some extent be explained by Colonel Richards, who reported that one officer responsible for issuing ammunition insisted on authority to do so from Headquarters, even though the German tanks were visible by that time.[71]

Such confusion regarding orders may be explained in part by a statement in Jack Mortlock's memoirs. According to Jack, the Germans advanced at such speed that by the time information and orders reached them, they were inaccurate or no longer relevant.[72] Jack's memoirs also provide some insight into the confusion regarding Klopper's decision to surrender or to fight on. He refers to a rumour, namely:

> It is said that General Klopper received, but did not succeed in transmitting to all units, the order to fight their way out if they could, and, if not to resist to the last. We certainly did not receive orders to this effect, even though General Klopper was at our Brigade Headquarters![73]

For many South Africans, a thick cloud of smoke, symbolic of the confusion of the preceding days, signified the end of the battle. In his memoirs, Dennis Mugglestone of the 6th Infantry Police Brigade described the smoke as the 'approach of death and destruction'.[74] AJ Cremer also mentioned the clouds of smoke which blotted out the sun late that afternoon.[75] Bill Hindshaw remembered that

> the conditions were terrible, there was no communication, there was nothing, nothing, nothing. No ammunition, nothing, nothing, I was 2 k's away and we sat and watched, we sat there and watched those stupid bombs, and the next minute the harbour of Tobruk was on fire.

Dennis Mugglestone in his new uniform, 9 May 1941.
COURTESY ELIZABETH MUGGLESTONE

In his memoirs, Ike Rosmarin, a war correspondent with the 2nd SA Division, described the German attack as 'terrifying [but] worst of all was the fact that we did not know what was happening as there were no orders from our officers. Confusion reigned with fear and panic.'[76]

The indecision and disagreements between those in command affected everyone at Tobruk. For instance, the Cape Town Highlanders received an order stating, 'if anyone leaves Tobruk now, they'll be classified as a deserter'. One of those Highlanders, Gordon Fry, believed that had an order of 'every man for himself' been given, he would have been able to escape capture. The idea of the lost opportunity for freedom haunted him throughout his time as a POW.[77] On the other hand, HL Wood, stationed with the HQ Company of the Umvoti Mounted Rifles, described the disappointment of Captain de Jager of the Umvoti Mounted Rifles, who 'with tear-filled eyes' conveyed the order to surrender.[78] Wood, however, simply took it for granted that it was now a case of every man for himself and attempted to escape, as did many others. The order of 'every man for himself' seems not to have been officially given, as none of the men could say reliably where it originated from – for example, in this statement from 1943, Colonel du Plessis declared that 'we who were at Divisional HQ were told that HQ staff were clearing out, and that it was "every man for himself".'[79]

Perhaps because the battle was so frightening, the misunderstandings so plentiful and the orders so confusing, it is no surprise that the men were so dumbstruck at their capture. They felt that because they had been so misinformed, they were not to blame. Some felt the extreme unfairness of having been taken prisoner, as they were not doing any fighting at the time of their capture. Clive Luyt, for example, stated his feelings in no uncertain terms: Klopper was 'straight from a desk in Pretoria,' he declared. 'We didn't have a commanding officer of any consequence. There was nothing wrong with Klopper, but he didn't know his foot from his elbow. [...] A lot of people blamed him.'

Fred van Alphen Stahl's account of his experience shows how perplexed he was by the events, even though he described it 70 years later:

> ... of course your first feelings as a prisoner of war ... this is the end, you imagined going to the Army you could lose an arm, you could lose your life, you could lose your legs, your sight, but you never gave prisoner of war a thought, and so this, this is the end ... I wasn't busy fighting at the time ... we had been fighting in the Gazala handicap and on the rearguard coming back, and they said right now you are all moving into a particular point, we didn't even realise it was Tobruk ... and the next morning we were getting ready, getting our guns in order again, and a signal just came in and they said destroy your guns, destroy your vehicles, Tobruk

Unknown swimmers near Tobruk. COURTESY ENID BATES

has fallen ... you are now prisoners of war.

Lieutenant Goldman of the Royal Durban Light Infantry recalled that when he was told that 'they have surrendered', he thought *they* were the German forces. When he realised that it was in fact the Allies he was 'astounded and flabbergasted. I had not for a moment thought that we would surrender. It seemed fantastic. We had not fired a shot.'[80]

Stanley Smollan was unfortunate enough to have returned to Tobruk after recovering from an injury in Cairo the day before it fell to the Germans, while David Brokensha was literally captured with his pants down. He was swimming naked in the sea after sharing a bottle of gin with his brother Paul and four others who believed they could swim to freedom following the surrender order. Brokensha's capture was therefore humiliating on many different levels; firstly he was part of a surrendering army, secondly they failed to escape, and thirdly he felt 'embarrassed, not only at being a *hands-upper*, but also because I was "starko" – as though this were not the right script; people did not get captured without clothes.'[81]

After experiencing heavy fighting in the week before the fall of Tobruk at Point 209, also known as Commonwealth Keep, Jack Mortlock simply stated that 'continued resistance appeared hopeless', and he and others obeyed the order to destroy their weapons and documents.[82] Surrender was synonymous with the destruction of weapons, and for everyone this was a difficult task to carry out, remembered starkly. Fred van Alphen Stahl's way of describing the destruction of their guns clearly illustrates his emotions:

> our trucks had to be destroyed and our guns, so we destroyed our gun first, that we had lovingly been cleaning all these years, and now we had to shoot down the barrel and a shot in the bridge and fire and blow the barrels to pieces and that was sort of bad enough and you are still just a youngster, eighteen, nineteen years old, well, prisoner of war …

The 2nd Anti-Aircraft Regiment had trouble destroying their guns. As Michael de Lisle described, the 'breech mechanism of beautifully engineered stainless steel was undamaged' after they fired at the muzzle into which they had placed a round. They were then forced to take the guns apart and bury the components in different places.[83]

Howard Bates, also in the 2nd Ack Ack, remembered the 'consternation' when he heard about Klopper's capitulation. He and a small group of friends decided to 'remain together for as long as possible', in this way hoping to ease the shock and confusion of becoming prisoners of war. Two days later, Howard's hopes were lifted marginally when he saw a Scottish regiment marching into the holding pen. The sound of the bagpipes

> lifted our hearts and gave a lift to our depression. We heard the 'skirl' of pipes in the distance and, then, over the hills marched the

> Scottish Regiment – 'The Cameroons' [sic] – in column of three and with fixed bayonets. I was extremely moved by this incident as the sound of pipes always affected me dramatically. They had held their sector and had fought on, refusing to surrender to the Italians. The Germans finally accepted their surrender and, in honour of their resistance, allowed them to march in full regalia under their own officers.[84]

Although large numbers of Allied men were taken prisoner by the Afrika Korps, many soldiers took matters into their own hands as they saw the German tanks coming closer. Gert van Zyl remembered that many men 'dispersed in all directions' before they were even aware that Tobruk had fallen, and that by the time the German tanks arrived at his position, there were only about 50 men left who were then informed by the Germans that Klopper had surrendered.[85]

Some escapees were lucky enough to find abandoned vehicles. These trucks, tanks and ambulances were driven at high speed towards Allied lines until they sputtered to a standstill when the petrol ran out. However, a few of these escape attempts were successful, as was the case with Lieutenant AN Goldman and Sergeant CH Spear of the Royal Durban Light Infantry, who, after a few close encounters with German forces, reached Allied lines eight days after Rommel's attack.[86]

In a letter to his family, John Davidson told of a Guards major who refused to surrender and escaped with a 'crowd of men'. In the same correspondence he also wrote about Allan Bird, who 'just dashed through a mine field path' with an ambulance and a truck. When the ambulance was blown up, he returned to clear the track for others who might have to use the same route to escape. In their desperation to get as far away from the Germans as possible, John and his fellow escapees actually drove through a few Italian camps. He remembered how, if 'you just drive through and wave and cheer – the Ites are usually so surprised that they just wave back'.[87] Lieutenant CR Featherstone of the Middellandse Regiment also escaped successfully with 46 men, as did Sergeant Woodley and nine others who escaped by hiding in caves and living on abandoned German rations.[88]

Dick Dickinson's escape attempt was less successful. Shortly after their capture by German forces he and his friend, Rollo van der Burg, came across an injured member of the Non-European Army Services and managed to convince two of their captors that the man's wounds needed urgent attention. The Germans agreed and, inexplicably, gave them a truck to take the man to hospital. Dickinson, Van der Burg and the injured soldier set off, quickly realising that they had enough diesel to cover a significant distance. Sadly, however, they had no idea where they were, and decided to stay on the road so as to avoid minefields. As they drove on, walking soldiers who were also trying to evade capture climbed onto their truck until it was completely overloaded. Dick and Rollo were eventually recaptured when they were stopped by a German patrol. It was only now that they realised that the injured soldier had somehow disappeared along the way. The furious German commandant did not believe a word of their humanitarian story and they were unceremoniously herded back towards the thousands of other captives. Although Dick was happy to be alive at this point, he now realised that he was a prisoner and no longer had the luxury of free will.[89]

In many more cases, men found themselves lost in the desert with diminishing food and water supplies, walking in circles searching for the Allies. When the Germans eventually caught up with them, they were mostly relieved, as they had come to realise that the desert was a far more deadly enemy than any Axis force could be.

Rommel considered the fall of Tobruk on 21 June 1942 as the high point of the war in North Africa. Hitler was delighted when he received the news and promoted him to Field Marshal.[90] For South Africa and the Allies, the fall of Tobruk was disastrous and rumours about South African incompetence threatened to sour military relations between South Africa and Britain.[91] Relations between the two countries had already become strained before the war, not least as a consequence of the creation of South Africa's Seaward Defence Force which eventually led to the setting up of the South African Naval Forces in 1942.[92] This and the Union neutrality crisis of 1938 and 1939 were evidence of a growing sense of nationalism that was not unique to South Africa, but was also gaining momentum in all wartime Dominions as they sought a greater sense of independence from their colonial masters.[93]

As Auchinleck was commander of the Middle East, he had to explain what had happened. His subsequent report was not favourable towards the role of the South Africans, something which the Union government obviously found unacceptable.[94] On 9 July 1942, the High Commissioner in London wrote to the Minister of External Affairs in Pretoria informing him that all correspondence containing uninformed speculation and criticism about the events at Tobruk would be censored. According to the High Commissioner, Churchill's remarks to Parliament and other comments made in the House of Lords were fuelling damaging rumours and the Germans were using the information to undermine Allied morale. In order to turn public opinion towards a less critical view of the situation, the High Commissioner suggested that 'authentic' accounts from survivors be made public in South Africa and in Britain, but only if these accounts exonerated Klopper, as it had been suggested that he was guilty of treachery and it was a fact that no government spokesman had made any 'appreciative or sympathetic reference' to him.[95]

Shortly after hearing the news about the surrender from his adjutant, Sir de Villiers Graaff, SG (Wally) Wolhuter, an intelligence sergeant with the Middellandse Regiment, was assured by the acting commanding officer that the rank and file were not at fault in the defeat. Because POWs were reluctant to accept responsibility for their capture, they also looked elsewhere to assign blame. In the days immediately after their capture, many of the POWs felt very little sympathy towards Klopper as they tried to make sense of their situation. Shortly after arriving at the POW camp in Derna, Ike Rosmarin described how the garrison commander was brought to the enclosure by German officers to address the prisoners:

> but the prisoners of war, especially those from the British forces, were in no mood to listen to someone whom they thought had betrayed them. They were in an angry and belligerent mood and, amid boos and hisses, Klopper did an about-turn without saying a word.[96]

Seeking a scapegoat for the disaster was a natural reaction. The Allies had suffered several serious setbacks since 1939, including 30 000 casualties at Dunkirk in 1940 and the capture of approximately 85 000 soldiers during the surrender of Singapore in February 1942.[97] The fall of Tobruk meant that a further 33 000 Allied soldiers – roughly a third of them South African – were taken prisoner.[98]

On 10 July 1942, the Ministerial Secretary announced that a Court of Inquiry would be appointed as it was believed that this would be the most effective way to put an end to the negative rumours. He also ventured that in his opinion the reason for the fall of Tobruk was the 'decision to hold Tobruk against the whole force of Rommel while Eighth Army disappeared eastwards into the blue and thus unable to assist the defence ...'[99] That opinion may have been a fair argument against the negative Tobruk rumours, but it also pointed towards the growing opinion in South Africa that Klopper had been abandoned by British forces, a feeling echoed in many POWs' statements and memoirs. A week later, the *Rand Daily Mail* reported that harmful reports of South African conduct at Tobruk were the result of Axis propaganda, and then sought to counteract this with its own morale-boosting efforts by insisting that the conduct of the South Africans during the battle had inspired their fellow soldiers as well as all who were fighting for freedom.[100]

For you the war is over

The young volunteers were now all POWs, defeated soldiers. At Sidi Rezegh and at Tobruk the men were captured by Germans uttering the famous phrase, '*handen hoch* – for you the war is over', as Fred van Alphen Stahl remembered. Once in enemy hands, the POWs were handed over to Italian control, as they were in an Italian colony. This did not sit well with the South Africans, whose first impressions of the Italians had been utterly negative. Strangely, the German forces felt the same. When David Brokensha was captured, the Germans admitted that they considered the South Africans, like themselves, to be good soldiers, but that the Italians were not, and therefore they felt obliged

Taking control of German guns at Bardia. COURTESY ANTHONY MORTLOCK

to apologise as they had orders to hand them over to their inferior allies. Apologies such as these were not limited to Tobruk, but also took place at Sidi Rezegh, where Bernard Schwikkard was captured:

> General Rommel, the famous German Commander, drove up to us and said he was sorry to be handing us over to the Italians, but he needed all his soldiers to do the fighting. He indicated that, as soldiers, the Italians were a miserable lot.[101]

It was earlier in the war, when UDF forces captured Italian soldiers, that the perceptions of the Italians as inferior were formed. Jack Mortlock described Italian POWs as behaving like animals while he thought German prisoners 'carried themselves with that characteristic air of superiority that seemed second nature to the German Army at that time'.[102] Derogatory opinions about Italians were also formed when South Africans raided abandoned dug-outs at Mersa Matruh, Sidi Barrani, Sollum, Halfaya Pass and Bardia. According to Rosmarin, it was 'no wonder that the "Ities" were looked on as inferior to the Germans' as they often found women's clothing and condoms in the dug-outs, supporting the allegation that prostitutes travelled with the Italian troops to the front.[103] Fred van Alphen Stahl also attested to finding condoms in Italian quarters in Abyssinia, but to him the hygiene of the Italians was of greater concern as they 'would rather cover themselves with scent and powder, than to use soap to wash [...] so they were probably used to being lousy from time to time'.

Rommel shared some of the frustrations which the POWs now experienced. He was known as someone who was seemingly unable to cooperate agreeably not only with the Italians but also with German high command. His initial annoyance at being placed under Italian command while in Africa obviously influenced his opinion of the Italian forces, just as the South Africans' respect for Rommel influenced their opinion of German soldiers in general. There is no doubt that he was a brilliant military strategist, and the opinions that some Allied soldiers held of him played a part in creating the superhuman myth surrounding him. Rommel became widely known as the Desert Fox, implying cunning and intelligence.[104]

Accordingly, for David Brokensha, who experienced no fighting before he was captured at Tobruk, Rommel 'was our favourite general, I won't say our only favourite German general, but for some reason we all ... He had a very good name as a proper soldier, and very efficient.' This sense of awe for Rommel and the Afrika Korps was shared by almost the entire Eighth Army. In some cases their admiration bordered on an inferiority complex, which no doubt affected them during combat situations.[105] Ike Rosmarin, for instance, noted in his memoirs that 'Eighth Army Command was simply out of its

Fighting in Bardia as portrayed from a soldier's point of view. COURTESY ANTHONY MORTLOCK

depth when faced with the quirky genius of the "Desert Fox".[106] Wally Wolhuter shared the same opinion of Rommel's prowess and blamed the fall of Tobruk on the fact that 'we had conveniently forgotten what an exceptional military commander Rommel was'.[107] However, from David Brokensha's point of view, at least, there were no such illusions, given the sense of a necessary cause. Any apparent respect which he may have held for Rommel did not temper his convictions in the slightest as he firmly believed that 'we were the British, the Allies; we were going to defeat the bastards'.

Many English-speaking South Africans probably found the German apology regarding the Italians mildly amusing. Many of the Afrikaans-speakers had German ancestry, however, and some of them had gone to Germany before the war to study or to work, so there was a distinct chance of a spark of fellow feeling. Shortly after his capture, AJ Cremer noticed a German soldier speaking Afrikaans to a group of South African POWs. The soldier had been a South African student in Germany before the war and 'to survive' he had joined the German Army in 1939 because the war saved him from having to go home.[108]

Dennis Mugglestone also remembered recognising two South Africans by the names of Van der Westhuizen and Le Roux among the German guards. He regarded them as traitors and was offended when they tried to enter into conversation with him.[109] Fred van Alphen Stahl did not identify with Germans in any way, though he did find it interesting that they did not seem to take any note of his own Germanic name. In complete contrast, Wessel Oosthuizen regarded the Germans as a proud nation and shared the German view of Italian soldiers as an unworthy enemy. His admiration for the German nation was reciprocated by young German soldiers who approached Wally and his fellow POWs as they were marched to a temporary camp. Wally remembered how the 'German soldiers, nearly all young boys, came and shook hands with us and called us "Kamerad".'[110]

While POWs had different opinions about the German soldiers they encountered, for some white South Africans, Germany held a greater significance as many of them identified with the Nazi ideology. It was especially among the Afrikaners such as Robey Leibbrandt and

Oswald Pirow that the Nazis saw an opportunity to create disunity in South African as well as within the British Empire. While Leibbrandt's assassination attempt on Smuts ended in his arrest in December 1941, other German agents had contact with Dr JFJ van Rensburg, the commandant-general of the Ossewabrandwag from 1941. All of this contributed towards a worrying 'fifth column' in the country. Pirow, however, had a far greater potential impact on South Africa's war effort as he was the Minister of Defence before Smuts and was accused of having tried to sabotage the internal security of the country.[111] Added to this were the Nazi radio broadcasts in the form of Radio Zeesen, which not only countered Union pro-war propaganda, but also had a substantial listenership among fascist-orientated white South Africans.[112]

The battles of Tobruk and Sidi Rezegh were in relatively close proximity and the thousands of POWs could not all be kept there. To make things worse, the Italians were in no way prepared to accommodate them and temporary holding pens had to suffice. Captured officers were transported to these pens, or POW cages, by car. Most of the Sidi Rezegh POWs had to walk to their camps in what became known as thirst marches. Some of those captured at Tobruk were lucky enough to be transported by truck but many had to endure long hours of walking. For Dick Dickinson, for instance, the march was completed in stages which he recalled as being 'dreadful dark days – of dysentery, very little food …'[113] The shortest distance, 172 kilometres, is from Tobruk to Derna. From Tobruk to Benghazi, where most UDF POWs seem to have been taken, the distance is 461 kilometres.[114]

Newman Robinson was part of a group of about 2 000 who marched for three days across the desert with almost no water or food. On the first day of the march, Germans were in control, but at the day's end they were handed over to Italians. Newman thought that the Germans treated them with 'cold efficiency' and that when the Italians took over, they 'introduced a more human element of slapdash and muddle'.[115] Throughout the march the prisoners were told they would receive water and food if they could continue for one more kilometre. After each kilometre the Italians would say they had to go one more, and so on until men started fainting from dehydration.

When a truck with a water tank did stop, Newman remembered the desperate scuffles and how at last the officers among them organised them into queues so that each man could receive half a biscuit and a cup of water. Newman realised the hopelessness of their situation when he saw that the

> Cape Corps and African sections had been left till last, and before their turn came the water finished. They would have been justified in making a protest. Instead, they turned away sadly with the angry look of beaten animals. I felt like crying with helpless rage.[116]

These thirst marches were very effective in making men aware of the hard reality of their new status as POWs, but it was not only the lack of food and water that they had to endure. It seemed that their captors thrived on humiliating their captives – and in such cases, the perception of Italians as inferior often made the acceptance of POW status harder to deal with. Refusal to accept Italian authority manifested itself in a few cases of blatant defiance of Italian guards. One such example was of Fred van Alphen Stahl who, together with Michael de Lisle, was transported by truck towards the transit camp near Derna. Fred's sense of frustration was exacerbated by the Italians who had the audacity, he recalled, to jeer at the prisoners. He described them as

> funny looking little people with great big helmets and clothes that didn't fit and unshaven … and one, but he was particularly annoying, laughing and jeering at us and waving his rifle, and I said to old Michael de Lisle, he was a bit of a linguist, I said to him what's ice-cream in Italian and he said *gelati* – and I pointed to this chap who was waving his rifle around and I said 'two *gelati* tingelingeling' and he got so mad that he put his rifle up and he was going to fire at us and one of the others came and knocked the rifle and he fired two shots in the air, or one shot in the air – and I just wondered whether my big mouth could have got us into trouble there – could have got somebody shot that day.

On another occasion, Fred used what he thought was reverse psychology against the Italians in an effort to protect prisoners' rights. When a bombardier had his watch taken by a guard, he flattered the Italian officer, saying:

> 'I thought you Italians were all the same, honourable people' and he said: 'So we are, so we are!', and I said: 'Well that man over there has taken my friend's watch.' And then he called this chap over, he got the watch back from him, gave him a slap through the face and handed the watch back.

Michael de Lisle described how POWs could buy two small loaves of bread for a watch and 20 cigarettes for £1. In his memoirs, Michael also pointed out how the Italian doctor at Benghazi spent most of his time debating prices for loot taken from captives by an Italian corporal instead of paying attention to the medical needs of the POWs.[117]

In some other instances, German guards even sided with the South African POWs against the Italians, as in an incident when a UDF man exchanged his watch for a helmet filled with water to revive a friend during a thirst march. A German soldier who witnessed the incident intervened by punching the Italian, replacing the brackish water with clean water from his own water can, and by finally returning the watch to the POW.[118] On another occasion, GH Collet, a soldier in the Middellandse Regiment who was captured at Tobruk, witnessed an Italian guard offering bread in exchange for watches or fountain pens. When a German saw this, he took the bag of loot from the Italian and threw it over the fence, humiliating the Italian to the enjoyment of the POWs. Collet notes in his memoirs that 'this incident epitomized the difference in the German and Italian behaviour to us as prisoners-of-war'.[119] By and large, in the eyes of the POWs, German soldiers exhibited admirable discipline and self-discipline, something that those South Africans with a stiff Calvinist upbringing could probably identify with.

To help them in the huge task of watching over thousands of prisoners, the Italians recruited the local Senussi population to help guard the POW camps. These guards seem to have displayed little mercy or humanity towards the prisoners. None of the available POW accounts reveals any signs of goodwill between the Senussi guards and their prisoners. In his memoirs, LG Tupper of the Kaffrarian Rifles described them as 'a lot of black Senussi bastards guarding us and they would shoot for the slightest provocation. I remember one chap who showed them the "V" for victory sign and was shot.'[120] This description probably reflects the general state of relations between POWs and Italy's local collaborators. For Ike Rosmarin, the Senussi guards at Benghazi were 'raw desert natives' whose behaviour only increased the tension between the captives and captors.[121] According to Jack Mortlock, the Senussi

> endeavoured to make their wishes known by bashing you about with a rifle butt. I believe there were cases of prisoners being shot by these creatures. Furthermore, if they noticed watches, fountain pens etc., these were immediately ripped off. It was indeed a lucky thing for the Senussis that none of the prisoners whom they handled were in the victorious Eighth Army advance in the latter part of 1942.[122]

In a letter following his capture at Sidi Rezegh, Lieutenant-Colonel Purchase's view of the Italians as actually inferior to the POWs becomes clear in his description of how the POWs jeered at the Italian guards when Allied artillery started firing at them: 'we stood and laughed at them. We were their prisoners, but we ordered them out of our shell slits, *and they obeyed*. They're funny.'[123] AJ Cremer's memoirs reveal a similar encounter. While being transported on a truck, the POWs became so irritated with their young guard who insisted on singing and whistling while firing shots at random targets in the desert, that one of the prisoners grabbed his rifle and threw it into bushes next to the road. The terrified guard banged on the roof to alert the driver but either he was ignored or the driver was too frightened himself to stop the truck. When the POWs arrived at their destination, they disappeared into the already crowded camp and no action was taken against them.[124]

A captive's sketch of the POW camp in Benghazi. COURTESY ANTHONY MORTLOCK

Dog-eat-dog

The capricious conduct of most of the Italian guards meant that they could hardly command respect and were therefore forced to continue using callous and demeaning methods to maintain order among prisoners. For POWs, this only served to highlight the difference between their German and Italian captors. A classic example of German insistence on respect was observed by Newman Robinson while in a transit camp following his capture at Sidi Rezegh. As a German officer was explaining to the prisoners why they were being handed over to the Italians, a South African POW, lying on the floor, asked the officer, 'Hey, you, what's the news?' Robinson, believing that 'Germans invariably did that sort of thing', was convinced that the German was going to shoot the man. However, the officer explained, tight-lipped, that

> in your army, [...] you do not address officers while you are sprawling on the ground. Now that you are a prisoner you will keep up the tradition of respect and self-respect which your army expects of you. I am nobody in particular, I am not as you English say, a

The reality of the POW camp in Benghazi. COURTESY ANTHONY MORTLOCK

'big shot', but I am an officer, and you will treat me as such.[125]

Many South Africans were deprived of water and food during the first few days in transit camps, and had to kowtow to their captors for the sake of survival. In Derna, the POWs were kept in a graveyard where there was virtually no water or food available. According to AJ Cremer, most of the guards there were Syrian and as the water taps were on the outside of the graveyard, the prisoners were reduced to begging for water. Apparently some of the guards became irritated by constant begging and started shouting insults at the prisoners, something which one of the captives could not stand and returned an insult. A guard reacted by shooting into the crowd, killing one of the prisoners. In response, the POWs stormed the fence and the guard fled. When the Italian officer asked the prisoners to bury the man, they refused as they felt that they had not been responsible for his death.[126]

In the Tobruk camp, POWs also died at the hands of more wilful Italians who seemed quick to take advantage of their position of power. Private Connelly was shot by an Italian commandant who ordered him to move away from the fence. Although Connelly obeyed, the commandant still shot him in the back. On another occasion, also at the Tobruk camp, Private Myles was severely injured when an Italian guard threw a bomb into the camp.[127]

David Brokensha felt pent-up resentment towards coarse guards at Derna where he was kept in crowded army barracks. Eventually, this could be bottled-up no longer. As prisoners were being counted, he and a friend became very impatient towards guards who seemed incapable of counting the captives without making mistakes:

> Fatigue, hunger, bewilderment and general misery all conspired to make me, and a fellow prisoner, careless. [...] each time we were counted, and recounted, a grimy Italian guard clapped his hand on our shoulders as we filed past. [We] watched with impatience, scorn and distaste as the inefficient guard messed up the counting yet again. We also involuntarily flinched away from his grubby paw. Apparently our refined reaction offended him ...[128]

David and his friend were taken to a small office, where an Italian lieutenant 'smelling of perfume and soap' pretentiously displayed his revolver. The guard then slapped both of them across their faces as punishment for their behaviour during the counting process. According to David 'the slaps didn't really hurt, what was hurt was our youthful pride. I was furious – and powerless.'[129]

For many, the blatant disregard of POW rights in medical and other matters increased their dislike of the Italians, but there were exceptions. Uys Krige was struck by the humanity displayed by one of the Italian guards who warned him that it would be harmful to drink too much water after he had gone without it during the long march from Sidi Rezegh to Gazala.[130] Equally, some other POWs also realised that the terrible conditions in the camps in North Africa were a result of the unexpectedly large numbers of prisoners taken and they even seemed to excuse the Italians as a result. Stanley Smollan, for instance, was shocked when he noticed the poor state of the Italians' uniforms, equipment, transport and rations. He was especially horrified when he realised that the Italian soldiers did not have socks, but were given pieces of cloth to wrap around their feet. Smollan emphasised that 'the Italians were a very kindly people ... in Africa it was very bad, things were very bad and I can't blame the Italians because I think they did what they could.' Michael de Lisle expressed similar views in his memoirs, declaring that their Italian captors 'proved inefficient, capricious, and unable to provide us with the necessities of life because they had very little for themselves'.[131]

As it happens, Stanley Smollan, Michael de Lisle and Uys Krige escaped in Italy following Mussolini's capitulation and depended for their survival on the generosity of Italian peasant families who risked their lives by providing food and shelter to escaped POWs for months thereafter.[132]

If the white POWs thought they had a difficult time adjusting to captivity under what they considered an inferior enemy, then experiences of the men in the Non-European Army Services and the coloured servicemen of the Cape Corps were beyond description. The 1929 Geneva Convention stipulated certain conditions regarding the rights of POWs. However, neither the Germans nor the Italians regarded the Convention as having any bearing on the rights of black POWs, as they did not view them as *regular* forces. These men were subjected to harsh treatment from the enemy forces with no regard for their rights of any kind.[133] Furthermore, the Red Cross, which became a lifeline to POWs later in the war, was unable to assist in any way in North Africa.[134]

African and coloured POWs were therefore in the worst possible position and had perhaps to rely on each other more than other POWs did. Black soldiers from different parts of the Commonwealth endured bad treatment from their captors, and several were shot if they were seen to be too much trouble.[135] In his memoirs, Mugglestone recalled how intoxicated black soldiers were shot by German guards while being marched to their POW camp. According to him, the black soldiers 'were too drunk to move any further, and the Jerries could not be worried. This was the result of the liquor they stole from Battalion HQ the previous night.'[136]

In the Tobruk camp, black South African POWs were forced 'under

IN ENEMY HANDS

The omnipresent cloud of smoke that to many signalled the fall of Tobruk on 21 June 1942.
COURTESY ANTHONY MORTLOCK

threat of death' to do war work, which was contrary to the Geneva Convention.[137] Their food was also totally inadequate as they were only given one packet of British Army biscuits per day and water rations were kept to a minimum.[138] Shortly after the fall of Tobruk, the RAF and the US Air Force carried out several air raids on the harbour. During these attacks, black POWs were not able to take cover as they were in wire 'cages'. While their captors sought out protection against the bombing, many black POWs took the opportunity to escape. In one such case, Privates Hermanus Chaka and Sprinkaan Masamudi broke out of Tobruk. Following a month in the desert with very little food and water, the two re-joined the UDF lines.[139]

It would seem that in many cases, black servicemen could also not rely on sympathy or assistance from fellow South Africans, as illustrated by AJ Cremer, who saw a black man shooting at the German Stuka dive-bombers, using a small Italian gun, in the chaos during the fall of Tobruk. AJ made no effort to help him or to take him to the headquarters, towards which he was heading. The black soldier was left in the desert, a solitary figure shooting up at the dive bombers, while AJ 'could only laugh' at the absurdity of the situation.[140]

At another level, while many white POWs expressed either paternalistic or blatantly racist views towards other races, genuinely decent and respectful relationships did exist, such as that between a medical officer, Harry Klein, and his batman, Nelson Koza, who had met before the war. The bureaucratic regulations of the day prevented these two men from working as equals, regardless of the status of their personal friendship. Harry even gave Nelson a Banda rifle which they found after an ambush in East Africa. Nelson cleaned the gun and made it usable again, but when he used it against the enemy, he was reproached for having secretly collected ammunition. Some time before the Battle of Sidi Rezegh, Harry was sent back to the Union and Nelson was left to fend for himself. He was captured along with 1 655 others from the members of the Native Military Corps at Sidi Rezegh in November 1941.[141] Another example of a medical officer and his batman was that of Ben Hermer, a medical officer with the 17th Field Ambulance, and his batman July Monaremi, who supported him throughout the battles in North Africa. When the two were captured at Tobruk, they were split into separate POW camps, with Ben describing their last conversation as a 'bitter goodbye. There were tears in July's eyes and in mine too ... my heart was heavy as I knew I would never see him again and I didn't.'[142]

Elsewhere, some black soldiers showed surprising loyalty towards their white fellow soldiers and country despite the discriminatory treatment they received. One such example was Job Maseko, who was captured at Tobruk and decided to sabotage the enemy 'because of our ill-treatment by the enemy, especially the Italians, and because I felt it a duty in this way to assist my own people'.[143]

Job was one of the soldiers who were off-loading military equipment in Tobruk harbour and as he had experience of working with explosives, he put it to use in assembling a bomb using jerry cans, straw and petrol. As he was the last to leave the hold of the ship, two of his friends distracted the guard and Job lit a fuse. Later that evening he saw smoke rising from the harbour as the vessel burned and sank. The next day, the POWs were questioned about smoking while on board ship, to which all answered that cigarettes were not included in their rations, an answer which their captors could not dispute.[144]

In another act of blatant defiance, Job got hold of a radio, which he set up in a cellar containing an unexploded bomb. He knew that the presence of the bomb would prevent the guards from finding the radio and thus was able to listen freely to broadcasts about the progress of the war. Thanks to this radio, Tobruk's POWs were able to distinguish between Axis propaganda and the truth – the Eighth Army had not been driven out of North Africa. Job Maseko, Hermanus Chaka and Sprinkaan Masamudi all received the Military Medal.[145]

The fact that African and coloured troops were being used to do war work on the docks also held an advantage as they occasionally had the opportunity to steal food, something white prisoners in camps could not do. Hunger seemed to help white POWs forget their ideas about race and as black soldiers returned from their work with stolen food, the white POWs begged shamelessly for whatever the black POWs were willing to part with. Michael de Lisle recalled how these prisoners would return from the harbour with haversacks filled with maize and other foodstuffs, and 'the unfortunate consequence was that hungry English and even S. Africans would lay siege to their tents at night to beg the crumbs of their charity'.[146]

The prisoners were ill-prepared for captivity, because although they were issued during training with instructions should they become prisoners of war, this guidance was wholly inadequate to prepare anyone for what to expect, especially in the desert of North Africa. Furthermore, preparatory instructions were only issued to the European ranks of the UDF. The information leaflet was probably largely ignored: UDF volunteers never considered that they would become POWs and had a flippant attitude regarding the instructions; in any case, the leaflet was vague and non-specific. Its only clear instruction was that soldiers were responsible to provide solely their name, rank and service number. Beyond this, the document gave no practical guidelines regarding living conditions and acceptable treatment by captors as it focused mainly on methods that the enemy may use to gather information from POWs. Soldiers were warned not to discuss things such as morale, arms and equipment, politics, food and liquor supplies. They were also warned that the enemy might use kind treatment, alcohol and bogus prisoners to gain military information from them.[147]

Although no evidence could be found of prisoners acting as enemy informers in North Africa, Germany did recruit a number of prisoners in an effort to influence POWs regarding the German cause, especially towards the end of the war. A number of treason cases were also instituted against South Africans following the war. However, the conditions in North Africa were probably too chaotic and the high number of prisoners taken by the Afrika Korps probably hindered Nazi indoctrination efforts this early on in the war. The message was more one of hardship and survival. For instance, Rommel was reported to have warned POWs captured following the Battle of Sidi Rezegh that they 'had a long way to go, and to be prepared for privation'.[148]

Survival was the priority in North Africa and disagreements and discrimination among the men did not last long when they were faced with the severe lack of food and clean water in what most of them referred to as the 'cages'. Most camps were simply fenced enclosures with tents as accommodation, but by mid-1942 some POWs were lucky enough to sleep in converted barracks which were equipped with electricity.[149]

POWs became acutely aware of what was needed to survive and without fail food in any form became immensely important. On average the men lost between 20 and 30 kilograms, and many recalled that the lack of female company was vastly overshadowed by hunger pains. Wally Wolhuter remembered that 'sex is way down on the list [of basic needs] and seldom discussed by hungry men'.[150]

Because there were so many prisoners, the distribution of food was a long process and after queuing for hours, the POWs were always disappointed when they received their rations. In Derna, hard biscuits were issued: when the Reverend Major Patrick J Nolan was unable to bite into his biscuit, he asked an Italian guard to break it with his bayonet. The guard instructed Nolan to soak the biscuit in water – but the water supply had run out.[151] At times POWs also received tins of bully beef to be shared between two or three of them.[152] The chronic shortage of food compelled prisoners to look for it elsewhere and on one occasion Collet was lucky and desperate enough to catch and eat a mole.[153] In another case, an unfortunate desert rat became the main ingredient in a 'magnificent stew'.[154] The fact that a POW was able to catch this desert rat, or jerboa, is an indication of how desperate the man must have been to find food. Jerboas are not only relatively small, they can also jump several feet at a time. As a result of its agility and speed, the jerboa came to be the mascot for the British Seventh Armoured Division, also known as the Desert Rats.[155]

Dick Dickinson's diary account of the time in North Africa probably gives the most accurate description of the food which POWs received from the Italians:

> Our daily ration is a tin of bully-beef and a small loaf of bread, the size of a large hot-cross bun, per man. The bully-beef is 300 grams. About every third day we are given a hot meal which is a pint and a half of stew, but which is mostly rice. When we get this meal, our bully is cut to half a tin.[156]

David Brokensha's bad feelings towards the Italians made him defiant and stubborn. When he was offered water by the guard who had slapped him earlier, he refused it, believing his treatment was the result of animosity towards South Africans in general. At this early point in his captivity, David had not yet realised that a crucial rule of captivity was sharing, and that rejecting the water would harm the others in his group. It was Paul, his older brother, who alerted him to this fact and, his youthful pride protesting, David then grudgingly accepted water from the guard and shared it among the others.[157]

Although pilfering what was available was accepted and even celebrated, strict codes of morality governed conduct among POWs themselves. Prisoners caught stealing from within their own ranks were severely punished by fellow POWs, as was the case with two British POWs who stole food in the Benghazi camp. They were chained to a gate for 24 hours without food or water.[158]

Food was not the only scarce commodity. Clothing was in short supply because most men had had very little time to gather their belongings when they were captured. Michael de Lisle remembered that the disappearance of boots in the Benghazi camp caused great unhappiness among the POWs. The guilty man, described as 'weak [and] lousier than most', was soon identified and when he was seen selling stolen boots to Italian guards, he and the Italians were confronted. Unfortunately for the culprit, it was a week before the Italian camp commander transferred him to the guard-tent.[159] In a contrasting incident, Stanley Smollan exchanged enough cigarettes to acquire a coat, which he then gave to David Brokensha who was struggling to cope with the colder nights when the season started to change. David recalled that when Stanley handed him the coat, he had to 'try hard not to weep, it was one of the most welcome presents I have ever had, and one of the most disinterested gestures I have known, a pure act of love'.[160] Thus POWs established codes of conduct and friendships that would last throughout their imprisonment.

Trust and sharing went hand in hand because food was so scarce that each morsel became extremely important. Fred van Alphen Stahl and Michael de Lisle were part of a group of four who supported each other during their stay in Benghazi and Derna. In his memoirs, Michael pointed out that during his days in the army he was never able to establish particularly close friendships, but that the 'need for mutual support' in POW camps made such close groups a necessity.[161]

Indeed, the experience of imprisonment could come to shape consciousness of what army life meant for individuals. For many, the Army may have become a place where firm friendships were formed, but not all men experienced that sense of camaraderie. For Dick, the Army was a place where, although he learnt to appreciate the value of 'good and simple things', he became embittered, especially towards those in positions of authority. His experiences led him to believe that the Army was a 'dictatorship' because an 'NCO should lead and set an example, not drive and give orders all day'.[162]

When strong-minded men such as these were taken prisoner, they saw their officers in a new light. Although men like General Klopper and De Villiers Graaff were separated from the masses of prisoners, other men of rank were not afforded superior treatment. Most of the rank and file were struck by the fact that officers and men suddenly became equal, as the Italians only separated them when they reached permanent camps. The transit camps therefore forced men of all ranks to live together and to undergo the same privations. For some on the battlefield it may have been a situation of 'every man for himself', but in the camp it became 'dog-eat-dog', regardless of rank, as they struggled to stay alive.[163] Rosmarin was amazed at how quickly 'Army Apartheid' evaporated when he saw his commanding officer at the transit camp in Tobruk 'too dispirited even to shoo away a mangy desert dog which was lifting his leg on his mackintosh'.[164]

Along with hunger and thirst came lice and dysentery. Toilet facilities were hopelessly inadequate – the Benghazi camp, for instance, only had one toilet – and there were more than 4 000 prisoners in the camp. To solve the dilemma, the men had to think creatively. A trench about four metres long was dug and a box with holes was placed over the trench. Although toilet paper was non-existent, POWs sometimes found paper in which an occasional lemon issue was wrapped, but this was a luxury reserved for POWs suffering from dysentery. At some camps POWs were not allowed to go to the toilets at night, and they had to use small tins that were placed outside the barracks. With dysentery, these tins were obviously entirely useless.[165]

But it was not all doom and gloom. As the initial shock of captivity started to fade, so a sense of humour appeared and although there was nothing funny about their situation, laughing became an important coping mechanism. Eric Hurst, a British POW, started *The Benghazi Forum*, a camp wall newspaper that endeavoured to lift everyone's spirits.[166] In the first edition of 4 November 1942, the editor recorded that 'there has been produced from chaos, law and order, efficient food and water supply; regular concerts with original material ... Arts and Crafts Exhibition; [and] a well organised Farmers' Association ...'[167] For the most part, the newspaper focused on organisational aspects of the camps, biographies of inmates and reports of concerts or sporting events. Michael de Lisle remembered that Bill Sykes, who worked for the *Cape Times* before the war, contributed numerous illustrations of British camp officials, and that this section in the *Forum* quickly became known as the 'Rogues Gallery'.[168]

The handwritten sheets were pinned up on the wire fences for POWs to read. Eric had the help of a few fellow POWs who contributed stories and illustrations. One such contributor was Ben Hermer, who also happened to be a talented artist. Ben was very popular among the Italian guards, who provided him with photographs of their girlfriends. Ben reproduced the girls' faces, but as for the rest, sensuous naked bodies resulted from his artistic licence. The grateful guards in turn provided Ben with jam, a welcome treat, and with paper and pencils which were used to produce *The Benghazi Forum*.[169]

I walked down the track I found at my feet

The majority of POWs spent about five months in Benghazi, but five months is a long time to live on rumour, hard biscuits and bully beef. A number of men ignored rumours of rescue and decided to escape and to take their chances in the desert instead. The lack of food and water, as well as uncertainties regarding the loyalties of the local population, deterred many, as did many failed escapes. Their Italian guards, always eager to demonstrate their position of power over the prisoners, used excessive force when dealing with escape attempts, as was the case with one POW who was shot at close range as he tried to cut through the wire fence. The guard left the dead prisoner hanging on the fence as a warning to others.[170]

Still, there were other strategies to be exploited. The Italians' lack of proper clothing, for example, afforded two South Africans, Sergeant Dawie van der Merwe and Gunner Louw, an opportunity to cut and run for it. These cunning accomplices offered to exchange a pair of boots for cigarettes and first threw one boot over the fence, received their cigarettes, then threw the second boot in between the multiple fences. This distracted the guards, who ran into the fenced enclosure to retrieve the boot, while at the same time Louw and Van der Merwe made their escape. Following a few days in the desert, however, the two were apparently betrayed by a Senussi tribesman and they found themselves back in camp, in shackles as punishment for escaping.[171]

Other attempts, however, were more successful. Lieutenant LH Bailie and Sergeant 'Toys' Norton of the Kaffrarian Rifles had escaped capture with some others during the battle at Tobruk, and a few days later were discovered by two men of the Second Battalion, Transvaal Scottish, who had escaped from the POW camp at Tobruk. The escapees were lucky as they had used up their food and water the previous day and might well have died had they not come across Bailie and Norton. Their good fortune continued when they met sympathetic Senussi travellers who gave them food and water and information about the whereabouts of the Eighth Army. Bailie and his group managed to reach the position of a New Zealand battalion at Ruweisat Ridge. Bailie's experience of the generosity of the Senussi prompted him to become quite philosophical when he told his story to the East London *Daily Dispatch* some time later:

> the friendship and charity extended to us by these four primitive souls was touching, and presented an object lesson which if studied and carried into effect by the so-called 'advanced' and civilized races of this world, would do much to put an end to avarice.[172]

Another successful escape was from a temporary camp at Mersa Matruh. Reuben Maloyi was captured with the 15 Field Ambulance at Tobruk and taken to various camps where he and other African soldiers were instructed to unload ammunition while the white prisoners were expected to provide medical care to soldiers. When the Allies bombed Mersa Matruh, the prisoners were moved to a camp surrounded by a minefield on its outskirts. Reuben and a friend, Shaw, escaped through a weak point in the fence, leaving behind a cautious fellow countryman as they believed the man's fear of escaping would delay their progress. After successfully negotiating the minefield, Maloyi and his friend parted ways because they wanted to follow different routes. Reuben was assisted by an Arab who provided him with water and directions to the Allied forces at El Alamein. On his way, he was confronted on two occasions by enemy forces, but in both cases managed to avoid capture. Following 17 nights in the desert living on Italian biscuits and water found in abandoned vehicles, Reuben eventually reached Allied forces in Alexandria.[173]

In the case of Ben Hermer, the doctor and sketch artist, escape and braving the desert was motivated by love as well as a desire for liberty. Following his capture at Tobruk, he found himself in one of the infamous Benghazi camps. At first, Ben tried to settle into camp life by petitioning the camp commander to provide better facilities in order to improve hygiene, but as the relationship between him and the commander deteriorated, he started to become involved in other camp activities, primarily using his medical knowledge to ease prisoners' suffering. As a devout Jew, he also organised religious services on Rosh Hashanah and Yom Kippur.

When the Italians started transporting POWs to Italy, Eric Hurst, founder of *The Benghazi Forum*, prepared a copy of its various editions for Ben as a memento of the Benghazi camp. Ben's newspaper colleagues left for Italy a day before he himself was due to leave, but he was desperate to remain in Africa as he believed that it would give him a better chance of getting back to South Africa. Once liberated, Ben felt he would be in a better position to find his fiancée, Olda Mehr, who had been held back somewhere in Germany when she visited family there shortly before the war started.

While he was eating bread in the officer's mess the evening before he was to be shipped to Italy, Ben's anxiety got the better of him and he asked to see the camp commander, saying that one of the POWs had contracted typhoid. The commander, although impatient with Ben, was obliged to investigate as a typhoid outbreak would be disastrous. As the alarmed Italians went looking for the non-existent patient, Hermer simply slipped out of the camp and 'walked down the track I found at my feet'.[174] His fortunes, like those of other POW escapees, depended on the goodwill of the local population. In his case, Ben spent several days with an accommodating Senussi family, recovering from dysentery and waiting for news of Allied advances. Eventually, news reached him that the area once again belonged to the Allies and he went to the Benghazi road once he had seen Allied vehicles travelling along it in both directions. Astonishingly, John Baird, a friend of his family, recognised him as he was passing and took him to Tmimi, from where he flew to Cairo. There, by another extraordinary coincidence, he came across Olda, who shortly before had fled Nazi Germany with her mother.[175] It was only in March 1943 that Ben's former POW mates heard about his successful escape when the *Tuturano Times* reported in a brief paragraph: 'It is believed Capt Hermer visited Cairo on his way to South Africa.'[176]

CHAPTER THREE

TREK OXEN IN AUGUST

As Ben Hermer enjoyed his newfound freedom and celebrated his reunion with Olda Mehr, thousands of POWs in the cages of North Africa were picking lice from their clothing and growing weaker as dysentery took its toll. Their misery, however, did not prevent them from remaining hopeful. Searching out morsels of truth from the propaganda-laden stories that infiltrated the camps came to occupy the minds of many men at this time.

The Allied forces were continuously bombing Benghazi harbour as it was an important supply line for the Axis forces in the desert.[1] While this may have worsened the situation for the POWs with regard to food supplies, it also kept their spirits up as they waited to be liberated. In reality, the Axis forces were preparing for a complete conquest of the Eighth Army and as the POWs were marching west towards Benghazi, Rommel's forces were making quick progress towards Egypt, taking Sollum and Mersa Matruh on their way to El Alamein.[2] Rumours in the camp flew almost as fast as the bombs in the harbour and in most cases only served to sow confusion. As LG Tupper recalled:

> one day we heard rumours that Alexandria was taken. The wogs were very excited and told us that they would soon be on holiday in that city. We were very down in the dumps but still had faith in that our bombers were still coming to bomb the harbour.[3]

Michael de Lisle, in Benghazi, recalled only one incident when the rumours were not false:

> every other day there'd be a story of an Arab trader passing a message through over the fence with a loaf of bread, I think the enemy fostered these rumours to try and break our morale, raise our hopes and then dash them.

As the toilet facilities afforded no privacy and were in constant use due to the dysentery epidemic, they became centres of information and rumour. Rumours known as 'latrinograms' travelled from one end of a toilet trench to the other.[4] It was impossible for POWs to determine their veracity, but Jack Mortlock recalled that they 'were generally reputed to have come from reliable sources from outside the camp, and that it would only be a matter of days before we would be released'.[5]

When the Italians started to transport POWs from Benghazi to Italy many tried to delay their departure, hoping to be liberated before they found themselves in Europe.[6] According to Michael de Lisle, he was transported to Italy in October 1942, only four days before the Allies reached Benghazi. Tupper too stated that he narrowly missed being liberated as 'on the 12th November we embarked for Italy ... little did we realize how close our troops were because they reached Benghazi on the 20th November'.[7] Although De Lisle and Tupper left Benghazi at different times, their belief that they were transported just as the Allies were advancing on Benghazi indicates their desperate optimism during the first phase of their confinement. The same could be true for HL Wood, who believed he missed being liberated by five days when he was transported to Tripoli, and again narrowly missed the Allies when he was sent from Tripoli to Italy two weeks later.[8]

While the POWs were optimistically waiting for liberation, the Allied forces in North Africa were concentrating on strengthening the morale of the Eighth Army and preparing for the El Alamein battles which took place between 23 October and 5 November 1942.[9] The POWs in Benghazi and other temporary camps in North Africa were certainly not a priority. However, the black POWs who were still doing war work in Tobruk at that time were the fortunate ones for whom the rumour became true: when Tobruk was recaptured in November 1943, approximately 1 200 Allied POWs were liberated.[10]

A Mediterranean cruise

Cyril Crompton had only spent two weeks in the Benghazi camp when the POWs were informed that 2 000 of them were to be transported to Italy. As the men approached the harbour they noticed the severe damage caused by Allied bombing. To get to the ship that would take them away from Africa, they had to climb over another that had partially sunk. Clearly the Mediterranean crossing would be hazardous, and when Cyril asked a German officer about protection, he was told that Stuka dive bombers would protect them from air attacks, but that there was nothing they could do about torpedoes. Cyril knew that the safest place would be in the middle of the ship and by chance that is exactly where he found himself as they were closed up in the holds.[11] Many chose to deal with constant fear in the cavernous darkness by trusting in luck: as Dick Dickinson declared in his diary, 'we make up our minds that this attack won't happen'.[12] A more pessimistic Wessel Oosthuizen, however, morbidly compared the hold of the ship to a coffin.

Most prisoners captured at Sidi Rezegh were transported to Italy in December 1941, usually from Benghazi to either Patras in Greece or Brindisi on the Italian east coast. The following year, the Italians started to move the Tobruk POWs, mostly from Benghazi to Tripoli and from there either to Naples or to Palermo. The majority were transported by cargo boat, but officers and those POWs who were considered valuable for negotiating reasons arrived in Italy either by aeroplane or by submarine.[13] For men of other ranks, the journey across the Mediterranean was nightmarish.

Cyril did not remember receiving any food before or during the journey, and there was very little water available. A 40-gallon drum cut in half served as a toilet, but most men with dysentery could not reach this drum in time as they struggled on weak legs through the pitch

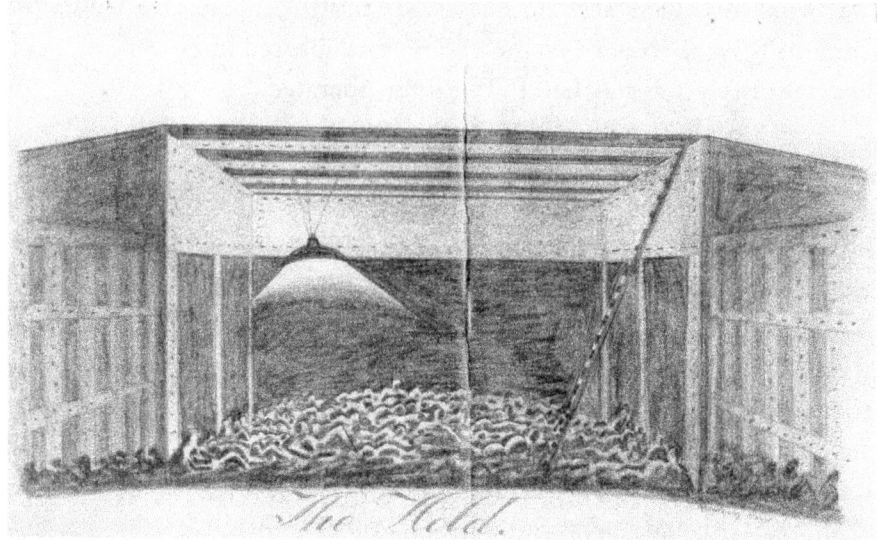

The hold of the *Rosalina Pilo* was packed with POWs on the trip from Benghazi to Tripoli.
COURTESY ANTHONY MORTLOCK

darkness of the hold.[14] Cargo spaces were packed with men, and movement was severely limited. Some were allowed to go on deck to use the toilet facilities there, but most dysentery cases were too weak to climb the ropes or rope ladders that were lowered into the hold. In any event, toilets on deck were not necessarily much better, as in some examples they were nothing more than a bucket system requiring men to balance on a pole suspended over the container.[15] At night, hatches over the holds were closed, which resulted in at least one death as a result of suffocation on the *Rosalina Pilo*, a ship that transported POWs from Benghazi to Tripoli in August 1942.[16]

As Ike Rosmarin recalled, tins of horse meat and dog biscuits were dropped through hatch openings and the POWs directly below the hatches were responsible for the distribution of food.[17] On the *Rosalina Pilo*, which transported Dennis Mugglestone, food was lowered into the cargo holds by rope.[18] This was a situation that could easily have led to fighting among prisoners, when one considers how they fought for food and water while on the thirst marches in the desert. Perhaps an equality of misery in acutely cramped conditions imposed its own form of restraint or self-discipline. On the other hand, it is possible that they were just too weak and despondent to put up a fight.

Michael de Lisle travelled to Italy in October 1942 on a ship that brought Christmas parcels to Italian soldiers. The prisoners boarded the ship at Benghazi and then went to Tripoli where these treats were to be delivered. However, once the POWs discovered the food, which included sugar and sweets, they wasted no time in helping themselves to it. By the time the vessel arrived in Tripoli, the POWs were 'drunk on sugar', and had tied their trouser legs at the ankles and filled them up with sweets. When the Italians discovered this, they 'went wild', Michael recalled; 'tried to search us and take away the food we'd discovered. Shooting left and right and threatening us with all sorts of terrible tortures.'

During the journey to Palermo, Michael's ship experienced a near-miss when a British submarine torpedoed the Italian destroyer escort, resulting in overloading of the POW ship with survivors from the sunken warship. As the POWs were permitted short periods on deck, Michael, an anti-aircraft gunner, used the unexpected opportunity to compare notes with German anti-aircraft gunners who were also aboard.

Limited individual freedom to move around on deck was allowed, depending on the mood of the guards. Thus, David Brokensha and his friends were permitted to go on deck during daylight hours and to use the 'over the side privy', although this was stopped when the ship was attacked by RAF aircraft, injuring some Italians as the POWs cheered in support of the attackers.[19] While the stoical David sarcastically referred to this crossing in his memoirs as a 'Mediterranean cruise', his brother, Paul, suffered what was probably the lowest spiritual point of his POW experience, exclaiming, 'God? There is no God.' Spirituality certainly seemed to ease the trip for some POWs, as was the case with the Sikh men 'who stayed in a corner, prayed, talked quietly, and remained imperturbable while ignoring the incredible squalor and filth all around them'.[20]

A sudden sickening sensation

> Early in the afternoon we were roused from our listlessness by a sudden sickening sensation – the ship seemed to be rising right out of the water, as if some giant hand had picked her up. This was followed immediately by a horrible sound of crashing and rending, and at first we thought we had been bombed.[21]

In December 1941 the *San Sebastian*[22] was torpedoed by the submarine HMS *Porpoise*. Between 350 and 450 men died as a result of this attack.[23] Private Vivian Rees-Bevan of the Regiment Botha was on the ship, as were Bernard Schwikkard, Newman Robinson, Cyril Crompton and Aussie Hammond, along with between 2 000 and 2 500 others who were being transported to Italy.[24] Although most POWs did not know what had hit them, their instincts told them to get out of the holds of the ship. In the hold where Vivian was, they could not reach the hatch and panic broke out. It was not until someone dropped a rope down to them that they were able to climb out one by one.

In a statement made after the war, Private Whittaker insisted that the ship's captain and most of the officers used the lifeboats to save themselves while many of the POWs were being sucked underwater by the ship's propellers as they tried to swim to shore. This view was shared by Bernard Schwikkard, and it is also corroborated by recent research.[25] Yet the pandemonium following the blast seemed to have distorted historical evidence because in contrast to Whittaker and Bernard Schwikkard, Aussie Hammond's memoirs have the ship's crew under the command of a German captain, who 'from the moment of disaster had kept to his post, and did his best to inspire the crew to remain on board'.[26] Bernard believed that a German captain took control of the situation when the Italian crew had abandoned their posts, ordering the men to remain calm as he steered the ship towards the shoreline. Newman Robinson, on the other hand, stipulated in his memoirs that German engineers took control of the situation, while Whittaker stated that a South African, Sergeant Tillard of the 1st South African Irish, took over once the captain and his officers had gone.[27] In all likelihood, there would have been different persons seizing control in different areas of the ship, as some tried to restore order while others tried merely to save themselves.

Uppermost in all POWs' minds was survival, but the way they approached the challenge differed vastly. Most men wanted to get off the ship as soon as possible, and Newman Robinson saw a number of POWs jumping overboard in an attempt to reach what they thought was the safety of the nearby Italian destroyers. The Italian crews apparently ignored these desperate men.[28] In an effort to destroy the submarine, the destroyers were dropping depth charges, and many POWs were killed by these explosions. Cyril Crompton, however, viewed the depth charging as a life-saving eventuality, as it deterred the British attacker from closing in again with another torpedo.[29]

Being a medical orderly, Newman Robinson's sense of responsibility compelled him to help the many injured men and he

> asked everyone whose face registered the slightest gleam of intelligence to help me carry the patients into the cabins and saloon [...] We parked the shock and exposure cases on the platforms of the engine room, which was ideal for them, and made the wounded as comfortable as possible [...] I then went on a marauding expedition [for] blankets, coats and curtains for cover, and towels and pillowslips for bandages, and got to work splinting broken limbs. The work was hurried and shockingly bad; I probably did more harm than good. But it was a relief to be doing something.[30]

In an effort to dispel fears about the ship sinking, Newman invented a story that the Italians had radioed for a hospital ship and that it was on its way to collect them.[31]

For those Italian guards who did not manage to escape along with their captain, the situation quickly became very frightening. Vivian Rees-Bevan's most persistent memory of the incident was of the Italians 'running all over the place, shouting and cursing'. For some POWs this was an ideal opportunity to take revenge for the harsh treatment they had received in North Africa, and a number of guards were thrown overboard by prisoners, 'without any qualms at all'.[32] Even so, in the midst of mounting chaos and panic, Italian guards appeared to find it difficult to break their routine habit of demanding an exchange of goods for services. Whittaker, for instance, was forced to trade a pair of riding gloves for a lifebelt from one of the remaining guards who had hidden the lifebelts away.[33]

All the while, those who had taken over control of the ship were making frantic efforts to save it from sinking. As the Greek coast was not very far away, the ship was steered towards it. Many POWs started jumping overboard and were killed as they were dashed against the rocks.[34] Witnessing this mayhem, Cyril also saw how many of those who were in the water at that time were killed by the ship's churning propellers.[35] However, the close proximity to the shoreline offered a chance of escape and an unidentified South African POW swam to shore with a rope still attached to the ship, allowing many others to reach safety by using the ropes. Bernard Schwikkard knew the man as Bernie Friedlander, who:

> took a long rope from the deck, and bravely lowered himself into the sea. He was able to attach the rope onto some rocks below, and this enabled the rest of us to slide down the rope, wait for an incoming wave, drop in front of it, and get carried to the shore by the wave. I got ashore in this way …[36]

The fact that Friedlander was recommended after the war for a George Medal with the support of a German officer may also provide some verification of Bernard and Newman's claims that a German officer or engineer had taken control when the Italian crew abandoned their ship.[37] That aside, it would also seem that Friedlander was not the only POW who swam to shore in an effort to secure a system of ropes with which to save others. Cyril Crompton describes how he, being a strong swimmer as a result of his childhood river swimming experience in Natal, volunteered for the job. Securing his rope to a rock, it 'became part of a network of other ropes down which the men could climb and swing ashore'.[38]

In the meantime, a wonderful discovery had been made by those who had not yet jumped overboard. The galley was loaded with edible luxuries and once this news spread, men rushed there to wolf down as much food and drink as possible. Aussie Hammond, who had been asked by the medical orderlies to find brandy for the injured men, came upon 'several nonchalant types frying a large supply of sausages and eggs':

> Innumerable little rolls of bread had been left behind in the ovens. These were now baked to perfection. 'Climb in Aussie!' one of my fellow prisoners shouted, waving a sausage at me and trying to stuff a bread roll into his mouth at the same time. 'If it's gonna be our last meal it'll be a darn' good one!'[39]

Aussie took time to deliver brandy to the medical orderlies first before he 'dashed back to join the feast in the galley'. Later he saw POWs appearing on deck in their newly looted Italian clothing.[40]

Even now, when the drenched POWs reached the shore, Italian guards searched them and confiscated personal effects. The loss of Bernard's pocket watch, a gift from his mother, embittered him towards the Italians. When those still on the ship saw what was happening to the survivors on shore, they decided to remain aboard, perhaps hoping somehow to avoid recapture and extend their brief period of freedom. Bernard's brother was one of those who remained behind, choosing the food and drink in the galley over the Italian looting on the beach. However, in time all the POWs were removed from the ship and were forced to join the ranks of the drenched on land.

The next day, an Italian hospital ship arrived and started to remove the wounded.[41] Newman Robinson was still on board, and remained with the wounded until they were all removed and taken to the Military Hospital at Caserta in Naples, where by common consensus they received excellent treatment.[42]

The ship was torpedoed near Greece and the POWs now found themselves at Cape Methoni, in weather considerably colder than in North Africa. Most men were still dressed in their desert uniforms of shorts and short-sleeved shirts. Some of those who had raided the galley for food had also found blankets, which they brought ashore with them. The shared severity of common experiences, now worsened by cold, had an unexpected social consequence as it brought POWs together across the customary racial boundaries. Bernard Schwikkard recalled that there was 'a coloured from Cape Town who had a blanket, so we smooched up to him, and said look, come on man, let us share, and he was very kind, he agreed, but provided that he had the middle, and so four of us had a blanket …'

Others had got rid of their clothes while still on the ship as they prepared to swim ashore, leaving them with only the bare minimum.[43] In Vivian Rees-Bevan's case, the ship's oil which covered him following his swim to shore is what he believed saved him from becoming very ill.[44] From the shoreline, the POWs were taken to a barn near a submarine base, and they were then marched to Pylos Castle where they were kept in its dungeons. The next destinations were Kalamata and then Akhaia, where they were put into a wire enclosure, similar to the transit camps in North Africa.[45]

The entire episode left Newman Robinson with a changed perspective on the idea of war and its futility. In witnessing the chaos and horror on the ship, he did not distinguish between friend and enemy, but thought

> bitterly of the smug announcement which would report this and a thousand incidents like it: 'one of our submarines torpedoed an enemy merchantman off the coast of … When last seen she appeared to be sinking by the bows.' If people could see what it was like they would never have applauded such news. If they knew what it was really like, I thought, they would say nothing on earth justified the torpedoing of ships at sea.[46]

As the POWs were marched to their varying destinations, local Greeks lined the streets attempting to hand food, wine or cigarettes to the prisoners. Vivian encountered two Greek women who tried to give him currants and raisins, but this was stopped when the Italian guards shot at the women.[47] In other instances, the Italians kept the locals away from the prisoners with bayonets and rifle butts.[48] When Newman Robinson saw Italian guards throwing stones at a Greek boy who was trying to hand cigarettes to the POWs, he lost all respect for what he sarcastically referred to as the 'Second Roman Empire'. Yet, in a simultaneous reflection he seemed also to lay some blame at the feet of the Germans for leaving the policing of occupied Greece to Italian forces.[49]

At Akhaia the POWs were given small blankets, but conditions in the camp were so unhygienic that it soon became known among prisoners as 'Dysentery Acre'.[50] When they were moved to warehouses near the Patras harbour, a severe lice plague forced them all to spend their days 'like monkeys catching fleas'.[51] A 45-gallon drum served as a toilet in each warehouse that housed approximately 300 men. The sheds were so crowded that the men had to take turns to fetch their food when it arrived, as the floor space was too small to occupy all of them simultaneously.[52]

By February 1942 the last of the shipwrecked POWs had been taken to Italy where they joined the others who had arrived from North Africa.

One for the record books

Towards the end of 1942, another ship with South African POWs on board arrived at Patras harbour. Fred Geldenhuis was one of the prisoner passengers and he assumed that the ship was diverted from its original route towards Italy to avoid submarines.[53] Once they had disembarked, the POWs found themselves in an improvised and far from secure prison camp in the grounds of a castle. The boundary wall was six feet high – Fred was taller. The prisoners were given biscuits and watery soup, and made to sit in the rain. Fred was fed up, and

> by midnight I felt I had had enough so I looked at the guards, they were all sitting under their ground sheets, probably half asleep. In the darkness I managed to climb over the wall which was easy and made for the bush.[54]

Thanks to the assistance of a sympathetic Greek family whose daughter could speak English, Fred enjoyed a good meal on the first night of his escape. The next day, he left the town and managed to live under cover in Greece for two to three months with the support of a helpful local population and a basic knowledge of the language. Becoming over-confident in his linguistic ability, however, led to him being detected and recaptured in Athens, from where he was despatched to join the rest of the South African POWs in Italy. Fred's reputation as a determined escapee seemed to have preceded him: he had been in Italy for less than a week when he was approached by a group of Royal Marines, asking him to join them in their plans to escape.

Fred Geldenhuis and the Marines planned to escape by cutting through the camp fences and stealing a boat with which they were going to sail to Greece. Once there, Fred knew that the Greek resistance fighters would be able to help them reach Cairo. Fred believed that 'it was a well-planned escape, if it did come off it would have been one for the record books'.[55] However, most of their group was captured while still within the perimeter of the camp, while Fred and a Royal Marines officer, Captain Nixon-Eckersol, were apprehended just as they reached the harbour.

As punishment, Fred was placed in solitary confinement for 12 days. This was followed by a comical interview with the camp commander who, 'like a father, point[ed] out the dangers of escaping and [I] had to promise him that I would not escape again'.[56] Years later Fred still thought of the Italian commander as 'alright'.

Throughout the war, POWs from various other Commonwealth countries were regularly on the run in Greece, often aided by the local underground resistance. They either sought to exist in the guise of Greek civilians or else tried to make their way out to re-join Allied forces in North Africa or in Turkey.[57]

Of Lice and Men[58]

Following their dreadful experiences in Libya and on the cargo ships, the hopes for improved conditions were high amongst the POWs.

Although they blamed the Italians for the deprivation they suffered in North Africa, many also realised that their situation was temporary. They all assumed that once they arrived in Europe, better and more permanent arrangements would have been made to accommodate them. Italian guards, being proud of their home country, also boasted to the POWs about the ample food and other luxuries that were to be found in Italy.[59] Once they disembarked on Italian soil, the beautiful scenery added to their optimism. Wally Wolhuter wrote about their expectations, saying they

> feasted our desert-weary eyes on the beautiful scenery until the train stopped and we were ordered to get out at a small station named Laterina. So we were to stay in this paradise of green vegetation, sun-kissed hills and peacefulness. The prospect was most attractive and our anticipation keen. It is unfortunately often the best-looking apple that contains the worm![60]

Newman had similar feelings when he wrote in his memoirs about the Italian troops singing of beautiful Italy, 'and the plentitude [sic] of food and other delights there. We were soon disillusioned. And perhaps they were too.'[61]

The Swiss Protecting Power and the Swiss-funded International Committee of the Red Cross (ICRC) had access to POW camps across Europe. It was the responsibility of Switzerland, acting as the Protecting Power, to ensure that the Geneva Convention was upheld in all prison camps. To do this, inspectors visited camps on a regular basis and as the war situation allowed. The reports that these inspectors compiled described camp conditions under headings such as *general conditions, interior arrangements, camp capacity, toilet facilities, food and cooking facilities, medical attention and sickness among POWs, clothing, laundry, money and pay, canteen, religious activity, recreation and exercise, mail, welfare work* and *complaints*. Reports on camps with satellite work or hospital camps included conditions in these camps, although the inspectors often relied on the statements from the POW camp leader, also known as the Man of Confidence, as it was not always possible for inspectors to personally visit all the work and hospital camps.

The work of the Protecting Power and the Red Cross undoubtedly helped to improve conditions and also ensured that prisoners in Western Europe generally received better treatment than those in the Pacific and in Eastern and Central Europe.[62] Switzerland was also responsible for representing South African interests in enemy and enemy-occupied countries.[63] Because all agreements regarding POWs were of a reciprocal nature, on paper Italy and Germany were mostly careful to adhere to the Geneva Convention with regard to the circumstances of all prisoners. In practice, however, things were often very different. Early in 1942, when the first of the Battle of Benghazi captives started to arrive in Italy, the country was still relatively new to the war and it would seem that accommodation for POWs was very low on its list of priorities. Red Cross inspection reports revealed many instances of Italian camps not conforming to the Geneva Convention.[64]

Even before the POWs arrived at their Italian camps, disillusionment started to set in. Many of those disembarking from the POW transport ships were still suffering from dysentery and virtually all were fighting a losing battle against severe lice epidemics. Their first experience after landing at Bari, Brindisi or Naples was of being deloused, hair shaved and enjoying hot showers, for some the first wash in five months.[65] The hot showers, intended to rid POWs of lice, were not always effective, however, and in some instances clothing – as in Bill Hindshaw's experience – was not disinfected but left in a pile for naked prisoners to sort out once they emerged from the water. As Jack Mortlock remembered, the soap that they were given was also ineffective in ridding them of lice as 'it was more of a scouring compound closely resembling "Monkeybrand".[66]

When the men were transported, or marched, from the harbours to their transit camps, they got their first glimpse of the Italian local population. For many it was a shock to see their poverty. However, the sight of the deprivation did not stir in all POWs a sense of sympathy. When Dennis Mugglestone and his fellow POWs disembarked from the *Rosalina Pilo*, they were filthy, but in his view they were 'nevertheless a picture of cleanliness in comparison to some of the civilians of Naples'.[67] After his arrival at Camp 82, his opinion of its commander – a 'big stout man, with so many ribbons on his bioscope commissionaire uniform, that it made Goering look like an amateur' – was equally sneering.[68] The squalor that POWs witnessed in the streets of Italy spilled over into their camps: AJ Cremer sarcastically remarked in his memoirs that all Italians must have been fly farmers, judging by the millions of flies that swarmed the camp at Bari.[69]

The flies were very often accompanied by lice, which reappeared very soon after the ineffective disinfection routines. For many POWs the discovery that they carried lice was at first a personal embarrassment and an indication of the pathetic state they found themselves in. Jack Mortlock was mortified when he first discovered lice. He remembered how he at first

> found two peculiar insects in my trousers, three more in my shirt, and also a row of tiny little grey dots that could be nothing else but nits. My face was hot with shame, I had lice, and how could I face the rest of the tent? I need not have worried. It was only a day or two later that most of the others also confessed that they had also found lice.[70]

'Reading' – the meticulous inspection of every piece of clothing, especially the seams, to remove lice and nits – became a communal activity.[71] Although they were self-consciously repelled by becoming infested with lice, as a common plight it could not be a dirty secret. Men congregated in sunny spots where they discussed all manner of subjects while slaughtering 'thousands upon thousands of lice'.[72] In some camps the plague was worsened by the lack of water, which spread infestation. Thus, in Camp 54, at Fara Sabina, about 50 kilometres north-east of Rome, Dick Dickinson recorded in his diary that 'the showers are often dry. Whenever the water comes on, the cry of "water" goes up, and we make a dash for cleanliness. It is too real to be a good joke, but the showers can become so full that one is never quite sure whether you are scrubbing yourself or the man standing next to you.'[73]

'Shirt reading', ostensibly to find and eliminate lice from clothing also served to combat boredom and exchange news. COURTESY ANTHONY MORTLOCK

However, life in Italy during the winter of 1942/43 was particularly harsh. The barracks in most camps were insufficient to accommodate all the POWs: Michael de Lisle remembered that many were forced to live in tents pitched in mud and snow. When AJ Cremer was transferred further north, he escaped the flies, but was now faced with a camp that was built on hastily reclaimed marshland. The soil remained wet, and to make matters worse, they did not receive any mattresses; each morning their blankets were soaked.[74] The ICRC report on Camp 85 near Tuturano also noted that many POWs who had arrived from North Africa had to make do with only 'a pair of shorts, a pair of boots, and sometimes a shirt'.[75] In other camps conditions were equally dismal. When Jack Mortlock arrived in Camp 54 in August 1942, he and others had to drag in their own sleeping bunks from a nearby camp, and sleep in tents. Issued with a blanket, Jack dismissed it as 'suitable for short miserable Italians, but … certainly far too small for the average South African'.[76]

Many POWs who arrived from North Africa had supplemented their clothing on the journey. Fred Geldenhuis, for instance, arrived in Italy with a pair of trousers made from two blankets,[77] but as Bill Hindshaw remembered, for the extreme weather and the constant hunger there was little by way of comfort at Camp 65 once winter had set in. 'Very few of us had enough warm clothing, and the blankets were also very thin ... We were cold and very hungry and the Red Cross food parcels were very irregular.'[78]

Later in the year, when the prisoners from Tobruk started to arrive, conditions had improved marginally, although they were still far from what the Geneva Convention required. For Michael de Lisle, Camp 85 was 'fairly well organized', and it may well have been, compared to the chaos that was the order of the day in Africa. The truth, however, was that Italy was unable to adhere to the Geneva Convention. A poor country, it was involved in a war that it could not afford – and the POWs from Africa were arriving in such numbers that the authorities simply could not cope. Transit camps were hastily converted to permanent camps as more and more POWs arrived. This was the case with Camp 85, which was listed as a transit camp in the third issue of the list of prison camps, but described as a permanent camp by the Red Cross inspector when writing a report only a month later.[79] Camp 85 later had 13 smaller work camps under its control when reported on by the Red Cross.[80]

In due course, as South African authorities started receiving reports from the Protecting Power, they became aware that Italy was unable to provide sufficiently for all its POWs. The Union's Secretary for External Affairs believed there was little that could be done about this state of affairs, as he admitted to the High Commissioner in 1943: 'as regards clothing we would I think be able to claim with justification that the Italians are not carrying out the terms of the Convention, but the pity of it is that they would be able to return the compliment'.[81]

The main responsibility for improving matters fell once again on the Red Cross and in December 1942, when the two Brokensha brothers arrived in Camp 54, conditions there had changed to a considerable extent. It was certainly sufficient for David Brokensha to be able to state in his memoirs that they were now impressed by the 'well-organised camp, with beds, blankets, new uniforms, showers, reasonable food and our first mail, as well as our first Red Cross parcels'.[82] A month later, Camp 82, where Dennis Mugglestone found himself, also received winter battle dress uniforms which provided considerable relief as many of the POWs were still housed in tents at that time.[83]

While the Red Cross was doing what was possible to improve circumstances, each camp was still dependent on the camp commanders and the degree of gravity they attached to their responsibilities. Preventing escape often took precedence over living conditions: where POW camps were located near the borders of non-Axis countries, Italian commanders and guards became obsessed with POWs fleeing captivity. At one camp near Bergamo, close to the Swiss border, POWs' trousers and boots were confiscated at night, regardless of the temperature. POWs were constantly searched at this camp, a chance for guards to confiscate clothes, blankets and anything of value. 'Spare boots, blankets, cigarettes and groundsheets, plus countless other priceless items (to the owners) were simply confiscated' when Bill Hindshaw and fellow POWs were made to line up outside the barracks and present their personal items to the guards. When the POWs objected to this blatant abuse of power, they were simply ignored.[84]

Although the Pretoria authorities tried to ensure that UDF prisoners were treated according to the Geneva Convention, they were mostly powerless to act diplomatically as a national interest, as any Dominion representations were made through British authorities. Another factor that impeded South Africa's ability to do anything about conditions was the fact that by the time it had received Red Cross reports, the increasingly unstable Italian political situation had changed to such a degree that representations concerning camp conditions would have had little practical force.

Although the South African authorities were more or less powerless to play an active role in ameliorating circumstances for POWs, they nevertheless remained informed about the circumstances surrounding the camps. As a result of early reports by the Protecting Power on Italian camps, the South African government became very concerned about the provision of food and clothing to South African POWs in Italian camps. As early as December 1942 a report by the

Senior Dietician stated that the Italian rations to POWs were 'grossly deficient in all respects'.[85] The calories allocated to each prisoner were of great concern as the Italian rations provided less than half of the daily requirement. According to a Red Cross report, the basic rations in Italy were as follows:

Bread	150 grams per day
Pastas (such as macaroni etc) or rice	66 grams per day
Oil or fat	6 grams per day
Sugar	15 grams per day
Dry vegetables (peas, broad beans etc)	30 grams per day
Concentrated puree of tomatoes	6 grams per day
Coffee substitute	7 grams per day
Cheese for grating (cooking)	8 grams per day
Cheese for eating raw at table	30 grams – 5 times per week, on days when meat is not served
Meat	120 grams twice a week

In January 1943, arrangements were made for the local packing of South African Red Cross food parcels and examples of their contents were sent to the Red Cross. By April of that year, however, it emerged that the British Red Cross preferred cash from South Africa to fund parcels packed in Britain and the Red Cross in South Africa was advised to 'discontinue the preparations' for the packing of food.[87] For most South African POWs, the fact that the Union did not dispatch the relief packages was of little concern, except for the smokers among them, who preferred the prized Springbok cigarettes as these were considered to be of better quality than English and American products.

Most parcels packed in Canada, England, Scotland and New Zealand contained similar foodstuffs. The Canadian version, for instance contained 14 000 calories, 400 g protein, 5 000 mg calcium, 30 mg iron, and sufficient levels of Vitamins A, B and C. The Red Cross was also advised of foodstuffs that were popular among prisoners, and these included dried eggs, oatmeal, sweets, salt, mustard, pepper, pancake batter and vegetable seeds. The South African Red Cross was also asked to send Springbok cigarettes to supplement British cigarettes.[88]

For some POWs these foodstuffs were not only favourites, but also life-savers. Oatmeal, for instance, was used at the POW hospital at Bari in an effort to cure dysentery. When Clive Luyt arrived at the Bari camp he found that the 'conditions were bad there, the food was bad, my, everything was rotten and disorganised'. He soon contracted dysentery and spent a month in the camp hospital. His condition did not improve until Carl van Heerden, a doctor with the Middellandse Regiment, started treating him with 'special oats' which had arrived in Red Cross parcels. Clive survived and was discharged from the camp hospital ten days later.

On the other hand, when Bernard Schwikkard received his first Red Cross parcel at the camp near Brindisi, a few mouthfuls of uncooked oats swallowed with spoonfuls of condensed milk almost caused his death. Feeling full for the first time in months, Bernard went to sleep after his meal but woke up a few hours later with a swollen stomach. As the size of his stomach grew and his pain increased, fellow POWs gave advice on how to solve the problem, including sticking his finger down his throat in order to vomit. When the guards refused to call a doctor, Van der Westhuizen, a farmer from the Orange Free State, offered to stick a knife into Bernard's stomach to let the air out, just as his father used to do with cows that ate too much maize. When Schwikkard saw the farmer approach with a rusty knife, 'the sight of this chap with his knife, I thank God, I vomited and crapped, I did everything. And afterwards, I was so sorry I had lost all those wonderful foods, gone to waste. I learned a lesson.'

Regardless of the Red Cross's contribution to food rations, the South African authorities believed that it was important for the Italians to increase the provisioning of POWs as the transport of parcels could be delayed or stopped as a result of deteriorating European war conditions. In the view of Pretoria, POWs in Italy would endure 'great hardship owing to lack of adequate food and clothing if anything should happen to cause a serious dislocation of Red Cross parcel supplies'. They were also concerned 'that it be established beyond doubt that Italian Government are in fact carrying out their obligations under the Prisoners of War Convention'.[89] The vulnerability of the Union's POWs was underlined by comparison of their circumstances with those of Italian POWs in South Africa who were, according to Squadron Leader Keeling of the British Red Cross Society, 'receiving, quantitatively, three times as much food as our men in Italy are receiving'.[90]

A further factor which impacted on the value of Red Cross packs, and one which the authorities may not have been aware of at the time, was the fact that parcels had often to be shared between a number of men, diluting their nutritional value as that was based on the formula of single use. So, the joy of receiving the first food parcel in Italy was soon replaced by extreme disappointment when Bill Hindshaw and his fellow POWs were told that each parcel had to be shared between ten men.[91] According to Dennis Mugglestone, the first Red Cross parcels that arrived at Camp 82 had to be shared between 18 men. Nevertheless, the prisoners were so happy to receive their consignments that their applause caused those guards who were unaware of the arrival of parcels to assume that the war had ended, for 'they slung their rifles away and started dancing and cheering with the prisoners'.[92]

At other times, cheering died away. Although the Red Cross packed a week's provisions, when the Italians handed them out they punctured tins to prevent POWs from storing food in preparation for escape. This meant that tinned food had to be eaten sooner than otherwise. To avoid eating contaminated food, Fred Geldenhuis would always eat tinned salmon on the day of issue, leaving the canned sardines for up to three days before eating them, with 'no ill effects of poisoning as we had been told as children'.[93] When, in December 1942, Christmas parcels arrived in the Bari camp, famished POWs could not contain their excitement and consumed the entire parcel in one sitting, causing many to become ill. The joy of receiving these items was not even tempered by the fact that most of the food ended up in the toilets. As Fred heard from a fellow POW, 'Hell Gellie! When that pudding went out it tasted just as nice as when it went in.'[94]

The manner in which POWs approached food was of course determined by the state of malnutrition they were in. For some though, a man's behaviour, especially regarding food and personal hygiene, determined his respectability amongst fellow POWs. When Fred van

Alphen Stahl noticed that American POWs did not bother to cook their oats, to wash their hair or shave, he regarded them as having been spoilt by the American Army and as having grown psychologically too weak to cope in camp conditions. Even in the difficult conditions in the ill-equipped camps, many POWs considered personal hygiene as a sign of self-respect. Personal sloppiness signified an absence of shame and these men earned the scorn of those who had to endure the mess they left. Aussie Hammond was especially critical:

> Having so degenerated, men of this particular type thought nothing of urinating in their bunks, irrespective of their unfortunate companions below. During the cold weather they defecated on the floor rather than go outside, and some could not be bothered to go even as far as the floor but simply messed in their own beds where they lay and then pushed the stuff out by hand or foot.[95]

In other cases, men became obsessed with food and did not realise the effect their resulting bizarre behaviour had on their own health. In Camp 52, one disturbed man became so fanatical about the idea of starving should Red Cross distribution not reach the camps, that he stored all of his food instead of eating it. As the rest of the POWs in the barracks were unaware of what he was doing, they assumed that he was lying on his bed, depressed, as he was 'loafing or lost in melancholy'. It was only later that they realised that he was ill, and when he was moved to hospital, they found six Red Cross parcels hidden with his kit. He refused the offer of food from a priest and died of malnutrition a few days later.[96]

A similar incident took place in Camp 65, where a South African POW became convinced that 'a Higher Power' had ordered him to give his rations to others. As he wasted away, he seemed to become more delusional and tried to climb the high fences surrounding the camp. When placed in the infirmary he could not be convinced to eat, insisting that he wanted 'strength to resist the temptation of this devil's disciple ... climb the fences and be saved!'[97]

Peter Ogilvie – the man who had been tasked with persuading the delusional POW to eat – had been was among the first group of POWs to be placed in Camp 65, who were forced to endure long months of hunger before the first Red Cross parcels arrived. During this time they received rations from the Italians, but came near to starvation during the first two months, as their arrival in Italy coincided with a 50 per cent cut in camp food. Although the camp commander tried to supplement their rations with dandelion leaves and turnip tops, there was not much that could be done as the food situation in Italy deteriorated; between 1939 and 1942, food prices had risen from an index of 100 to 172, and by April 1943, even Mussolini had serious doubts that Italy would be able to continue to feed its army.[98]

AJ Cremer was unlucky enough to be sent to a camp where the Red Cross parcels were delayed even longer. He spent four months in dreadful circumstances before his camp received its first delivery. During this time, they were given a 16 ounce tin of soup and a small bread bun daily. As a result of their weakened states, the men fell victim to dysentery. For AJ the situation became unbearable when at the height of the epidemic, rain started pouring down, leaving the camp in a muddy state. As men struggled to get to the toilets, their frail bodies fell into the mud and the best their mates could do was to turn these unfortunate men's faces sideways so that they did not suffocate in the mud. AJ counted 26 coffins that left the camp on trucks. When the parcels eventually arrived, the cigarettes were missing from each one. The guards had pilfered the entire supply.[99]

Newman Robinson's description of hunger in Camp 65 is among the most terrible of all POW memoirs. As a consequence of the severe hunger, Newman observed, 'the British were becoming quarrelsome; the South Africans lethargic and morbid; the New Zealanders whined'. Matters turned explosive when a group of Palestinian and Cypriot POWs started to accost the vegetable cart, depriving the rest of the camp of the food, leaving Newman and his friends to consider 'leaving their last vestiges of pride and joining in the anarchic scramble'.[100]

When an Italian interpreter one day announced that, 'tomorrow you eat better than we do' he seemed genuinely pleased to inform his captives that from the following day Red Cross parcels would arrive, bringing relief to starving POWs. Their issue was, however, beset by bureaucracy as the Italians first deliberately awaited orders from Rome, and then delayed the process further by inspecting each tin for, as Ogilvie wrote sarcastically, 'hand grenades or Spitfire parts'. Frustration at the delays reached a high point when one POW tried to commit suicide before parcels were eventually handed out.[101]

Food preoccupied the thoughts of captives day and night and many consoled themselves in fantasies, absorbed in visualisations of the food they planned to consume once free. For Michael de Lisle, this coping mechanism kept him optimistic, as boredom was relieved by 'food, collecting recipes, it was a popular game. Talking about food. Thinking about lovely food after the war.' In a similar way, thoughts of food helped Dick Dickinson to cope with extreme nutritional deficiency and the mental adaptation required of POWs as the importance of sex and female companionship diminished and was replaced by feverish thoughts of food. In September 1942 Dick wrote in his diary that he

> Heard only one discussion on women, and that a very brief one. Women and sex are forgotten and there is only one topic of conversation – food. To all intents and purposes I am as sexless as a block of wood. To eat is the extreme fundamental of living.

Neither women nor adequate food were available to POWs, yet Dickinson and his friend Frank chose to make their torment worse 'by recording each day an item of food that we would like, and we are determined to eat through the list when we get out! Some examples: fried eggs; Castle ale; fried kidneys on toast; *koeksusters*; fish and chips ...'[102] Fred van Alphen Stahl even suggested that one could determine the state of food in any POW camp by listening to what its men were talking about; if they were talking about women, it could be assumed that the camp had sufficient food supplies.

In the Union, the Adjutant-General agreed with the High Commissioner in London that there was enough cause to make representations to the Italian government regarding the provision of food and clothing to South Africans, but also reminded him:

> it is true our men are badly fed in Italy and without the Red Cross parcels they would be in dire circumstances. But then, according to our information, the Italian depot troops are not fed any better and that will be the reply [from the Italians]. We are feeding the Italian prisoners of war here [in South Africa] on a princely scale in comparison with what our prisoners of war are getting in Italy, but we have to do that in terms of the Convention, so long as we apply a like measure towards our depot troops.[103]

He added that the matter should be dealt with by the 'Imperial Prisoners of War Committee "A" in which all the Dominions are represented' and that the Protecting Power should be asked for a report on camp conditions in Italy.[104] Article 11 of chapter two of the Geneva Convention states that 'food ration of prisoners of war shall be equivalent in quantity and quality to that of the depot troops' and as it was impossible for any outside authority to determine the veracity of the situation in Italy, the South African authorities had to accept the Italian response. In this way, the Geneva Convention, despite its humanitarian intentions towards the treatment of POWs, placed the South Africa authorities in an impossible position. They were unable to protest about the level of food provision to POWs as the Italians were adhering to the Convention in that they were providing the same rations to their own troops. South African concern was, of course, well-founded as the Red Cross inspectors' reports showed that all POWs faced the grim prospects of starvation.[105]

As POWs adapted to their new circumstances and became more familiar with their surroundings, they became more aware that Italian guards and civilians also experienced hardship as a result of the lack of food. In some ways, this knowledge led to POWs viewing Italians in a new light. While still in North Africa, most POWs blamed guards for their terrible conditions and shortages, and open aggression and physical conflict between POWs and guards appears to have been fairly common. In Italy, however, many POWs came to regard Italians merely as weaklings, unable – as Clive Luyt put it – to 'organise three beans in a row'. Equally, while on the surface relations between POWs and captors seemed to have improved somewhat in Italy, animosity and contempt were still the dominant emotions at this time. Still, some Union POWs looked to find positive interpretations of their circumstances and they believed that the Italians were trying to adhere to the Geneva Convention despite common hardships. As Stanley Smollan said, 'they had no food for themselves, let alone us but in the camps, in Fara Sabina in Camp 54, there were Red Cross parcels, everything was okay, they observed the Convention'.

In this respect, much depended on uneven circumstances. Michael de Lisle, for instance, was convinced that POWs were fed worse than Italian troops, a view shared by Wessel Oosthuizen, who saw men in the Fara Sabina camp sifting through straw intended for bedding in an effort to find a few grains of wheat, while others waited at kitchens for cooking water to be thrown out as sometimes a cabbage leaf could be found in this way. Waiting for scraps of food at the kitchen door was also a feature of life at Camp 82 near Laterina, where Dennis Mugglestone remembered food being delivered by cart, and men storming the kitchen once it had been off-loaded, hoping to find leaves that had fallen on the ground. Even the horse pulling the wagon became a victim of POW desperation, as Dennis once witnessed a prisoner pulling a head of celery from its mouth.[106] Jack Mortlock saw similar acts of desperation and remembered how, when they received their bowls of 'swill' they would take it back to their tent and

> either gulp it down ravenously, gloat over it, add some lucerne leaves and cook it again over a small smoky fire, or do something else with it, depending upon the individual concerned. Looking back upon those awful months it is surprising that we retained any degree of sanity at all; there were exceptions of course. We all had our whims; some would eat their rations as they received them; others felt that they would get more satisfaction by re cooking them and adding lucerne leaves. Even snails or rotten turnip leaves

Being last in line had the advantage of being served the thicker soup at the bottom of the pot.
COURTESY ANTHONY MORTLOCK

that they had scrounged from the refuse bins, others just sat and looked at their food and kept it until it was entirely unfit for human consumption.[107]

The men at Camp 52 found another unique way of bulking up their soup. They added a roll of toilet paper to each pot, which made them feel fuller.[108] For some, hunger gained greater significance than that of any physical condition. Wessel Oosthuizen, for instance, believed it changed his mental outlook on life. When missing home, he did not miss the people as much as he missed his mother's Sunday roast, something which remains a difficult guilty memory today. For Mathys Beukes, the way in which men dealt with constant hunger was also an indication of willpower and character. Hunger caused some POWs to steal boots and other essential items from each other to sell to the Italians for extra food. Although Mathys, who was 26 when he was captured, believed that older POWs fared better than younger captives, it was willpower which kept many going in the months before the first Red Cross parcels arrived. A young English POW had a particularly poignant effect on Beukes. The young man ritually licked the last of his food from the container with the words, 'now that's my breakfast, lunch and dinner and God help me'. The crucial importance of food and some sense of the effect it had is apparent from a sardonic extract from Dick Dickinson's diary, written in one of his many philosophical moods:

> The man who professes principles of virtue is quietly regarded sometimes as the fool. The man without scruples, without pride, without dignity, lives superficially better than the man possessing those attributes. His conscience or lack of it, allows him to scrounge, to hang around the Italians or the cooks, to barter, to make a bit on the side, to steal. And what is the loss of a little pride or dignity compared with a full stomach or smoke-filled lungs?[109]

By then, smoke-filled lungs had already begun to play a major role in daily existence. In North Africa, cigarettes had become an important camp commodity, as they not only relieved hunger pains, but also became a currency for trading amongst POWs. Red Cross parcels contained foodstuffs and cigarettes that were scarce in Italy, and as soon as POWs started receiving these, they were in a superior position to their guards. To Stanley Smollan, the POWs 'were the wealthy ones with Red Cross parcels and the Italians were the really poor ones because they had very little to feed themselves'.

In January 1943, the British Red Cross was able to supply 50 cigarettes per week to each prisoner, and as it wanted to make an effort to supply familiar brands to each nationality, the South Africa Red Cross was asked to supply Springbok cigarettes for camps containing South African POWs.[110] POWs could use this commodity to trade in all kinds of goods with their Italian captors. Bernard Schwikkard recalls how some POWs regarded trading with the enemy as disloyal to the Allied cause, but that he and others regarded it as doing their bit in the war, especially as they were exchanging non-nutritious goods – not only cigarettes, but also tea and coffee – for nutritious food. (Fred van Alphen Stahl added that, because tobacco was so valuable, most of it would be removed and replaced with dried tea leaves before being bartered.) Moreover, Bernard and others also soon realised that trading with civilians would be more profitable and they made it a priority to get selected for work parties which would allow them outside the main camp and provide more opportunity for exchanges.

One such deal took place between Aussie Hammond and a young woman, who was going to provide Aussie with cheese in exchange for a watch. Although keen to conclude the transaction with extra benefits, as the girl 'proved to be a hot little number', he was deflated when he realised that months of malnutrition had taken its toll on his body. The girl was no less disappointed as she quickly realised the watch was also out of order.[111] In Camp 54 in Fara Sabina, tea was also used as a trading currency, but only after it had been brewed, dried in the sun and repacked. Stanley Smollan remembered that they would 'throw [the tea] over the fence ... a peculiar sight, we'd throw over a packet of tea and they'd send over a couple of loaves of bread and what they didn't know was that the tea had been brewed to its last and dried out on the roof and repacked, that was one of the things we did ...'

In general, smokers suffered more physically than others as many of them would trade Red Cross foods for cigarettes, something which non-smokers found incomprehensible. Clive Luyt, a non-smoker, would store up his cigarettes and when he had 20 or 30, depending on the price, he would trade them for a tin of bully beef. Springbok cigarettes were evidently very popular, with one Springbok equalling ten Italian cigarettes. David Brokensha ingeniously compared the use of cigarettes with Gresham's law in economics, with bad money (Italian cigarettes) driving out good money (Springbok cigarettes).[112] Union cigarettes were a high-value acquisition, and when he won a pack of Springbok in a bridge tournament, 'it was like a gold bar'.

Thoughts of food were uppermost in the minds of the hungry men, but as Jack Mortlock said, this was made worse by the fact that, especially during the first few months, there was nothing to do but sit around and think about food. In his memoirs, Jack describes their hunger as being aggravated by boredom because

> To aggravate matters even more, we had nothing to do apart from routine searches and numerous roll-calls. I had a dictionary that I had picked up in Benghazi. Unfortunately it was only from A to M. The other portion had been torn off, and that was all that I had to read. Some of the more fortunate ones had playing cards, whilst one poor chap had a portion of 'Good Housekeeping'. He spent hours gloating over the beautifully illustrated dishes, which did him no good at all.[113]

Once conditions in Italy stabilised, the Red Cross and the YMCA started providing sports equipment, indoor games, musical instruments and books, but until then, POWs had to think creatively to keep themselves occupied and their minds off food.[114] Bill Hindshaw remembered that in some instances, initiative and creativity eased the monotony and even drew in the interest of their enemy captors:

> Perhaps the biggest bugbear of being a POW was trying to kill time. Trying to instil some enthusiasm, the camp leaders decided to have an exhibition in one of the bungalows of what anyone wished to show. This involved the whole camp. It was amazing. One person had actually made a working clock from empty jam tins, etc. Others had carved in stone or modelled clay. The drawings were in some cases exceptional. Many of these were purchased by the guards. In spite of this brief respite, life was too awful for words.[115]

Michael de Lisle remembered that they did not play any sport while at Camp 85 near Tuturano and that 'walking around the camp that was about all the exercise we got [...] we didn't play games like football or anything like that'. A report of March 1943 by the Protecting Power confirmed that Camp 85 'covers such a big area that there is plenty of space inside the fences for taking exercise,' but that the camp was in need of all manner of sports equipment, and especially educational books. Nevertheless, in due course there were some other diversions. These included a band whose members consisted mostly of members of the South African police band, which entertained POWs in a makeshift theatre.[116] In May 1943, the camp newspaper, the *Tuturano Times,* reported that in Camp 85 'food, though important, is no longer the be all and end all of our existence' and that POWs were pursuing other interests such as sport, literature, education and music. In some instances, performances by camp bands were even attended by senior Italian officers, such as a Colonel Pallotta, who attended a concert in March 1943.[117]

Whatever Michael's grumpy experience, few individual aspects of POW recreational experience can be wholly generalised, as it was up to each captive to decide on the extent of his participation in the activities. In Michael's case he obviously preferred to improve his knowledge of the Italian language rather than to play sport or try music. He also spent time in Camp 82 near Laterina in the few months before the Armistice, and here the Protecting Power report noted that prisoners wanted permission to remove vines and fruit trees as these were growing on the only available land that would be suitable for games such as rugby and soccer. It would seem as if the need to relieve boredom had surpassed the significance of food, as a few months earlier these same men would have scrambled to get at the fruit of these trees. The inspectorate did in fact advise against the removal of the trees but also remarked that there was 'no lack of intellectual entertainment [in the camp] and instruction is given in various subjects'.[118] In this case, Michael probably participated, as he was teaching Italian to other prisoners: 'I just realised I was good with language and I enjoyed teaching and so that set me off on my career as a teacher.'

Just as *The Benghazi Forum* provided moral support to the men in the North African desert, camp newspapers in Italy were a form of entertainment and kept many busy with reporting especially on sports meetings, a popular pastime between different nationalities. Rugby and cricket were popular among most POWs and there were regular games between British Commonwealth nations. David Brokensha remembered those between Australia and South Africa being of particular interest, as there was always competitive national rivalry. Even those who did not participate directly benefited as spectators or as gamblers, risking precious commodities in the process. A particularly competitive match between the Springbok and Tommie teams occurred at the Tuturano camp in July 1943, with the Tommies winning 2-1. A detailed description of the game in the *Tuturano Times* was followed by an 'In Memoriam' section with the following announcement:

> In Memoriam of many sad losses resulting from Sunday's match; parcels, tins, cigarettes galore, multi lire (including one bet of L480). Not forgetting late lamented apple pudding placed by an artist who should have known better.[119]

In Camp 54, cricket and soccer seemed to have been the games of choice – Clive Luyt recalled that shorter games were played in quick succession so as to give as many POWs as possible a chance to play, 'as part of keeping us from going gaga'.

Camp 52 near Chiavari seemed to have been where the performing arts proliferated. Here the Camp Amateur Dramatic Society, known as the CADS, staged many performances which were presented as if they were professional productions. Aussie Hammond remembered singers, stage managers, costumiers, comedians, show poster artists, and last but not least, 'Harold Pullen who played many a charming "leading lady".' Productions included *Pygmalion, Charley's Aunt, The Importance of Being Ernest* and *Of Mice and Men*, a play some believed should have been entitled, '*Of Lice and Men*'.[120]

Although the POWs were very creative in finding ways to deal with boredom, they still needed some equipment for their leisure activities. Camp inspectors regularly reported on the needs of each camp, but it seems as if bureaucracy in the Red Cross system and in some cases the unsympathetic attitude of the Italians delayed delivery of entertainment apparatus to camps. In October 1942, on his first visit to Camp 122 in Cinecittà near Rome, the inspector noted that 'little opportunity is offered for sport [...] it is the intention of the camp commander to procure footballs, the game which the inmates of the camp prefer'.[121] By April 1943, a further report showed that POWs were still asking for sporting equipment as 'the censor destroyed many of the articles which were intended for use in sports'.[122]

The destruction of Red Cross equipment may be explained by the fact that Italians viewed these items as possible escape aids. Their fears were indeed justified, but British intelligence did not use the Red Cross as a cover to aid POWs in their escape plans, they created fictitious charity organisations as a front. In December 1939 a new branch was established in Britain's Military Intelligence. A function of this branch, known as MI9, was to inform fighting men on how to avoid capture and how to behave if they were captured. However, the main function of MI9 was to obtain intelligence about the enemy from those who had escaped successfully. Therefore their main aim was to assist POWs in their efforts to escape.[123]

An MI9 operative, Christopher Hutton, for instance developed many tiny devices that could help POWs in escapes. These devices included compasses, maps printed on silk and an 'escaper's knife', which consisted of a blade, a screwdriver, three saws, a lock pick, a forcing tool and a wire cutter. The employees of Waddington's, the manufacturer of the Monopoly game, became involved in a top secret operation when they were asked to print silk maps of Italy and Germany which were concealed in the playing pieces. In this case the games were sent to POW camps in Red Cross parcels, which in fact was against the regulations of the Geneva Convention.[124]

Requests for reading material were similarly ignored by both the Red Cross and the camp command, which was of the opinion that only a third of prisoners in Camp 122 were literate, even though POWs asked for books in English, Afrikaans and Sesotho as early as October 1942.[125] Accordingly, in Camp 122 at least, most POWs had to devise their own entertainment and many kept busy with what the camp inspectors referred to as 'national games'. These included variants of *Morabaraba*, which is similar to Nine Men's Morris, a game played in the British Isles.[126] In contrast to Camp 122, which significantly contained mostly African prisoners, reports on Camp 75, an officers' transit camp, show that although a request for 2 000 additional books was made in March 1943, the library still only had 500 volumes by June 1943, as the Allies prepared to land in Italy. Nonetheless, it was far better equipped for recreation than Camp 122 as it had workshops for a variety of trade occupations, a theatre, an orchestra and a canteen.[127]

Labour detachments were a welcome reprieve from camp life. Captured officers were accommodated in separate camps, along with those other ranks who were suffering from ill-health. They had nothing much to do but wait for the war to end, or to amuse themselves with sport or other entertaining activities. For the rank and file, however, the option of work detachments was a way out of the camp, to gain temporary and limited freedom and extra food. Bill Hindshaw and fellow POWs worked on a farm near Tuturano where they got the opportunity to mix with local Italian men and women. They also used the chance to have their subtle revenge on their captors when they involved the accompanying guards in a game of *bok-bok*, always making sure that the Italians 'were bucked down first!'[128]

The experience of having fun and of acting in a free manner while on farms was something that had become a remote dream for many since capture. Indeed, Bill Hindshaw considered working 'a Godsend, because in the prisoner of war camps, the food was too ghastly'. For David Brokensha's group, too, farm work came as a blessing:

> Persuaded our easy-going guards to let us swim in the river during their midday siesta [...] we would strip and place our clothes and shoes in a big pile, which provided the guards with a comfortable pillow for their siesta [...] we had no chance of escaping: naked, and with at best a rudimentary knowledge of Italian, we would not have got far. Twenty of us would dive into the swift-flowing Tiber [...] and swim to the end of the field, the rapid current carrying us swiftly along. Then we would run back along the bank of the river, a half-mile, to repeat the process again and again until it was time to dress and start work. What wild whoops there were when an unsuspecting peasant girl entered the field during our midday revels; once, I distinctly saw one girl covering her face with her hands, but discreetly gazing at us through the lattice of her fingers. Lovely carefree moments, these plunges in the Tiber are among the happier memories of my captivity.[129]

For others, though, farm work became boring after a while and in at least one case, a relieved POW was 'given temporary sack from farming work'.¹³⁰ In another case, POWs on a work detachment near Torre Allemanna were unhappy about the amount of food they received on the farm and the fact that the Italians withheld their Red Cross parcels while they were working. Michael de Lisle was one of these men and as he had some knowledge of the Geneva Convention, he knew that their rights as POWs were being neglected. Following long discussions with the Italians, the POWs decided on a 'no parcels, no work' policy and went on strike. In response the Italian lieutenant tied a man to a tree and threatened to shoot him at noon if the men still refused to work. In return, Michael agreed that the men would return to work if he could speak to the camp commander at the base camp in Bari. Michael was taken to the lieutenant's office where he spoke to the commander on the telephone about the missing parcels. The men returned to work and their parcels arrived.¹³¹

Although agricultural work was the most common labour for POWs, there is data that shows Italian authorities may have used this screen to cover the controversial employment of POWs in war labour. This was prohibited by Article 31 of Chapter Three in the Geneva Convention, that 'work done by prisoners of war shall have no direct connection with the operations of the war'.¹³² On 17 August 1943, Clara Urquhart of the South Africa Red Cross Society wrote to the Prisoner of War Directorate in Pretoria asking for advice on how to deal with information received from repatriated POWs that prisoners from Camp 85 were made to work on Aero Porto 456 in the Italian south. (Anglo/Italian exchanges of POWs had started in early 1942.)¹³³ The Red Cross believed that the lack of letters from this camp to family in the Union confirmed the fact that POWs were doing war work and that their letters were being confiscated or censored by the Italian authorities. In a reply from the Border Centre, Urquhart was informed that a repatriated POW had confirmed 'a previous statement that prisoners-of-war from Camps 75 and 85 were *definitely* taken to work on an aerodrome near these two camps'.¹³⁴

In fact, the authorities were already quite aware of the work on the airfield as they had been sent secret information in July 1943 which had gone to British and American authorities, as well as to South Africa House in London, on 'South Africans made to make Foggia aerodrome'.[135] Sensitive to potential risks, cautious Union authorities treated the entire matter with complete secrecy, even warning that repatriated POWs could be court-martialled if they spoke openly about the issue. It was believed that if it became known to Italian authorities that repatriated soldiers were revealing such information, there could be harsh consequences for vulnerable POWs still in camps.[136]

Michael de Lisle and Fred van Alphen Stahl were both at Camp 85. Here they volunteered for a labour camp near San Pancrazio Salentino. However, this time they were not taken to a farm, but were put to work on an aerodrome, which Michael, of course, knew was against the Geneva Convention. There were, he recalls, 'enormous amounts of sabotage there, there were 800 of us in that camp, working for the Germans, the Italians were in charge of us but we were working for the Germans'. In his own way, Michael, acting as interpreter between the Germans and Italians, tried to sabotage the efforts of his captors by causing confusion through his translations, something that brought him great pleasure, as he remembered the 'Germans scorned the Italians and the Italians hated the German arrogance and yet they still had to treat each other politely, it was such fun watching them'.

In his memoirs, Michael mentioned that the aerodrome was 'roughly between Taranto and Lecce',[137] which would indicate the military airport at Manduria. He was happy to hear that the Allies bombed the aerodrome shortly after they returned to the base camp for POWs at Tuturano: this meant that the 'war work' they had been doing would not be to the benefit of the Axis after all.[138] Following the Italian Armistice of 1943, the Manduria airport became the base for the American 47th Bomb Wing of the Fifteenth Air Force Heavy Bomber Unit.[139]

They would let you die

For those unlucky POWs who remained behind in the base camps as a result of illness, things seemed only to worsen when they were sent to

POW hospital camps. Article 14 of the Geneva Convention stipulates that each camp 'shall possess an infirmary, where prisoners of war shall receive attention of any kind of which they may be in need'.[140] While it was clear that the intention of the Convention was to ensure humanitarian treatment for POWs, given the circumstances of the war and the practicalities involved, the provision seemed to be at odds with stark realities, especially when one considers the experience of POWs who saw friends die needlessly or who themselves required medical treatment. So, while those shipwrecked prisoners at the Caserta hospital viewed their treatment in a positive light, most other POWs did not experience such good treatment at Italian hospital camps.[141]

Indeed, there were so many complaints about costs in Italian POW hospitals that the Directorate of Prisoners of War formally protested against the 'financial exactions in Italian hospitals, on dental treatment, and confiscations of shirts and of shoes'.[142] This protest was entirely justified, because according to Article 14 of the Geneva Convention, the Detaining Power was responsible for all expenses related to medical treatment and the provision of remedial equipment. The Geneva Convention also declared that medical inspections by mixed medical commissions would take place on a monthly basis,[143] and while these visits did occur, inspectors could usually only reach camps every three or four months.[144]

Although most independent reports considered medical treatment to be reasonably adequate, many referred to a less than ideal situation, primarily as a result of the difficult circumstances brought about by the war in Italy as well as the drought experienced during the summer of 1943. For instance, in a report on the Military Hospitals of Giuliano and Monteluce at Perugia, the inspector, George Bonnant, wrote, 'treatment of the prisoners is very good [...] the general complaint has been the lack of Red Cross parcels [...] these defects are naturally accentuated at the moment by the difficulties of communication'.[145] The fact that the inspection was done on 4 September 1943 explained the 'difficulties of communication', but also meant that the promised representation to improve conditions was most probably stymied by the Armistice, leaving the patients in a perilous position.

Following the peace agreement between Italy and the Allies, some of the hospitals in Italy remained under Italian administration, such as the one at Celio, which was visited by Captain L Trippi on 21 January 1944. At the time of his visit, there were ten South African POWs along with five Englishmen and one Indian. The rest of the more than 1 500 patients included Italian soldiers and civilians who were victims of bombing raids. Although Trippi's report states that none of the POWs died while in hospital, it also mentions that three of the men were eligible for repatriation as a result of their illness, but that the Armistice prevented this. The Trippi inspection concluded that the 'prisoners of war are very appreciative of their treatment they receive'.[146] It is unlikely that warm statements such as these conveyed the actual state of affairs in POW hospitals.

When Lieutenant Colonel JS Alexander returned to South Africa from the Moriji hospital camp at Piacenza, his impression of the Italian medical commission which visited the camp to determine POWs' eligibility for repatriation illustrated how bureaucracy and an unsympathetic attitude affected the lives of patients. Alexander's view also made it clear that Italian authorities interfered to such an extent that their actions resulted in contravening the Geneva Convention. According to the Convention, POWs who suffered from paralysis and 'grave chronic affections of the circulatory organs', among others, were eligible for repatriation,[147] but Alexander found that the authorities 'were continually pressing to send the less severe cases to camp'.[148] While it is obviously impossible to know the severity of their illnesses, the fact that the Italian medical commission also did not see patients with serious wounds which could later result in septicaemia and cause permanent disabilities, shows that the method by which it functioned was largely ineffective.

Moreover, Alexander observed that the commission declined to see cases other than those listed by the Italian medical officers, making the appointment of 'neutral officers' to serve on these bodies futile. The reality for many POW patients was that they were overlooked for repatriation, and then, as was the case at the Moriji hospital, had to wait many months for another inspection, hoping that the Italian medical officer would place them on the list. In many instances, repatriation at an opportune time could save a limb or prevent a long-term illness, and here Alexander's assessment showed that officers had a significant status advantage over other ranks. Thus, 'the senior member of the commission [...] refused to see any other cases as it was outside his instructions [but] amongst the cases repatriated with the last batch were a number of officers seen at their own request'.[149]

Vulnerable POWs were not passive, adopting a posture of medical helplessness. As soon as men realised that they could not rely on Italian medical care, they accepted responsibility for their own health as far as possible, something that started even before they reached Italy. In Benghazi, for instance, Michael de Lisle recalled that one of the first camp rules made by POWs was that no one was allowed to use any medical supplies for trading purposes, not even to obtain extra food. It was also at Benghazi that POWs realised that individual arrangements would sometimes have to be made so that many could benefit, as was the case when Michael grasped that despite the bad treatment, a trip to the dentist could bring certain advantages. His first visit to the camp dentist was as a result of a legitimately severe toothache. Yet once the tooth was pulled (without anaesthesia), he spotted fence poles along the way back, and collected some precious firewood. The next time he and his friends needed firewood, 'another tooth started giving trouble [...] but this time I knew that I could take the pain, and I got another fence pole'.

Fred van Alphen Stahl, who suffered from recurring bouts of malaria and pneumonia, found that the Italians, in addition to lacking medical supplies, showed little sympathy towards POWs. As he remembered, in 'Italy, they would let you die, because they would say *Domani* but they didn't have doctors, they didn't have medicine themselves. Or they couldn't really be bothered. We were working on a farm on one occasion [...] out of the five of us who got malaria, two of them went to hospital and they both died.' Dick Dickinson's diary reveals a similar situation when he recorded that 'Pvte J (Jim) Maddocks died on 23 February. He had pneumonia and a weak heart. The last we saw of him was being taken away on a donkey cart. He didn't make it.'[150] Dick's phlegmatic tone showed no outrage at the ill POW being carted away and the shrug at his 'not making it' reflected that death was probably not an unusual occurrence in the camp.

While efforts at medical relief were clearly limited, some improvisations were not entirely without some beneficial impact. As early as March 1941, belligerents agreed that medical personnel and army chaplains could remain in POW camps to assist in medical and spiritual matters on a voluntary basis.[151] While a large number of medical officers volunteered to remain with the rank and file, their work was hampered by insufficient medical supplies and they were often forced to improvise when treating patients,[152] as in the case of Dr van Heerden treating Clive Luyt ingeniously with 'special oats'. In other cases, the fact that the doctor was South African and could speak Afrikaans to fellow Afrikaans-speaking POWs provided social and cultural comfort, as Mathys Beukes found when he became ill and had a visit from an Afrikaans-speaking doctor who talked to him about his perceptions of the war.[153]

For a brave boy

Whether they were ill or not, POWs were eager to receive news from their families. However, they were often disappointed, not only because the letters and parcels took a very long time to reach them, but also because their families and friends were clearly ill-informed about conditions in POW camps or what it meant to be a POW. One such obvious example was a letter which Aussie Hammond received from an acquaintance in Durban, asking him to make a few business deals while in Italy. Other letters clearly showed that those at home considered POWs to be cowards and unworthy of any sympathy. Writing to thank a patriotic lady in South Africa for the socks she had knitted and sent, Aussie got a curt reply from the woman saying that the socks he received were 'meant for a brave boy fighting at the front, not for a prisoner'.[154]

When he returned home after the Armistice, Uys Krige pleaded with the families of POWs to write often, as letters were their most important link to domestic normality. Although rejection letters from girlfriends and fiancées could cause such extreme depression that in some cases former POWs would not even relate the event in their memoirs, others viewed these more with dark humour, pinning rejections on notice boards for all to read.[155] Another sore point arising from the letters POWs received from home had to do with the government system of holding back 'key men' in the Union. Key men were usually artisans with specific skills, but many POWs resented them as they were safe in the Union and free to continue with their careers and personal lives.[156] News of the promotions or marriages of their friends at home created similar feelings of resentment. Dick Dickinson remembered receiving a letter from his mother informing him 'of a wonderful job Keith Clarke has in Cape Town. I saw red when I saw that. There is only *one* job for a man in wartime.'[157]

However, communication between POWs and their families had a significant impact on morale, as Bill Hindshaw well expressed:

> I cannot recall whether I received anything, although I am certain that those at home would have made every possible effort! The point I want to make is the contrast in the joy of the lucky ones and the sadness of those who didn't receive anything. The feeling was unbearable. The lucky ones soon came to realise the situation and in many instances tried to buck up the others – even sharing the good news as best they could.[158]

POWs were naturally aware of the fact that letters to their families were strictly controlled to prevent enemy countries from obtaining information, but many were determined to bypass the censors. Some contrived to let their families know in coded ways about the shortages of food by referring to images that they knew the Italians would not understand. Thus, on 17 April 1943, Newman Robinson wrote 'we are very fit and the rations keep us in the condition of trek oxen in August', obviously implying that they were starving.[159] Howard Bates admitted that they were not allowed to write anything 'detrimental' about their Italian captors, but that they used 'innuendo' in their letters to let their families know the true state of the conditions they were living in.[160]

Afrikaans-speaking POWs had an advantage over the Italian censors, as their language was obviously not understood. Some indicated their state of affairs with examples such as 'give my regards to *Ons Lyhonger* [We are starving]'; 'Our best friend is *Uys Koud* [Ice Cold]'; and 'Don't forget to remember me to *Niksti Vreet* [Nothing to Eat].'161 The Cape Town branch of the Prisoners-of-War Association published these quotes in the local press, as it believed that their sardonic tone would help to raise the morale of the families and friends. However, the Adjutant-General was not amused and warned that the Italians might stop all mail between South Africa and POW camps if they became aware that captives were hoodwinking censors in this way.162

Codes were also used by families and friends writing from the Union to inform POWs about the progress of the war. When the Allies recaptured Tobruk, Wally Wolhuter's mother used a play on words in her letter to tell him about this victory. This was one of the very few times that Wally could believe what he read, as rumours, or what his group referred to as 'shit-reps' were rife and the propaganda in the Italian state-produced *POW News* was 'so feeble and transparent that [POWs] regarded it as an insult to the intelligence'.163

Howard Bates also remembered the *POW News* and that it was 'all propaganda and was treated with much contempt'. Another propaganda news sheet was the *Ripley News*, which Howard came across in Camp 85 in Tuturano. News in this publication was merely translated from the Italian newspapers, but it did benefit the POWs in that they could derive information from it, for instance that the Alamein battles were going mostly in favour of the Allies. As conditions improved in the Tuturano camp, the POWs there developed their own news sheet, entitled *The Griff*. This was a daily paper, edited by English POWs, with John Wilson producing the unique *Springbok* version.164

Most UDF prisoners were convinced that they did not receive all the letters and parcels that were meant for them, but a June 1943 telegraph from the London Committee of the South African Red Cross contradicted this idea. The telegraph contained an extract from a report by Monsieur Zollinger, the Head of Prisoner of War Parcels Department in the International Red Cross. It created a picture of preferential

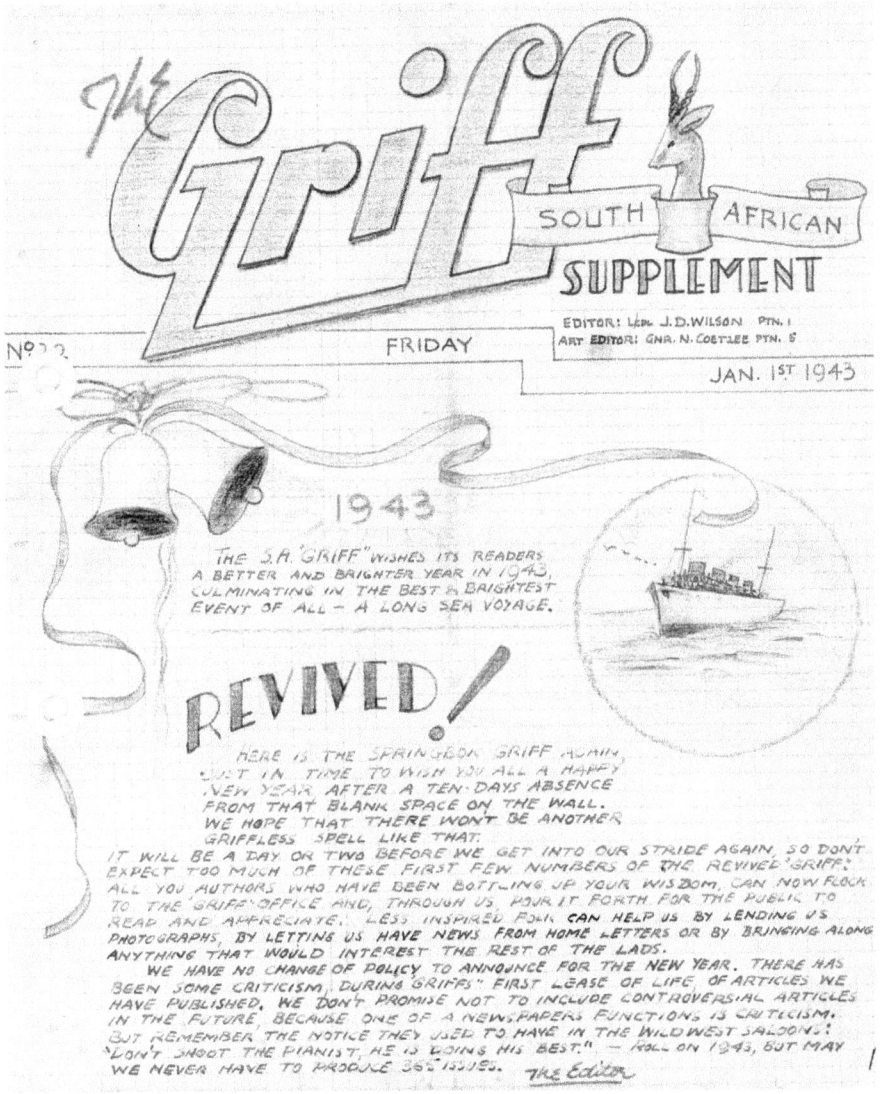

The first edition of the POW newspaper, *The Griff*, on Italian soil. COURTESY ENID BATES

treatment of South African consignments, despite the fact that many POWs evidently received no or very few parcels and letters from the Union. The following statement on Camp 82 was included:

> *Confidentially:* However much South African Prisoners may

complain that they have not got this or that, for propaganda reasons they, both white and native, are treated better than any of the other Prisoners. When parcels are marked from South Africa, or for South African Prisoners of War, they are pushed forward first.[165]

CHAPTER FOUR

WIRE HAPPY

Without a doubt, the first few months in Italy were absolute hell for the captives. Yet, POWs were soon describing certain aspects of their experience as 'carefree' and 'a Godsend'.[1] Adapting to life in Italian prison camps seemed unproblematic, at least on the surface, though punctuated by hunger pangs and boredom as well as moments of humour. In general, living conditions improved and a sense of routine helped many to become accustomed to their environment. For most of them, it was in Italy that they had to accept the fact that rescue had become a remote possibility, if not an impossibility. The relative comfort of the Italian camps also allowed POWs to focus less on pure survival and more on the emotional aspects of their situation, leading in some cases to complete acceptance and in others to a renewed desire to gain liberty.

Viktor Frankl, an Auschwitz survivor and psychiatrist, believed that prisoners experienced three mental phases during captivity, the first being that of consignment to prison, with the resultant shock, the second stage including acceptance of camp routine and, third, that of liberation.[2] In the case of POWs, similar phases may be identified, such as that of capture and dealing with its shock as well as for some the shame of surrender, followed by adaptation to camp routine, and then liberation. For those POWs captured at Sidi Rezegh and Tobruk, their experience in North Africa may be viewed as representing capture, shock and shame. Italy represented the second phase, although accepting the routine of imprisonment in the knowledge that these were not death camps may also have meant a greater self-acceptance and grasp of survival rights on the part of each POW. Frankl noted that during the second phase, in order to survive mentally, concentration camp prisoners became insensitive and uncaring towards themselves and fellow victims as a result of extreme experiences.[3] By contrast, by far the majority of POWs developed a sense of mutual cooperation in the interest of survival, while at the same time they placed significant emphasis on self-care. Exceptions to these unwritten rules of POW behaviour included those who neglected personal hygiene, those who stole from fellow POWs and those who became alienated from the group.

Although British Commonwealth POWs did not experience the extreme conditions of the concentration camps or the prison camps in the Eastern theatre of war, still, their mental experiences of shock, fear and humiliation cannot be discounted as insignificant. Thus, in Frankl's experience, the extreme loss of hope often preceded camp suicides, and in an effort to prevent hopelessness he attempted to provide his fellow prisoners with something to look forward to – each one 'had to be reminded that life still waited for him'.[4] Frankl's view was echoed by Bernard Schwikkard's consideration of how to cope with POW life. For him, age was a conditioning factor:

> You see when you are young there's a lot of life to look forward to [...] you've never had sex, you've never eaten caviar, there's a lot of things you've never had, and experienced, you never travelled, [...] and I found that frankly the older men didn't stand up to the hardships, they have lived, they've experienced many of these things, they didn't have so much to look forward to as we youngsters had to still see and experience, so to me there was a stronger will to see it through, but never, never would I like to go through it again, once was enough, because it was extreme, I went through some extreme conditions mainly due to hunger, to hunger.

In *The Great Escape*, a film about the mass escape attempt from Stalag Luft III under the leadership of a South African, Squadron Leader Roger Bushell, POW life is portrayed as an adventure where the ever-optimistic captives continually strive to outwit their captors. Their actions are characterised by episodes of humour and an atmosphere of goodwill between the captives. Films such as these are romanticised representations of POW life.[5] In reality, maintaining morale in POW camps was far more problematic than the films suggest. Getting along with others was critical to all POWs, as was the importance of one's group of close friends.

Similarly each POW had to accept and make peace with his own strengths and weaknesses, all of which were emphasised in these extreme situations. Each POW had to accept his new captive identity as well as craft a way in which to respond to his externally imposed circumstances. While high morale and optimism were a positive characteristic, it was difficult to maintain without support from close friends and active participation in activities in the camp. In a number of memoirs, former POWs describe how many of them were subject to mood swings and short tempers, demystifying to a degree the myth of unflappability in the face of adversity. For instance, Aussie Hammond recalled, 'moodiness was a common feature of prison life. A man's mind might rise swiftly to elation, or sink down to the depths of despair with equal rapidity. Bitter quarrels broke out during card games, and best friends frequently fell out over the merest trifle of conversation.'[6] In his diary, Dick Dickinson identified the type who, through noncompliant behaviour, harmed the sense of camaraderie and morale among the men; however, he added that 'in all truth, he is in the minority'.[7]

For those who found it difficult to accept their situation, it also became difficult to control their depression and many isolated themselves as a result. Among POWs the common term for this state of mind was 'wire happy' and in some cases the behaviour bordered on the abnormal, as was the case with those who were 'given to delusions of grandeur [...] and would only speak to their fellows in an effort to convince them that they were none other than Alexander, Churchill, or Montgomery in disguise'.[8] It is indeed so that those subjected to extreme deprivation and other acute experiences during captivity, including malnutrition, isolation, lack of medical care and humiliation, could suffer from psychiatric and unstable mental-health effects that remained prevalent among POWs years after their liberation.[9]

Long hours of boredom led some to re-evaluate their place in life, and to consider philosophical aspects that they previously dismissed as insignificant. For many prisoners, boredom itself became an enemy and often led to periods of severe depression. For Dick Dickinson, for instance, who considered himself an intellectual figure, the lack of books added to his frustration and he regarded 'the cost of [his] experience too great in time'.[10] He was aware of the impact of his depressive moods on his friends, but was unable to prevent himself from succumbing to them. Cheering one another up was important, because low morale seemed to act as an instigator that set a chain of events in action. For David Brokensha the link between friendship, trust, morale and personal hygiene was obvious. The support of his group, led by his brother Paul, was of vital importance to him. David remembered that

> Paul always had his little groups of pals, five or six of us, we shared things and then the wider unit was South Africans and we reinforced one another and little things which becomes big things that even when it was difficult in the desert we shaved every day, even though some guys hardly had a beard but that was important, you know, once you stop shaving then you stop washing and then you sort of fall apart.

Within all of this, there were also high-minded reflections on what captivity meant, with perhaps the best example from Eric Hurst, who in the June 1943 edition of the *Tuturano Times*, wrote of the personal changes experienced during the first year of captivity:

> We have seen a disorderly mob grow into a civilized community, and we know how much civilisation is worth and how it needs to be protected. And most of all we have learned how we ourselves change according to the external factors bearing on us. For me, who freely confess to having gone through the whole gamut of consciousness from that of a monk to a monkey, the result of it, I like to think, has been an increased perception and understanding, a

new humility and tolerance; a real faith, despite the side issues of politics, in our way of life, our laws, and customs [...] it has yielded a more proper understanding of the teachings of the great philosophers: Among all the peoples of the earth there is so much in common ...'[11]

'I thought all South Africans were black'

The men who were largely responsible for the 'laws and customs' in POW camps were the Men of Confidence, or camp leaders. Red Cross inspectors compiled their reports based largely on the information they received from these men, who made them aware of prisoners' grievances. Camp leaders were also responsible for communicating with Italian or German camp commanders regarding living conditions and other occasional matters. The election of camp leaders put in place a system which helped to establish order and a united front against their captors. In camps for men of other ranks, leaders were elected based on their popularity, leadership qualities and linguistic ability, as being able to communicate with camp commanders in their own language often determined the outcome of negotiations. In officers' camps, those with the highest rank most often assumed leadership, but in some cases animosity towards them as a result of incidents on the battlefield led to others being elected, thereby changing the military hierarchical structure once men entered POW camp.[12]

The role of the camp leader was crucial to ensure good morale and harmony between men of many different nationalities. One such leader was Regimental Sergeant Major BR Cockcroft of the Second Transvaal Scottish. Among the POWs he was known as Snakebite and he made a big impression on almost all the men who spent time at Laterina, Camp 82. Dennis Mugglestone, for instance, held Snakebite in very high regard and viewed his leadership as 'super efficient'.[13] According to Michael de Lisle, it was Snakebite's 'harsh discipline' that saw to it that all the nationalities lived together peacefully in the camp. Yet, as he often had to act as interpreter between Snakebite and the Italian commander, the camp leader's short temper often made life difficult when he insisted on everything being translated. In one instance Snakebite insisted Michael tell the Italian that he was 'a bloody Itie bastard!'[14]

Bernard Schwikkard remembered that Snakebite did not tolerate any opposition from POWs, and on an occasion when Australian POWs tried to replace him, he quickly stared down the challenge by climbing on a table, exclaiming, 'if any of you bloody Australians think you can do the job better than I can, get up here and put yourself forward, and see whether the men think you are soldiers or rabble'. No one put themselves up after Snakebite's outburst. It was clear that his bluff leadership style was imposingly effective, yet no one seemed to mind that he was dictatorial. All who recalled Snakebite seemed to have great respect for him, perhaps suggesting that a well-run camp was more important than a democratically run one.

However, Snakebite also had a softer side. Following a long spell without Red Cross parcels during which the men started to relive the hardships of Benghazi, Wally Wolhuter recalled that if it had not been for Snakebite's 'pep talk', many would have succumbed to the utter despair that always accompanied extreme hunger. Wally remembered Snakebite telling them:

> I know you have suffered and what you are going through, I was with you at Benghazi and the hell's kitchen of Derna! Don't let the Italians get you down; show these miserable people the stuff you are made of! This is only a phase in your lives, a stern test of your characters.[15]

Lower down on the POW hierarchy were hut leaders and group leaders. At Camp 52, Aussie Hammond was a hut leader, and very aware that he had to earn the respect of the men. One of his first responsibilities was to create a system whereby the bread issue could be distributed fairly and to everyone's satisfaction. On another occasion he was forced to act when a newly arrived American POW, nicknamed 'Beetle-Brows', ignored the line for the bread issue and 'swaggered slowly to the head of the queue'. Knowing that the men's eyes were on him to take action, Aussie at first asked the man to get in line; however, his polite request was ignored. Although Beetle-Brows was taller, Aussie sprang into action with 'a left to his jaw [...] and a plank cracking across his exposed neck'. Wanting to make sure that Beetle-Brows got the message, Aussie followed up with his 'knee up and into his side, jumping on him as he fell and bashing his head hard against the floor several times'. The American retreated, leaving Aussie with his authority intact. Apparently this was not the only unpleasant incident involving American POWs at Camp 52 and the idea took hold that the Americans were deliberately trying to antagonise them, 'for the sole purpose of stirring up anti-American sentiments among the British prisoners'. Shortly after the incident between Aussie and Beetle-Brows, the entire group of American POWs was removed to another camp.[16]

By the time that American POWs started to arrive in the camps, having entered the war only at the end of 1941, the British and Commonwealth POWs had already established a way of life. Many POW camp rules were unwritten and based on shared hardships during the early months of the war and of captivity. While in some cases relations between British and American POWs were positive, the arrival of the Americans was for the most part disruptive and many Commonwealth captives were reluctant to embrace them.[17]

Initially, David Brokensha, too, was critical of Americans in his camp, as in his opinion most of them did not seem able to cope with the stresses of POW life, and were too inclined, in a sense, to let themselves go – 'they didn't immediately leap into the showers, for instance'. Fred van Alphen Stahl was similarly appalled by Americans' apparent disregard for personal cleanliness. In his opinion, the Americans did not cope well in captivity because while still in fighting units they had been pampered too much. Fred believed that before their capture, American soldiers 'had laundry units, doughnut units, ice cream units, so they never did things for themselves'.

For Fred it was a point of pride that most British POWs tried to shave and wash as often as possible, even if they had to use their tin hats [as bowls]. Americans, on the other hand, had to be ordered to visit Dog Dead Evans, so called because he always said 'I'm a dog dead tired'. Evans was the camp barber, and he would send the Americans away to wash their hair before consenting to cut it.

George Tewkesbury and Wally Wolhuter both took a very positive view of the Americans. George was a member of the Black Watch Regiment, and he 'loved' the Americans, even though they were 'full of shit'. George was captured in 1944 during the Allied landings at Anzio, so he too entered POW life after certain rituals and routines had already been established – but in his case an accommodating and positive personality probably influenced the way he viewed others.

Wally only came to know American soldiers much later, once they poured into the German camps following the D-Day invasions, but in his view the South Africans and the Americans had a lot in common, including being 'fair-minded, tolerant and warm-hearted'.[18] George found the GI habit of boasting about the large size of all things American very entertaining, especially when a soldier from London's East End challenged an American to prove his boasting by parading his masculinity, saying, 'Well, if that's so, show me your willy and I'll show you mine!'

Taking controversial historical events into consideration, it may be expected of Afrikaans-speaking POWs to have held stereotypically negative views of British POWs, yet this was by no means the case. Mathys Beukes, for instance, viewed the British soldiers as stupid because, according to him, many were not fully literate. However, in the same breath he also declared that they mostly got along because they were all equal once they entered the POW camp. AJ Cremer, another Afrikaans-speaking POW, was both shocked and amused when greeted by a group of British POWs with the words, 'Goodness, chum, I thought all South Africans were black,' but his opinion of them ('friendly') was positive.[19]

Wessel Oosthuizen, on the other hand, had found it very difficult to fight alongside the British, as his grandmother had died in a South African War concentration camp. When obliged to live in a POW camp with British soldiers, his experience was that South Africans stayed together, and the British stayed together – 'like seeks like, you know' – yet he also believed that they were all in the same position and that no one nationality dealt with the hardships of POW life any better than another. Aussie Hammond also noticed how different nationalities 'tended naturally to segregate on a racial and national basis' when he arrived at Camp 52, which contained Britons, New Zealanders, Australians, South Africans and a small group of batmen from the Union's Non-European Army Services forces.[20]

Occasional dislike of British soldiers was not limited to Afrikaners, as some English-speaking South African POWs also held less than favourable views of their allies in captivity. Class was one issue. Dick Dickinson, for instance, admitted that he was very critical of British POWs because they 'were mostly lower class people, and they used the f-word far, far more than we did, every other word was f...' At the same time, some observations in his camp diary reflected more favourable sentiments. While in Fara Sabina, he shared in the joy of a young British POW devouring his entire Red Cross parcel in one sitting. On another occasion, he applauded Corporal Jock Spencer for raising morale as well as for his 'attractive Scottish accent, and the big smile across his face'.[21]

Something of the nature of the relations between POWs of different nationalities also emerges from the camp inspectorate reports of the Protecting Power. For instance, reports on Camp 85 noted that only South Africans POWs were being sent to work camps and that 'English prisoners in a way resented this because they think they are just as good for working on farms as the South Africans'.[22] South Africans may well have been selected due to Italian perceptions that they were better able to do farm work, but this perception did not take into consideration that the POWs had been subjected to bad conditions and poor food for months. When Howard Bates first arrived at his work camp, where his group was put to work harvesting broad beans, they were 'crippled with aching backs and blistered hands'. The living conditions on the farm itself were so poor and unhygienic that a sore Howard had obtained in the desert also flared up again at this time.[23]

Nevertheless, Bernard Schwikkard certainly believed that South Africans were more proficient in a rural work environment, as they

> were well experienced and we knew our way around [the farm], and

we felt that the English chaps were seeing that. Because we were better than them, and we started being friendly with the Italians, and we were able to find our way, and extra food.

The improved relationship that developed between Bernard's fellow prisoners and their guards went far enough for two South African POWs to convince their captors to share their marijuana seeds with them. Smoking enabled POWs to 'get through the work almost ten times quicker' than most others. However, the euphoria ended when the POWs realised that they were in fact digging a tank trench, and not an irrigation trench. When they complained about doing war work, Bernard recalled, they were all sent to Camp 82 near Milan where Snakebite Cockcroft was camp leader.

According to some testimony, South Africans were dissuaded from mixing with other nationalities, and were kept separate from British, Australian and New Zealand POWs owing to anti-South African attitudes following the military disasters in North Africa. For those who were captured during the Battle of Sidi Rezegh, the news about the fall of Tobruk resulted in new waves of despondency that affected their morale. For Newman Robinson the news was 'beyond belief'; he reasoned that it must have been a propaganda ploy by the Axis to cover up a defeat in Russia. When the Tobruk POWs started to arrive at his camp, Newman was horrified at the state they were in, saying 'I only once again ever saw anything comparable to them: films of Belsen survivors released by the Allies just after VE. They could only just walk.' Amazingly, the POWs who had endured months of starvation in the ill-prepared Italian camps agreed to share their meagre rations with the new arrivals.[24]

Ill-feeling between different nationalities over blame for lost battles could sour relationships, with Brokensha recalling that other POWs would often 'make snide remarks [about Tobruk] and it often led to fights when we were a bit stronger'. For Bill Hindshaw, the fall of Tobruk was also a sensitive issue, and he believed that blame for this military disaster was aimed at all South African POWs, regardless of where or when they were captured. Bernard Schwikkard, a Sidi Rezegh captive, experienced a more belligerent mood among Allied POWs from other nationalities even before the Tobruk prisoners arrived at his camp. Upon hearing the news about the defeat of the Allies at Tobruk, there was in his camp a

> deep hate, almost belligerent, against the South Africans, Why? The British. Because they felt that Klopper had surrendered, they should have gone on fighting. And they blamed South Africa for their predicament. And they felt that we were almost cowards, and they had this, there was this feeling [...] this anti-South Africa feeling.

When the Tobruk prisoners did arrive at Bernard's camp, they were told, 'We might as well tell you South Africans, that you might not find yourself very popular, because of the Tobruk saga. Behave yourselves and you'll be treated as soldiers, just be conscious of the fact that you're not liked.'

In Ike Rosmarin's perception, accusations against South Africans increased at times when camp conditions worsened, suggesting that rage at the loss of Tobruk could have served as an outlet for POW frustrations. It was easier to turn on their own than to vent anger against their captors. Ike felt that 'it was not until the end of the war that I could hold my head high' as he believed he was blamed, as a South African, for the Tobruk 'debacle'.[25] Again, experience seems rarely to have been uniform, or of one mind. Another inmate, Fred van Alphen Stahl, was emphatic that there was no Tobruk ill-feeling between different nationalities. References between POWs to events that took place during fighting were always made jokingly, and by and large 'there were no specific animosities'.

While some Commonwealth POWs blamed Union POWs for their predicament, feelings of discontent among South African POWs often led to them looking higher up in the ranks for scapegoats. The blame that was aimed at the officers and NCOs was often amplified by assumptions which may or may not have been based on the truth. In Camp 82 Dennis Mugglestone, for instance, was unhappy at what he believed was an unfair distinction between Imperial POWs and South Africans. According to him, all those who dealt with Red Cross parcels were on double rations, and all of them were Imperial 'RSMs, SCMs, Sgts and Corporals, all of whom got the jobs on the "jobs-for-pals" basis [...] We, as South Africans, were good enough to volunteer to fight for them, and when anything like this cropped up, we had to take a back seat and this will always be a bone of contention – the distinction that was always made between South African and Imperial.' To Dennis's mind, the fact that RSM Samuels, the leader in his section of the camp, was from an Imperial regiment justified his reasoning.[26]

According to a February 1943 inspectorate report, all officers received the same food as the camp's Italian officers, but were expected to pay some lire for their portion.[27] No independent reports on Camp 82 cited any POW group tensions, although these cannot be regarded as definitive as representatives mostly received information from the Man of Confidence and the camp commander, who may not have had all the facts at their disposal.

Although the Geneva Convention declared that 'belligerents shall as far as possible avoid bringing together in the same camp prisoners of different races or nationalities',[28] different races were often not separated until they reached permanent camps in Italy.[29] In response to the mix in North Africa, the British Directorate of Prisoners of War took up the matter in December 1942, when 'protests and representations were made to the Protecting Power against the continued detention of Imperial prisoners of war with prisoners of war of other nationalities'.[30] White Commonwealth soldiers of different nationalities were, however, not separated as all were classified as British forces. As Britain also viewed such Commonwealth soldiers as British, the POW directorate protest was in all likelihood aimed at preventing different races being grouped together in the same camps, or to prevent British POWs being detained in camps with POWs from countries who were not signatories to the Geneva Convention, such as Russia.

The exclusionary attitude towards black soldiers was not limited to British and South African authorities, but was also evident in reports by the Protecting Power. On Camp 82 in October 1942, one report noted that most of its 2 612 POWs were British or South African, but there was 'one nigger in the camp, probably sent by mistake: his transfer had already been requested'.[31] Italian authorities invariably separated POWs according to race once they were allocated to permanent camps. Officers were separated from other ranks to check any tendencies to take control and try to organise escapes.

A smell of garlick

While POWs established supporting networks amongst themselves, they were forced to rely heavily on their captors for their wellbeing. This placed them in the unique position of having to form cooperative relationships with the enemy. Because both Italy and Britain were signatories to the Geneva Convention, camp commanders were often careful in their dealings with Allied POWs because they knew any bad treatment could very possibly be reciprocated.

Because the Union of South Africa was a British Dominion, the principal arrangements regarding UDF POWs were made between the International Committee of the Red Cross and Britain. This meant that although the South African authorities were kept informed, the Union was powerless to act without first having its actions endorsed by British authorities. This often cumbersome process delayed the country's response to anything affecting UDF POWs. For instance, the British Political Secretary replied to a protest over poor camp conditions in Camp 85 and Camp 65 in October 1943, weeks after the Italian Armistice. Nevertheless, the South African authorities were assured that the 'Protecting Power achieve[d] their object in ameliorating conditions'.[32] South Africa was also assured that London would protest strongly if it felt that the Protecting Power did not act with 'sufficient vigour'[33] – as happened in February 1943 when the Directorate of Prisoners of War protested in its newsletter sent to the Protecting Power 'against the ill-treatment of prisoners of war in Libya in 1942, and the Protecting Power was requested to demand the punishment of officers and other ranks who were responsible for the outrages at Benghazi camp'.[34] Taking action against those who were guilty of acting in contradiction to the Geneva Convention may have been admirable, but by February 1943 the POWs who had suffered in the Benghazi camp had long since moved on, carrying the emotional scars of what they had endured with them.

The personality and political ideology of Italian camp commanders had far more direct effects on the daily life of POWs in prison camps. Among the commanders there were many committed fascists, and their race-conscious ideology resulted in treatment of black and white POWs that blatantly violated the stipulations of the Geneva Convention. Many POWs became victims of the propaganda campaigns of fascist ideology. Blacks were stigmatised as racially inferior, while others were simply treated as less than human. In Italy and Germany, fascists did not regard the Geneva Convention as applying to POWs who were not of European ancestry.[35]

An example of deliberate Italian disregard of the Geneva Convention was the use of Cape Corps POWs for war work. Howard Bates wrote of a group of between 200 and 300 Cape Corps POWs at the Foggia station who had been put to work on aerodromes in the vicinity.[36] In other cases, it is clear that black POWs suffered severe privations with regard to camp conditions and food. Private Andrews Dlamini wrote from Camp 85 that 'we got no food. Only three potatoes [...] we suffering very bad.'[37] Nelson Koza, the batman to whom Harry Klein said goodbye shortly after their capture at Sidi Rezegh in 1941, wrote to him on 18 August 1942 from Camp 22 near Rome. In his letter Nelson declared that he was still alive, but he also asked for any 'scrap' to be sent to him. By June 1944 he had written to Chief Mamitwa, through whom he had been recruited, saying that he was in Germany. However, on 16 August 1944 Harry's wife received a letter from the South African Red Cross stating that Nelson had died of tuberculosis. In response to the news, Harry wrote to Nelson's wife, saying that her husband 'has given his life for his country as much as in a prisoner-of-war camp as if he had died on the battlefield [...Nelson] was a good soldier and we honour him.' The blank period between Nelson's letters probably reflects how his living conditions began to demand more of him and reduced the time and energy he could spend on letter writing.[38]

Belligerent countries monitored letters from POWs in an effort to make sure that the Protecting Power was aware of cases where the Geneva Convention was not being adhered to. In May 1943 the Union Adjutant General received an incriminating document containing extracts from the (uncensored) correspondence of repatriated POWs which revealed an even starker picture of conditions and treatment than that sent from POW camps.[39] Extracts showed that ill treatment was not limited to black POWs and even included claims of murder. A Captain Crofts, for instance, wrote about an Italian officer who killed a POW by pushing him against a wall and stabbing his bayonet into the captive's stomach.[40] In another description, Crofts indicated that although the accounts of returning POWs were in some cases conflicting, it was clear that without Red Cross parcels they would not survive. He added that 'discipline is severe, and when opportunity occurs the guards are ruthless [...] the Itos are getting windy about our invasion but say they will fight to the end. There are I expect Mussolini's 6 million bayonets and only a smell of garlick [sic] behind them.'[41]

As an inmate at Camp 65 near Gravina, Mathys Beukes believed that at first the Italians were unnecessarily ruthless in their treatment of POWs, but as the war progressed and as conditions became worse in Italy, guards softened their attitudes towards captives and would not report as many incidents to commanders as before in an effort to be more lenient. Camp commanders and guards adopted an even milder attitude when the Allies invaded Sicily in July 1943 and they could see the writing on the wall. A Captain Theunissen wrote of his conversation with a repatriated POW, Corporal Jack Thring, who had informed him that 'the Italians are very considerate towards prisoners now, as they firmly believe that they shall be beaten soon by the Allied Forces'.[42]

The leniency shown by some camp commanders and guards towards POWs, however, barely altered opinions of the enemy formed while in North Africa. At first, POWs were in an obviously low position as they depended utterly on their captors for food and shelter. When Red Cross parcels started to arrive and as the war turned increasingly against Italy, captors now found themselves in a more vulnerable position. In January 1943, for instance, Italian guards became acutely aware of their country's shortcomings when the POWs received new battle dress uniforms from the Red Cross. The new woollen clothing not only did wonders for the mood of POWs who had been enduring the European winter in their desert uniforms until then, it also changed the balance of power between the captives and captors, albeit only in terms of resilience. Wally Wolhuter was especially struck by the reactions from the Italians with regard to their Red Cross clothing, because the items were 'of a quality unprocurable or unknown in Italy at the time'. According to Wally many POWs became aware of their privileged lifestyles, and they 'swore [they] would be more appreciative […] when we got back to our own country…'[43]

Interestingly, before the 1943 Armistice, prisoners seemed to make few distinctions between Italian forces and Italian civilians. Beyond generally abusive descriptions of all Italians, some contempt took on an emphatically racist tone. While still in North Africa, a race-based outlook could be detected in some POWs who judged Italians according to how dark-complexioned they were, and this thinking thrived in Italy among other POWs. In another example, Dick Dickinson wrote of a friendship that developed between him and a guard. The Italian was from

> Bologna in the north [who had] the intelligence of the northern Italian and doesn't look at you blankly when you talk about Michelangelo […] in the northern Italian it is not difficult to see the past power and glory of Italy. The southerners are very different – smaller, very much darker-skinned and more the peasant type.[44]

Ironically, the view held by POWs that the north was superior to the south was shared by many Italians, especially during the inter-war period when the north became known as 'civilised' while the south was seen as 'barbarous'.[45]

Because POWs had so dim a view of their captors, the order to salute Italian officers was something that grated. For Mathys Beukes, the only reason why POWs saluted Italian officers was because they were soldiers, and in any army privates were expected to salute officers. In the Italian context, however, this reflex was not based upon respect for any authority of rank. What Mathys found particularly humiliating was the fact that when POWs jumped up to salute, they could faint because of their weakened state, causing Italian officers to burst out laughing.

While most POWs seemed to respect military rules, it was not always the same with camp rules. One such example concerned Sergeant-Major Snyman, camp leader at Camp 54 at Fara Sabina. When Snyman wanted to discuss a matter with the camp commander, he would simply walk out of the camp to the office, causing the guards to run after him, as they were not allowed to let a POW out without an escort. Jack Mortlock remembered that Snyman demanded respect from the Italian guards and POWs alike, but that his tactics at getting the respect were somewhat unorthodox. Jack recalled that Snyman was responsible for a lot of amusement among the POWs who watched him

> surrounded by a lot of gesticulating, screaming Italian officers. He invariably appeared to be feet taller than the little Italians and he simply towered over them. This in itself was a tremendous psychological advantage in that no matter how important the Italian officer was, he still had to look up to Snyman. Furthermore, he always seemed to contrive to stand as close to his victim as possible, which meant that the poor little Italian would have to bend his neck back even further to see Snyman's face. I cannot recollect ever seeing him smile at an Italian. Instead I felt that he treated them with obvious contempt.[46]

Contact between POWs and Italian civilians was not entirely devoid of humour and at times provided entertainment for POWs, although not necessarily for the Italians concerned. When local women were sent to cut the grass near the camp, Aussie Hammond and his fellow POWs delighted in a betting game they devised while watching the women bending over and working with their scythes. Aussie described how 'three "spotters" were immediately elected, their role being to take up position as soon as the women arrived, lying flat on the ground near the fence; meanwhile, bookies wasted no time in taking bets on what colour knickers each woman would be wearing'.[47] Despite loud cheers from the POWs, especially when a woman was spotted wearing nothing under her dress, the humiliated grass cutters evidently remained aloof.

It won't be long now

Escape in Italy was, before the Armistice, not a viable option for many rank-and-file POWs, leaving repatriation as a last hope of freedom. Repatriation agreements between Italy and the Allies were beset by bureaucratic wrangling, delaying freedom for many and bypassing others entirely.

Shortly after the fall of Tobruk, the Union attempted to secure the repatriation of some of those who were captured. However, its efforts were fruitless as bureaucracy and perceived competition between Commonwealth nations got the upper hand. When the Secretary for External Affairs approached the High Commissioner in London regarding repatriation of POWs captured in North Africa, he was informed that the British authorities disapproved of 'uncoordinated action', as they did not want one part of the Commonwealth 'profiting at the expenses of others'. This was something they considered 'especially likely in relation to the Italians, whose inefficiency might lead them to hasten notifications in response to pressure from one quarter, while ignoring equal claims from other quarters merely because they were not represented'.[48]

Medical repatriation was another option to freedom, but this process was just as unwieldy and frustrating. To qualify for this, a POW's medical condition had to be such that he would not be able to return to the front as a fighting soldier.[49] The British authorities proposed guidelines because the stipulations in the Geneva Convention did not consider POWs who deteriorated after an initial medical examination or who in fact improved following a further medical examination. The guidelines included selection for medical examinations by captors, and if POWs had been examined within six months of capture, they also had some chance of being selected for repatriation. Once examined, men would be placed in Category A, which meant direct repatriation, or Category B, which meant that they would be repatriated to a neutral country. Within Category B, POWs could be classed, firstly, as never to be fit again for combat; and secondly, those whose cure within one year could not be medically foreseen and who would be re-examined again in six months. If they were still not expected to be cured in one year they would be transferred to Category A. Thirdly, if a POW's application failed they had to be examined again after six months.[50]

The Red Cross, though, viewed this complex system as impractical because there was insufficient accommodation in neutral countries for POWs. It proposed that all POWs in Category B should be repatriated directly and that no distinction should be made between Categories A or B.

To further complicate affairs, repatriation agreements between belligerents depended on reciprocity, and if no suitable accommodation was available in a neutral country, exchanges of POWs could not take place. Repatriations between Italy and South Africa were rare as it was generally accepted that 'Italian POWs in South Africa live under more ideal climatic conditions and receive better treatment than they would in a neutral country'.[51]

Repatriations could, furthermore, not occur if conditions in the captive's home country were not acceptable, and following the Armistice those POWs still in Italy lost all hope of repatriation when the 'Swiss Legation in London was informed that no examination of Italian internees in the United Kingdom by the Mixed Medical commission will take place for the present time as there is under the present conditions in Italy no prospect of repatriations.'[52] About one year before this correspondence, however, Newman Robinson found his name on a list of POWs to be repatriated. They were to be exchanged for Italian POWs who were at that time in the Zonderwater camp near Pretoria – six Italians for every two South Africans. Following a few anxious days on a hospital ship in Smyrna, Newman recalled how, when they passed the Italian POWs on barges between the two ships, he formed the distinct impression that the Italians 'were not as pleased to be going home as we were'. So Newman was on his way home, leaving behind his friend Peter Ogilvie, who had been captured along with him at Sidi Rezegh in 1941.[53]

For the majority, the idea of freedom seemed unattainable until the Italian Armistice took place and most camps were left abandoned by their guards. However, not all POWs were prepared to sit around and wait for political events to determine their fate. According to Michael de Lisle, all UDF volunteers had been given a 'standing instruction' during their training that it was their duty to escape if taken prisoner. However, for many such an instruction lost any meaning as they were confronted with the reality of their circumstances in Italy. Successful escapes were rare before the Armistice, with David Brokensha voicing the common view that it was easier for officers to get out as they were better organised and their camps were easier to escape from. Officers' escapes have featured prominently in both popular and academic literature, where ease of escape, skill and education or higher levels of motivation have counted as major factors.

Whatever the case, the highest percentage of escapes came from the ranks of the Royal Air Force, who were kept in officers' camps.[54] Unlike other ranks who were often accommodated in tents or in hastily built barracks, many officers were imprisoned in established buildings such as old castles, and it was from one of these, Camp 12, near Florence, that six POWs escaped before the Armistice. All of brigadier rank or above, they escaped through a tunnel in March 1943. Four were recaptured, and one died in Spain. The sixth escapee reached Britain, but he died in battle a year later.[55]

Successful escapes in pre-Armistice Italy by other ranks were exceptional, possibly as a result of improved conditions in permanent camps and resigned acceptance of status and subsequent acquiescence to a camp existence. Although tedious and defined by constant hunger, lice, rumour and longing for home, set daily routines and more liveable conditions helped to habituate men to POW status and some abandoned any escape plans – realistic or otherwise – that they may have had. As one Sidi Rezegh POW concluded from Camp 52 at Chiavari in March

1942, 'I have had enough of war, and am now sitting back critically, while the others do the dirty work.'[56]

Escape also demanded energy, and those who had ambitions of escaping had to put aside their plans until the first Red Cross parcels arrived to improve their physical condition. Equally, Red Cross rations could also have the effect of dissuading soldiers from thoughts of escape because camp life assured them of some food. Other POWs thought it more secure to stay put as any successful escape would involve a passable knowledgeable of Italian and reliance on the local population for food and shelter, a risky requirement as they were unsure of civilian attitudes.

In Newman Robinson's opinion, the longer men stayed in POW camp, the harder it became for them to escape, always believing that a better opportunity would present itself on another day or at another season. What they did not realise, though, was that the longer they postponed their bid for freedom, the more the captors' grip would tighten around them, while at the same time their 'resolve would weaken with inactivity and hunger'.[57]

Some POWs used escape not to attain freedom, but to infuriate the Italians. One man at Camp 65 did this quite effectively. Drunk on Italian wine, he would crawl through the fence and then call the guards to collect him.[58] In certain other camps, he would not have had a second chance to repeat his prank.

Ruthless action towards recaptured men often put POWs off trying to escape, as Bill Hindshaw witnessed in Camp 60, near Lucca. During the first three weeks of his stay, he witnessed two failed attempts, one by a South African who lost his nerve and, while running back to his tent was shot by guards, and another by a British POW who was shot and killed while climbing the fence. After these two costly incidents, an Italian priest was called to the camp who warned the assembled POWs that to escape in Italy would be pointless.[59]

Nevertheless, many POWs did believe that they would have a relatively good chance of successful escape. While in Camp 75 near Bari, Clive Luyt knew of a group who were digging a tunnel in order to escape, although he never considered joining it. The escape proved unsuccessful as the diggers misjudged the distance and their tunnel came up directly underneath the guard room, providing endless opportunity for discussion and humour among other inmates. When Fred Geldenhuis arrived at Camp 54, he immediately joined an escape committee which had already started on a tunnel. However, the peace talks between the Allies and Italy following Mussolini's fall progressed at a faster pace than the Fara Sabina tunnel and Fred and his committee never used it.[60] The more circumspect Dick Dickinson, also there at the time, was completely unaware of the escape activity and considered plans as 'more talk than action [...] there has to be outside contact and knowledge of the language. Then, too, there is always the uncertainty of reprisal or of being re-captured.'[61] In fact, recaptured POWs were usually placed in solitary confinement or in specific punishment camps for persistent escapers, such as Camp 5 at Gavi.[62]

At Camp 65 the so-called 'escape season' proved to be livelier than at most other camps. In the summer of 1942 four British POWs caused a commotion when they crawled under the fence. The last of these escapees was noticed by guards and recaptured. Following this incident the guards were especially vigilant and nervous. When two POWs walked towards the fence – apparently innocently – a guard started throwing stones at them to dissuade them from escaping. The two men however thought they were being attacked with grenades. Their shouts of warning caused panic in the entire camp and as the POWs rushed towards what they thought was a secure area, the guards in that area thought they were now being attacked by the POWs. The chaos ended when someone shot a burst of machine gun fire into the air. A while later, and in stark contrast to this pandemonium, one South African POW in the same camp simply put his kitbag on a wheelbarrow and walked towards the camp entrance. The guard assumed the man was part of a working party and opened the gate for him. The enterprising escapee walked to the nearest train station, but when his train stopped in Bari, he was caught and returned to the camp.[63]

David and Paul Brokensha, along with Dickinson at Camp 54, seemed to have been unaware of escape committees and tunnels. For the two brothers, escape plans were forgotten when they received a huge batch of letters from home shortly after arriving in Camp 54. Not bothering to put the letters in chronological order, they began reading. The tone of the news from home seemed slightly confusing at first, but gradually they realised that their elder brother, Guy, had disappeared while serving on the HMS *Formidable*. It was assumed that he had fallen overboard during the night after seeing the ship's surgeon about stomach pains earlier during the day. David was very reluctant to accept Guy's strange death as he had always seen his big brother as 'invincible ... for nearly thirty years he used to appear in my dreams, looking older, and asking, "Dave, don't you recognise me?".'[64]

Escape was not a priority for Dick Dickinson. Although he mentioned escape attempts from his camp, his diary shows that he was far more concerned with the frequency of Red Cross parcels and how many men were expected to share these parcels between them. The lack of letters from home also made Dick feel morose and to 'take a delight in being rude to people'.[65] Later rumours of Allied landings in Sicily and of Allied military advances made escape plans seem irrelevant to many POWs.

Others lacked the patience to wait for the Allies. Cyril Crompton's memoirs recall how POWs near Padua tried to escape from camp by pretending to be part of the work parties, while others looked for exit routes through sewers or over roofs. But the majority of those who escaped before the Armistice were recaptured, and this discouraged others. Cyril also found guards were very zealous sentries, as any mistakes on their part could result in them being sent to the front line as punishment, 'and that was a death warrant, they believed'.[66] In many instances, even though only a small minority of rank-and-file POWs put their escape plans into action, the elaborate plans and endless discussions about escape provided intellectual stimulation that alleviated boredom and even improved morale.[67]

All the while, there were more impulsive POWs who were determined to try to escape at any opportunity and at any cost, such as in the case of Fred Geldenhuis's earlier escape in Greece. Others repeatedly refused to accept being held against their will, as with Peter Johnson, who was one of the few UDF POWs who escaped several times before the Armistice. While working in a cement factory in Taranto in March 1943, as Peter recalled, 'speculation was rife that Italy, as soon as it was invaded, would probably surrender and we would be free, for our guards were all Italian and would disappear overnight'.[68] Invasion rumours and assumptions about the fragility of enemy forces convinced Peter and a friend to escape as soon as they heard that the Allies were making their way up Italy. They also feared that POWs would be handed over to the Germans and this was something they wanted to avoid at any cost.[69]

Peter's fear of being transported to Germany was well justified, as Berlin had been moving Allied POWs from Italy on to Germany since 1941.[70] In July 1943, for instance, a British POW wrote from Stalag IVB in Germany to the YMCA in Geneva, declaring that he was one of 2 500 POWs who had been transported from Italy to Germany. In his communication to the South African Red Cross, the Adjutant General in Pretoria commented that 'it would appear [...] that the above [transfer to Germany] was planned and probably carried out before Mussolini's fall [...] I consider for the present the less publicity given to the question of transfers from Italy the better.'[71] On the same day, the Italian Ministry of Foreign Affairs contacted the Swiss Minister in Rome to express indignation at Churchill's message to the King of Italy regarding the transfer of POWs from Italy to Germany. The Rome Ministry stated that Italy had no intention of transferring POWs to Germany and added that the transfer of 2 400 POWs from Italy to Germany between 20 and 22 July had been carried out by military authorities before they had received communication from Britain that no prisoners were to be transferred to Germany 'in present circumstances',[72] referring no doubt to the *coup d'état* against Mussolini on 25 July and negotiations between the Allies and the new government of Marshal Pietro Badoglio.

Peter Johnson's flight included a few close shaves with enemy forces and injuries from running into barbed wire while under fire. His friend lost his nerve, eventually leaving him alone. Recaptured when physically unable to carry on, he was taken for interrogation about his escape methods, as the Italian command was puzzled as to how he had been able to evade hundreds of troops. As he left the interrogation room, an officer 'touched [him] on the arm, and from a large grin, exclaimed, "it won't be long now".⁷³ Peter understood the reference to the Allied invasion and pending liberation of Allied POWs. He now knew, too, of the officers' opinion of Italy's fate, which could not be revealed openly. Peter was even more surprised when one of the Italian guards suggested that they escape together as the guard had plans to emigrate to South Africa.

Peter was taken to Tuturano and placed in a punishment cell along with other failed escapees with whom he immediately bonded. Their sharing of escape stories had the effect of motivating them to try again.⁷⁴ Meanwhile, the Italians were supposed to prevent German forces from taking control of Allied POW camps during the Armistice negotiations,⁷⁵ and all inmates were to be handed over to the Allies once the Armistice had been signed.⁷⁶ But there is evidence pointing to Germans taking control of POW camps and evacuating prisoners to Germany between the date of the *coup d'état* and the Armistice agreement, to which Peter's escape attempt observations from Camp 82 provide vivid testimony.

Peter and a friend had been working on an escape tunnel when their camp commander informed POWs that Mussolini had been deposed and that guards would probably 'no longer take seriously their duties of guarding [and] would probably desert their posts and go home',⁷⁷ confirming Peter's belief that Italian forces had lost faith in the war. When informed of the *coup d'état*, POWs were instructed to remain in their camp to be provided with food and shelter while they awaited the Allies' arrival, but Peter nevertheless decided to break out again. Escape was now much easier, as he and two other South Africans found that they could simply walk out past smiling Italian guards.⁷⁸ That effortlessness may have made the fleeing POWs too confident, and they were soon betrayed to fascist forces by a 'middle-aged gentleman who spoke a little broken English'.⁷⁹

This time, however, Peter's recapture did not bring him into contact with friendly Italian officers, but with German police officers. These he assumed to be Gestapo. Despite their fear of the alleged 'brutal tactics' used by Germans, the escapees spent a restful night in a jail cell and were then transported back to their camp, which was now under German control. As soon as Peter arrived, he swiftly joined an escape committee and in July 1943 escaped again through a hole in the fence, along with a larger group of prisoners. Observing the camp from a distance the next morning, he spotted how its entire population was being removed, 'destined, no doubt, for another prison camp in Germany'.[80] Being near Arezzo, this removal was most probably from Camp 38 near Poppi. If Peter's eyewitness account is to be relied on, this suggests that in the pre-Armistice period, there were more transfers of POWs than the listed removal of the 2 400 men which took place between 20 and 22 July 1943.[81] Peter managed to evade recapture by the Germans and spent the next year living in caves, helping the partisans, falling in love, and working as a lumberjack while trying to make his way to the Allied lines. He managed this finally in June 1944 when he reached L'Aguila along with a British reconnaissance party.[82]

Every single bloody Itie wants peace

Peter Johnson was the exception: by far the majority of the rank-and-file POWs remained in their camps. These men mostly heard about Mussolini's fall from guards, but prior to this they relied on rumours, pamphlets and hidden radios for news of Allied landings in Italy. These rumours would later have a significant effect on their fate.

Before the fall of Mussolini, the Allies made numerous efforts at establishing peace with Rome, and news of these would often reach camps, raising premature hopes of liberation. When Churchill and Roosevelt attempted to convince the civilian population of the benefits of peace by writing an open letter explaining that surrender was their only option, it created a particular rumour-filled stir.[83] Michael de Lisle, in an agricultural work camp near Foggia at the time, remembered that the newspapers containing this message cost two cakes of soap, instead of the usual cigarette or two. As camp translator, he carefully translated Churchill's and Roosevelt's words to be read out to all POWs, helping to raise morale.

Many camps were near cities and intensifying RAF activity and anti-aircraft fire enabled some fairly accurate assumptions to be made. In Dick Dickinson's camp, a pamphlet drop informed POWs of Allied victories in North Africa. Shortly after a bombing raid on Rome in July 1943, Allied aircraft dropped more pamphlets into camps which the guards scrambled to collect so that they could sell them for soap and cigarettes, illustrating the state of shortages in Italy by that stage. Propaganda pamphlets also stressed the deterioration of the relationship between Italy and Germany since the overthrow of Mussolini. One of them, as Dickinson noted, 'tells the Italians that Rome is going to be bombed by daylight so that the Ities can see we are not bombing their valuable antiques – a thing Germany would do at night and blame it on us'.[84]

Camp 52 prisoners had access to a hidden radio and news was written down which specially appointed readers would carry to different huts. Readers carried lecture notes as cover, to which they could switch should any guards make an appearance. When camp command prohibited newspapers, which POWs had been exchanging for cigarettes, it seemed to confirm that Italy was losing its battle against the Allies. Rumours abounded in the pre-Armistice period: in Camp 54 it was even predicted that Berlin itself would fall within weeks. The phase between Mussolini's toppling and the Armistice was one of widening optimism for POWs, with conversation centred increasingly on Allied victories. Inevitably, a favourite pastime became betting, usually cigarettes, on how long Italy would be able to hold out.[85]

The prospect of imminent Italian collapse was greeted with oddly mixed feelings on the part of some individual POWs. Towards the end of July 1943, Dick Dickinson, for one, observed that he agreed with the Badoglio government about continuing with the war. By not giving in immediately to Allied demands of unconditional surrender, Italy would be able to emerge from hostilities with some honour intact. Dick sought to distinguish British views from a more romanticised colonial view – and distinguishing turncoats from upstanding nationalists, he suggested that:

> On a question like this the colonial sees things differently from the Englishman; the latter seems to lose sight of the fact that a great number of Italian scum have turned pro-British and there are still decent Italians who are proud and pro-Italian.[86]

That opinion did not, however, last long. With Italy still failing to capitulate following the fall of Sicily and the bombing of Rome, Dickinson's view of the Italian diehards deteriorated markedly:

> the fall of Sicily has been claimed by Italy as a military victory! [...] they say that from Addis Ababa to Messina the Italians have met with numerically superior forces and tremendous odds! God, what tripe! The stupidity of these Italians is unbelievable![87]

By then, he had grown so impatient about the expected peace agreement that his criticisms extended to the Allies, as his diary noted on 1 September, 'Churchill makes a waffling speech and the Pope blabbers about world peace. Every single bloody Itie wants peace, and we do nothing about it. I am really browned off.'[88]

After the *coup d'état*, the Allies had demanded unconditional surrender from Badoglio's new government, although it would not be until 3 September 1943 that the Armistice would be settled.[89] It was during this period, between the fall of Mussolini and the Armistice, that the already troubled Axis relationship between the Italians and the Germans worsened, with many Italian soldiers expressing hostility towards their new enemy.[90] At the same time, as experienced by Mathys Beukes and Jack Thring, many guards became more sympathetic towards their captives.

In some camps the circulation of news was so advanced that it was the POWs who were able to inform their guards reliably that Italy had fallen. As Aussie Hammond remembered, 'our guards laughed when we gave them the news first, but they accepted the official confirmation shortly afterwards with their usual shrug of the shoulders'.[91]

Stay put

Following the *coup d'état*, Clive Luyt remembers being told, 'don't go running around the countryside, because certainly in Italy you don't know who is a fascist, or who was not a fascist'. What Clive heard was in fact a coded message by MI9: an attempt to prevent thousands of Allied POWs from escaping after the Armistice. Mass escapes by POWs forming guerrilla fighting units could lead to reprisals by the Axis forces. To inform them of the possible implications of such escapes, an order was sent by Brigadier Richard Crockatt of Military Intelligence to POW camps in early June 1943.[92] This coded MI9 instruction was read in camps by registered readers, and included a warning of 'disciplinary action to prevent individual prisoners-of-war attempting to rejoin their own units'.[93]

MI9 had by this time expanded to include the Intelligence School 9 (IS9), whose task was to aid escape and gather intelligence from escapees. In August 1943 MI9 and IS9 decided that 'there should be a big speed up, especially in the amount of [escape] material despatched to Camps'; however, the main destination of these escape aids was camps in German-occupied territory and the POWs in Italy did not benefit from this decision.[94] The military situation and the risk of German reprisals against escapees in Italy must have been seen to be too great, and the 'stay put' order was given as a precaution.

Michael de Lisle recalls the message from registered camp readers advising all POWs to remain in their camps when British forces took over. In his opinion, obeying the order was not 'as easy as that, [as there were] tremendous rumours of five point landing up the coasts of Italy on both sides'. The Allies had indeed landed on the Italian coast in September 1943, with Montgomery leading the Eighth Army and the American General Alexander in charge of the entire campaign. Monty was sceptical from the start, believing that their plan was flawed. He was right; the war in Italy was characterised by extreme difficulties, the first of which were the drawn-out battles around Monte Cassino that started in January 1944 and only came to an end in May that year. The propaganda on the BBC World Service, to which many POWs had access, contributed to the high, but fatally flawed hopes of the prisoners. Its aim was to create the impression that the Eighth Army was moving north quickly, conquering Germans in its path. In fact, Monty and his men were moving far too slowly in the opinion of the American Fifth Army.[95] By December 1943 Monty had lost interest in the Italian Campaign and left the Eighth Army to command the 21st Army on the Second Front.

If the POWs were waiting for their fellow countrymen to liberate them, they would be even more disappointed. It would not be until the next year that the 6th South Africa Armoured Division would land in Taranto. They played an important part in this campaign, but although they were known as the 'Tobruk Avengers', their focus was not on liberating POWs, but on gaining ground and expelling the Germans from the land.[96] Alas, the 6th Division would become caught up at Monte Cassino, along with the Americans, Indians and New Zealanders.[97] Rome was captured at the beginning of June 1944, but it was not until May the following year that the war would be over in Italy.[98]

Most POWs had no way of verifying the rumours; they could only speculate on the landings and if they would mean the end of the war or their liberation. Confirmation of the Allies' arrival in Italy reached them at the same time as the instruction that all POWs should remain in their camps, waiting for the advancing Allies to liberate them. Ike Rosmarin's excitement was boundless as he pictured the Allies 'hedge-hopping across Italy'. In a week or two they would be free: 'freedom was a possibility, no longer an improbability'.[99] It would seem that Ike too had been listening to the BBC World Service.

At Armistice, of the thousands of Allied POWs in Italy, all could have had a chance at liberty had negotiations between the Badoglio government and the Allies reached a swift conclusion and had orders from the London War Office and MI9 not been so confusing for captives. While the Middle East Defence Committee in Cairo believed that mass escapes would aid the Allied advance by creating difficulties for the German Army, and the head of the Cairo office, Lieutenant-Colonel Simonds, had already devised escape instructions that involved POWs being aided and evacuated by invading Allied forces, London, however, believed that mass escapes would cause organisational problems and slow down the Allied advance.

These disagreements resulted in Simonds being left with four officers – one American and three British – to coordinate the assistance of the thousands of POWs following Armistice.[100] On 6 September, the Italian authorities attempted to honour their agreement to protect Allied POWs from German control and instructed commandants to defend the camps, failing which all white prisoners were to be released while black POWs were to remain interned. To the end, a racial pecking order was adhered to. The camp order also required, rather impractically, that freed POWs be given 'reserve rations' and helped to reach either Switzerland or the Adriatic coast.[101]

The commandant of Camp 49, an officers' camp near Reggio Fontanello, apparently obeyed the order to assist POWs to attain freedom, but at Villa Orsini, where General Klopper was held, his counterpart refused, although Klopper and those with him decided to leave as they rejected the War Office 'stay put' order.[102]

When he returned to South Africa, Klopper featured in a radio broadcast in which he related his experiences in North Africa and in POW camps. All POWs, Klopper reported, had had high hopes of escape following the Armistice, but 'it soon became apparent that any organised large-scale escape of prisoners of war was out of the question due to lack of supplies, transport, arms and assistance [...] the only chance of getting away would have to be through individual effort.' He stressed that Allied forces were 'up against a determined enemy [and] over-optimism among the POWs was cleverly exploited by the Nazis, who let false information trickle to the prisoners.'[103]

As Uys Krige stood watching a German patrol nearing his camp, he became aware of 'the fear that is the worst of all fears, the fear verging on panic'. Uys and three others from Camp 78 had spent the previous night on the outside of the camp, but were stuck as they could not find a path over the mountain that lay directly behind the camp. From where they were they could clearly see the Germans enter the camp, followed seconds later by the loud sound of machine gun fire. The sight of the Germans brought these four face to face with reality and they quickly found a route over the top of the mountain. At one point they ran alongside two of their erstwhile Italian guards who had discarded their guns and were also trying to get as far away from the Germans as possible.[104]

At other camps containing rank-and-file POWs, commandants appeared to have responded generally to the Armistice and to the order to protect POWs against Germans, but according to their political inclinations. Therefore, committed fascist commandants held POWs back until German forces arrived, while those who had become disillusioned with the fascist cause often assisted POWs to flee or simply abandoned their positions, leaving camps with no control structure. Ordinary guards reacted in a similar way, and most seemed relieved to be freed of their military duties. Bill Hindshaw remembered that at first guards became very friendly when they heard of Mussolini's toppling, and then, when Armistice was finally agreed, 'every sentry bar one changed into civvies and destroyed his rifle'.[105] Following the disappearance of the most of the guards at AJ Cremer's camp, the POWs were informed by the Italian commander that Italy had surrendered and that the POWs were now free to do whatever they wanted.[106]

Kouldn't Get Frough

At the same time, Bill Hindshaw was working on a farm with 50 other POWs, all of whom escaped when they heard the news of the capitulation. After a few confusing days looking for shelter, Bill and four others eventually found refuge with an Italian farmer. Here they stayed for the next 13 months, working as farm labourers, making cheese, playing cards and waiting eagerly for news of the Allies' progress in Italy. When they heard that the Allies were near Genoa, they decided to take the risk to reach them. Their journey towards the Allied lines was marked by narrow escapes, hunger, sore feet and severe cold. However, Bill's group were successful; with the help of Italian partisans they joined up with the Allies at Belvedere in France in January 1945. They had walked for 39 days, but the reward was great. They received clean clothes, had proper baths and were presented with a 'five star' meal by the Americans with whom they were housed before they started

Stanley Smollan (far right) and his fellow escapees in Italy, 1943. COURTESY STANLEY SMOLLAN

their journey back to the Union.[107] As far as Bill could ascertain subsequently, only three of the original 50 POWs on the farm reached Allied lines, while the rest were recaptured by the Germans.

Many of the mass escapes took place from Camp 54 near Fara Sabina. Stanley Smollan was part of a group of six who decided to ignore the 'stay put' order. Fortunately for them, Berchina and Attilio Venetonni, who lived near Montorio Ramano, provided them with food. The escapees spent most of their days hiding in caves. It was only at night that they emerged from cover to go into town and listen to the BBC. The Venetonnis also had contact with partisans who supplied the men with civilian clothing. Stanley and his fellow escapees lived like that for 13 weeks, but when 'one day the Germans arrived and they caught a family with some prisoners, the people were shot and the homes destroyed. So we said this is enough for us.' Not wanting to subject the Venetonnis to risk such as this, the men left for the village of Gerano. Here they were helped once again by the underground and by the De Lellis family, whose son, Tammaso, was a POW in South Africa's Zonderwater prison camp at the time.

Berchina and Attilio Venetonni were among the many Italians who provided a safe haven to South African escapees. COURTESY STANLEY SMOLLAN

By now it was early 1944 and the Allies had landed at Anzio, only 130 kilometres from where Stanley and his friends were in hiding. They made it, and 'nearly mobbed the sentry in [their] excitement' when they finally reached safety. A few days later, Stanley's mother received a telegram with the news that her son had arrived in Cairo. From June 1942 until that time, she had only known that he was 'missing'.[108] As soon as he got home, Stanley tried to secure early repatriation for Tammaso, but to his amazement, Tammaso declined his help, saying 'thank you, very much. But I am a fascist and I am an officer.'[109]

Clive Luyt's main motivation in escaping was to avoid being captured by the Germans. As he warned companions:

those Germans fought a war in North Africa to catch guys like you and me, they're not going to give up, [...] give them just a couple of days to reorganise and we'll be in a truck and off to Germany, which is exactly what happened to a lot of chaps, I said let's get out while we can.

Still, he did not rush. Only when the guards had thrown away their rifles on 11 September and left POWs to their own devices in Camp 54 did Clive and a companion decide to leave, ignoring instructions from senior NCOs that all POWs were to remain in the camp. Clive and his friend John Barclay remained in the area around Marcellina and Monte Gennaro for the rest of the war, living off the land, stealing sheep, eating snails, ricotta, fresh fruit and whatever else they could scrounge. They did not attempt to join up with the Allied lines, nor did they attempt to reach Switzerland. The two of them adopted the names of Carlo and Giovanni and immersed themselves in the Italian peasant lifestyle. It was during this time that Clive befriended an Italian by the name of Mariano, who regularly pointed out sheep that belonged to a certain Dmitri, who, according to Mariano, 'was a *Fascista* so it was okay if we stole his sheep [...] we didn't argue and we stole quite a lot of his sheep from time to time, at one stage we had our own private flock of 14'. On 8 June 1944 they heard that the Allied line had moved past them towards the north and that they were 'no longer on the wrong side of the German Army'. By 21 June they were on their way home.[110]

When Clive returned to Italy years after the war, he found that Mariano had died and that his family could not afford a gravestone. Clive and John offered to pay for a stone, but by this time their Italian language skills had deteriorated and the stone was inscribed with Mariano's date of birth and date of death, followed by 'Carlo and Giovanni.'

Another yet more stubborn escapee was Fred Geldenhuis. Like Stanley and Clive, Fred and a few others simply walked out of their camp at Fara Sabina on the morning of 10 September. POWs had cut a hole in the camp fence 'big enough for an ox wagon to go through' and waving at the Italian guards, they started their journey to freedom optimistically. At first they hid near the villages of Montorio Romano and Scandriglia, where they were cared for by an Italian girl, Lina, who supplied them with food and informed them of what the Germans were up to in the surrounding area. Eventually Lina's mother decided to take her daughter to Rome as the town's people were starting to talk about Lina's 'association' with Fred. Their friendship was significant to both of them, with Fred visiting Lina in Rome and then Lina returning to the village. Fred felt so strongly about her that he gave her a ring that was a gift from his father. Eventually the poverty of the Italian peasants became too much for him to deal with, especially when a family killed their pet rabbits so as to prepare a meal for him. Fred decided to go. He successfully reached the Allies, who promptly sent him back to join the partisans.

Fred was an active and successful partisan, but sadly for him, it was not to remain this way. Following a few daring escapades with his Italian companions, including one operation in France, he was recaptured by the Germans in Monteflavio when he was betrayed by fascist Italians. The Germans did not realise that they had captured one of the most determined escapees of the war, and Fred jumped from the truck which transported him while the guards were half asleep. This time his freedom was very short lived and when he inadvertently walked into a trap, he found himself being transported back to the POW camp near Fara Sabina.

Amazingly, Fred immediately joined an escape committee. Their first attempt was foiled when their plans were betrayed to the Germans by a spy amongst them. Their second attempt at freedom ended in chaos when about 50 men stormed the fence. The Germans opened fire and one South African, Vincent Freeman, was killed.[111]

Mathys Beukes grabbed a Red Cross parcel when he heard about the Armistice, and he and four friends at first stayed with an Italian family less than a mile from their camp near Mortara, south of the Swiss border. When Mathys's fellow escapees decided to stay with the family, he moved on alone. He occasionally exchanged his labour for food, avoiding contact with the local population as far as possible. Eventually he joined up with two British escapees and together they managed to reach the safety of neutral Switzerland. Of the estimated 13 868 Union

POWs in Italy at that time, Mathys was one of 896 South Africans who successfully escaped to Switzerland.[112]

Unlike Fred Geldenhuis, Clive Luyt, Bill Hindshaw, Mathys Beukes and Stanley Smollan, many POWs obeyed the 'stay put' order, although many could not resist at least exploring the surrounding countryside. The men went on what they called 'curiosity walks', looking for food or just enjoying the ability to walk past the gates of the camps.[113] Most of them returned to their camps at sunset, having made sure during the day that they gathered enough food. Dick Dickinson estimated that about 700 POWs left the camp when the Italian guards disappeared. He was part of a smaller group who, when they reached Montorio, became 'the centre of attraction' when young Italian girls showed great interest in them. Dick's group was offered a large meal of spaghetti, bread and wine. Despite the abundance of food, of which Dick could not finish his second helping, he regarded 'the poverty of these people [as] terrible, but still they are proud and want nothing from us. We, the English, are their friends. [...] Any malice I have borne the Italians is gone.'[114] It was a far cry from his pre-Armistice contempt for Italians as 'scum [and] cowardly'.[115]

Dennis Mugglestone remembered how the Italian peasants offered food and shelter if they wished to escape, yet the POWs returned to camp for three nights, 'with rabbits, poultry, and even full-grown pigs'.[116] No doubt these luxuries were from the local population. During these short interludes of freedom, many POWs found that as they were now dependent on the rural Italian population for survival, their opinions of the Italians became markedly more positive.

David Brokensha, his brother Paul and Jack Mortlock did not get much of a chance to form opinions about the local population because they were apprehended just over a week after leaving Camp 54. For years David believed that his group was betrayed underhandedly by a local farmer, but when Paul visited Italy after the war, he learnt that the farmer had been forced to betray them to a group of German soldiers who were rounding up escapees. As they were taken back to the camp under German guard, David and Jack briefly considered overpowering their captors, but decided against it: 'Paul, he told us wisely it wasn't a good plan, but I had nightmares about that for years afterwards, 20, 30 years, guard dogs and lights behind me.'

Uncertainty and confusion reigned during this time and many POWs were victims of false information, rumours and to an extent, their own preconceptions. Some in Peter Ogilvie's camp believed that the Italians invented the 'stay put' instruction to punish POWs for handing out spare tins of food carrying anti-fascist messages to local civilians. Ogilvie himself believed that the order from the War Office was in fact a hoax invented by the Italians to keep the POWs – already suffering three weeks without their Red Cross parcels as punishment – in their camps until the Germans arrived.[117]

Just as in North Africa, hope of an Allied liberation – for these prisoners at least – came to an abrupt end. After the war, MI9 compiled a report on its work, and listed several reasons why its efforts to aid escape in Italy were less successful than in Germany. These reasons were as follows:

> The inefficiency of the Italian administration handicapped our communications to such an extent that code messages and escape equipment often took more than a year to reach the P/W Camps. In addition, much of the mail was lost or destroyed by the Italian censors, probably through laziness on their part. Prisoners of war were guarded with much greater care than those in Germany. The Italian collapse came just as IS9 was getting into full stride.[118]

For those who took matters into their own hands and escaped but who were unlucky enough to be recaptured by the Germans, the disappointment was made conspicuous when the letters 'KGF' were painted in yellow onto their clothes. This abbreviation stood for *Kriegsgefangenen*, or prisoner of war, which some POWs turned into a rueful joke, claiming that it stood for 'Kouldn't Get Frough' to the Allied lines.[119]

CHAPTER FIVE

UNEASY INERTIA

While Clive Luyt, Bill Hindshaw, Stanley Smollan and Mathys Beukes were finding their way across Italy, thousands of POWs remained in their prison camps, hoping for the best. Those South Africans who were captured at Sidi Rezegh and Tobruk had by now been under Italian control for 22 months and 15 months respectively. With the passing of time, and general acceptance of their captivity, it is possible that many of them had retained their initial perceptions about the German forces as the more honourable of the two enemies. This idea was based on favourable first impressions of their German captors while still in North Africa, and, however ironic, it was shaped largely by the German habit of apologising for the fact that they had to be handed over to the Italians. Many of these rank-and-file POWs had been working on Italian farms and although some had ways and means of obtaining information about the progress of the war, the news they received was generally viewed with cynicism as they suspected it to be enemy propaganda. By the end of 1943, therefore, the men had become largely detached from the war and were not aware of the details regarding Nazi warfare techniques and atrocities.

Those Union POWs who waited in their Italian camps for the Allied forces to liberate them did not realise the enormity of the risk they were taking. Many regarded the Italians as being fickle in their political ideologies, and felt they would not be able to rely on Italian support once they escaped. In this way, however, they unknowingly gambled their freedom, because at that moment the German forces were already scouring the Italian countryside for escaped POWs. Those POWs who ventured into nearby towns exploring and looking for food, and perhaps hoping to meet up with Allies, were in for a similar shock. The idea among many Union POWs that the Germans were, as Fred van Alphen Stahl said, 'bastards, but they were *just* bastards', was particularly naïve and misinformed at that point of their captivity.

The meticulous ruthlessness with which Germany prosecuted the war was evident from the beginning. On the eve of the Polish invasion, Hitler emphasised 'that the aim of the war lies not in reaching particular lines but in the physical annihilation of the enemy'.[1] Education officers and frontline newspapers helped to disseminate and reinforce Nazi ideology among ordinary German soldiers, many of whom had been exposed to fascist ideals since childhood through the Hitler Youth movement. Characteristics such as sacrifice, endurance, obedience and loyalty were underpinned by the sense of Aryan race supremacy.[2] The first years of war were marked, as is well known, by Nazi military successes. By June 1940, the French had yielded to the German offensive, splitting into an occupied zone and the self-ruling Vichy Government. Across Europe, German invasions were characterised by civilian panic as populations tried to flee oncoming forces, some driven by memories of the previous world war, with others now experiencing atrocities at first hand.

Following their initial victories, the Nazis now anticipated the taking of Russia and on 22 June 1941, a year before the fall of Tobruk, the Operation Barbarossa offensive of Hitlerian 'annihilation' was launched.[3] Within the first three weeks of the campaign, the Soviet Union suffered 2 million casualties, with about 1 million of them taken prisoner. Towards the end of the campaign 5 700 000 Russian soldiers had been captured, of whom 3 300 000 died in prison camps. Regarding Russians as *Tiermenschen* or *Untermenschen*, and also because Russia was not a signatory of the Geneva Convention, the Nazis felt enabled to unleash the full force of their race-based wrath on Russian soldiers and POWs alike.[4]

The atrocities meted out by the Soviet Union against German POWs were equally ruthless. Many German prisoners were summarily shot by their Russian captors, who ironically also viewed their enemy as non-human. Later German POWs were used as slave labour and accommodated in horrendous conditions. Of the 3 150 000 German POWs captured by the Red Army, about 1 million died in camps. Germany and the Soviet Union both forbade the Red Cross from visiting any of their camps in the Eastern theatre of the war.[5]

Towards the mid-1940s, the Nazis were losing their grip on Europe and the Middle East. The Allies defeated Rommel's forces at El Alamein towards the end of 1942 and by February 1943, the German Army had surrendered in Stalingrad. As if this were not enough, Mussolini lost power in Italy and by September of that year the Germans had to take over the fighting in Italy, stretching their campaigning resources even further. By this time many Germans, soldiers and citizens, had begun to realise that Hitler's frenzied warmongering would lead to the ultimate destruction of Germany. As their morale eroded, some Germans defiantly criticised their leader, while others became more determined to put Nazi ideology into practice.[6] Throughout the war, however, Hitler remained unwavering in his pursuit of German military goals. In warfare, the position of 'inferior' enemy POWs became precarious, with the Führer classifying them in much the same way he did the Jews. Hitler had no sympathy for those suffering in prison camps, saying that 'in the POW camps many are dying. It's not my fault. I didn't want either the war or the POW camps. Why did the Jew provoke this war?'[7]

The fact that Allied POWs were protected by the Geneva Convention counted for something, although that did not mean that its terms were not liable to be manipulated. In September 1942, Berlin announced that Germany held many more POWs than the Allies, placing the balance of power regarding reciprocal agreements and retaliatory acts in its hands. Nazi propaganda also asserted that, since the Allies were 'indifferent' towards the rank and file, all Allied POWs would be housed with Russians, where Geneva Convention guidelines did not apply. In that calculation, Germany had no need to fear Allied retaliation as the only measure the Allies could have taken was to make German POWs reside with Italian POWs, with both their countries being signatories to the convention.

Inevitably, though, as Germany's fighting fortunes fluctuated, an increasing number of its soldiers fell into Allied hands. In the Mediterranean, for instance, 500 000 Italians and a 'significant number' of German soldiers had been taken prisoner by the middle of 1943. The consequence was two-fold. On the one hand, the German command became more desperate to secure military victories, but on the other, it was also pushed into a weaker negotiating position on POW matters as the political issue of reciprocity regarding their treatment became an issue of greater concern.[8]

Those POWs who did not escape following the Italian Armistice would soon find themselves caught up in the struggles of a dictatorship increasingly desperate to prevail. Yet, for all the critical situation in Western Europe, few Union POWs recalled having been fearful of the conduct of German soldiers or of German treatment of their enemy, based on their desert war experience. However, when Germans arrived at Italian camps, it brought a rude awakening to harsh realities.

Scared stiff

Like many other camp leaders, the celebrated Snakebite Cockcroft of Camp 82 also received the MI9 'stay put' order and he told the men, including Bernard Schwikkard, to remain in camp. Bernard trusted Snakebite and did not believe that he would give them anything but 'good advice'; however, not even Snakebite could have foreseen that the Germans would reach the camp before the Allies did. Bernard knew that a large number of POWs in his camp ignored Snakebite's instructions and escaped – and when the Germans arrived, he blamed himself for not having taken that initiative. In his memoirs Bernard exonerated Snakebite, stating that he 'never felt any resentment towards Snakebite for his decision, but regret not having relied on my own common sense instead. My only excuse was that I was an ignorant but obedient soldier.'[9] Clearly Bernard was unaware that Snakebite's 'advice' to them was in fact an order from MI9.

The Germans imposed strict discipline in the camps and did not tolerate the slightest disobedience or disrespect from POWs. Under this new form of imprisonment, POWs were deprived of even reflecting on the missed opportunities of freedom. Aussie Hammond remembered that their 'state of confused thinking and uneasy inertia was rudely shattered by harsh shouting'.[10] The voices they heard were German, and their camp had been surrounded by efficient-looking German soldiers who sent away the dispirited Italians. As Aussie and his fellow POWs were ordered back to their huts they discussed amongst themselves their lost opportunity of obtaining freedom. Aussie recalled that:

> Stupefied and resentful, the prisoners began ambling towards their huts, all talking at once [...] Such leisurely and half-hearted compliance with orders may have been good enough for our easy going Italian guards, but it certainly was not good enough for the Germans. Accustomed to instant obedience, they shook up their ideas by firing an overhead burst from their Bredas [machine guns]. We scattered like rabbits.[11]

Yet again, as in North Africa, their hope of imminent liberation was thwarted. All over Italy, German forces were taking control of POW camps and hunting down escapees. From his Laterina camp, a dejected Michael de Lisle reflected that, 'our disappointment was acute, on our own account and also for the failure of what had seemed such an obvious design for the capture of peninsular Italy'. They had 'obeyed orders which were definite and seemed reasonable, and had been badly let down. No parachutists dropped to conduct us to Leghorn. The house of cards collapsed and left us feeling dreadfully flat.'[12]

Up to the eve of the Germans' arrival at Camp 52, Ike Rosmarin and others had also been eagerly waiting for their liberation.[13] Yet, they were 'rudely awakened at dawn by young SS troops who had replaced the Italian guards along the wire'.[14] Ike knew now that they had misjudged the determination of the Germans to achieve victory. In a state of panic, many POWs tried to escape the camp through the storm water drains, but they were all caught and punished by their new captors. Ike described the German takeover of his camp as 'a display of jack-boot terror tactics to intimidate us and put the fear of God into our hearts. The trigger-happy SS spraying bullets around the camp succeeded in doing just that.' Ike knew of at least one POW who was killed by machine gun fire that day.

It was only now, faced with German soldiers for the first time since their capture in North Africa, that POWs became gripped by real apprehension of the enemy, and in describing their takeover of camps it is the emotion of fear that becomes a core part of the experience.

For Ike Rosmarin, the thought of going to Germany was especially frightening as he was Jewish and 'scared stiff'.[15] Others, most notably Fred van Alphen Stahl, had encountered German conduct even before the Armistice. As he was being moved to a camp in the north of Italy, his group came across retreating Germans and in an impulsive moment of bravado, he shouted *'arrivederci dedesci' [tedeschi]*, 'whereupon a sergeant and

> two of his *handlangers* pulled me out of the ranks and they started pistol-whipping me, hitting me with their pistols and fists and I dropped and I dropped my bag and they kicked me and as I got up they beat me with the pistol again and having this malaria I was in a pretty poor state and finally I thought no – people say, or some people say they know the moment of truth and I was at peace with the world and I said 'alright I'm going I'm going' and I got up to face them for the last time and that chap gave me another crack across the face and I dropped … and that was the end of it, I was unconscious.

Following this brutal experience, Fred tried to escape on the journey to Germany, leaping from a train with others, but this attempt was unsuccessful as malaria prevented him from keeping up with the rest of his escape group.

However, not everybody's initial German encounter was entirely harrowing. Four days after the Italians left Dennis Mugglestone's camp, German soldiers arrived and apparently told Dennis and his friends that they were obstructing the German Army's work by 'walking all over the show'. Shortly afterwards, they were marched to a train station where they were loaded onto cattle trucks, along with the horses that drew the carts of their rations. They were now on their way to Germany.[16]

For David Brokensha and Dick Dickinson the experience was one that they recalled many years later almost with fondness and nostalgia. Just before they were transported, Dick recorded in his diary 'there was plenty of *vino* in the camp last night, and we also had a parcel between four'.[17] David's memoirs furnish a more exact depiction. While awaiting their transport from Frascati, a German officer informed the POWs that he would make sure that their last Italian meal would be good, as he could not tell what lay ahead for them:

> Sure enough, a lavish dinner was produced [...] that was my first taste of Frascati wine, which has remained one of my favourite Italian wines. Paul, Jake and I were seated at a long table of about twenty-five POWs, including Australians and British as well as South Africans. As it was a warm evening in late September we removed our shirts. Towards the end of the dinner, we were joined by a group of friendly young German soldiers who also took off their shirts because of the heat; I have tipsy memories of a jolly evening with loud conversations and much singing and not being sure who was friend and who was foe: for a brief interlude, it did not seem to matter. It was good that we had that merry evening because grim times lay ahead.[18]

Those 'grim times' awaited a large number of POWs transported by train to Germany across the Brenner Pass. For most the journey resembled the terrible experiences endured on the sea voyage from North Africa to Italy. This time, however, the threat came not from below through torpedo attacks, but from above, through Allied air raids.

Faced with the reality of captivity under German control, a number of POWs realised that they would have to take a last and desperate chance at freedom before they reached German-occupied territory.

Harry Rose-Innes before his capture and subsequent daring escape COURTESY ENID BATES

Harry Rose-Innes was one such a man. He remembered nothing positive about his time under the Italians in Camp 60, describing it as a 'Hell Camp.' By August 1942 he had been admitted to a hospital in Lucca where he found improved conditions and was able to gain physical strength and mental resolve. The news of the Armistice broke while he was attending a lecture in hospital. Even though this information held life-changing possibilities for all the prisoners in the hospital, they all sat quietly until the lecture was over before they dispersed and discussed the news in small groups.[19] On 10 September the Germans arrived, and the prisoners were put on standby to 'evacuate at a moment's notice'. However, it was only on 26 September that all patients who were considered fit enough were loaded onto a train for transportation to Germany. Arrangements had been made to accommodate 200 men on the train, but it was loaded with 580 POWs. As a result, their rations were severely affected and they had to make do with one loaf of bread between three men for two days.

From the start Harry was determined to escape before they reached German-occupied territory. Waiting for the train to slow down, he squeezed through a small window, only to realise with a shock, once he was clinging to the roof gutter on the outside of the train, that it had in fact not slowed down. He remained there for what felt like half an hour before he determined the time was right to jump. He hit the ground and came to a standstill with the 'train rolling past two feet from my head'. The train then stopped and guards emerged, obviously looking for something. Luckily for him, he was not seen and shortly afterwards the train continued on its journey. Harry was elated, revelling in the fact that 'after more than a year's captivity, I was alone – truly alone'. His thoughts were interrupted by the sound of footsteps on the gravel – it was Taffy, a friend and fellow POW. They were shortly joined by Frank who had also leapt from the train. As they assessed their situation, they became aware of more jumpers emerging from the dark. All in all, eight POWs had jumped from the train when it stopped briefly at a signal post. Harry, Taffy and Frank were joined by two more South Africans, two Greeks and one American, all of them officers.

The group managed to survive in Italy for a month before being recaptured and kept in the German headquarters in Florence. Harry managed to escape again but was caught once more and interrogated by a German officer in Padua who, interestingly, was curious to know why the Union was fighting against Germany, as 'this is not *your* war'. Following his second recapture, Harry was finally on his way to Germany. He never found out what happened to those POWs who were considered to be too ill for transportation to Germany from the hospital in Lucca.[20]

For Michael de Lisle the thought of going to Germany was just as unbearable. Even before his group reached the station to board the train, Michael slipped away from the marching men, remembering how in a

> moonlight night, tumbling down the slope, dry thorn bushes ... I thought surely the German guard must have heard me but tramp, tramp, tramp they went on, on the road and I was free, you know

> I had to drop down the slope and there was this river Arno, which is no small river, and I waded through that, luckily it wasn't deep, and up the other side and out into a vineyard with high trellis in the moonlight and lovely ripe grapes, oh I just enjoyed those grapes that were my first real touch of freedom.

He estimated that of the 50 POWs who were on their way to the train, only about 14 of them actually reached the station, the bulk making their escape along the way. Having been a translator between the Italians and Germans in the Laterina camp, Michael was confident that his language skills would help him find his way in Italy. He was recaptured once by the Germans, but escaped again.

Michael remained in Italy for 15 months, during which time he joined a communist partisan group for four months. He regarded the partisans as an organisation which 'justified their existence by raiding German convoys' for the sake of their own survival, not necessarily aiming to overthrow the enemy. When he heard about a guide who could take him across to the Allied line, he left the partisans to find, quite worryingly, that his guide wore 'pebbled lenses to his spectacles, he couldn't see where he was going – he stumbled and fell and broke his glasses and we had to see him over the lines'. They reached the Allies near Lucca in November 1944. His first night of freedom was, however, spent with the enemy in a POW camp because a British officer would not believe that he was South African, having no papers to prove his status as an Allied POW. Two weeks later he was interrogated by a South African unit, and although Michael still did not have the necessary papers for identification, his interrogator turned out to be a fellow student from the University of Cape Town. Between the two of them they remembered mutual friends, and in this way the interrogator was satisfied that Michael was in fact South African. At last he was on his way home.

As growing numbers of captives were transported, the Germans took more precautions against escapes from trains. When the persistent escaper, Fred Geldenhuis, eventually found himself on his way to Germany, his train was repeatedly inspected as the enemy suspected that POWs were removing floorboards to escape. There were also guards on the roof of the train. Fred's cynical view of German warnings that one out of every five POWs would be shot if it was found that someone had escaped, was that this was 'just another way to kill some of us'.[21]

The journey to German territory was slow, uncomfortable and repeatedly interrupted by stops to repair tracks that had been damaged during Allied air raids. More often than not, Allied airmen would target these trains, unaware that they were carrying POWs. With most raids, the trains were stopped as German guards scrambled for shelter in nearby fields. POWs were left in their enclosed cattle trucks exposed to the danger of bombing. AB Smith, a South African POW transported with 800 others from Fara Sabina, had a harrowing experience when their train was left on a bridge during an air raid, exposing it to fire from above. He believed that the train was left intentionally vulnerable by their captors, as

> Jerry knew damn well that the bridge was going to be bombed. The Itys knew and he knew. It was the tenth time it had been bombed and as always the recce plane had been over the day before. Yet as soon as the planes came in sight they shunted the train squarely onto the bridge [...] and left us.[22]

Later, Captain DS Harrison investigated the matter and concluded that he was

> satisfied that the account of the bombing as given by Pte Smith [...] is incorrect in that the train was not deliberately left on the bridge at the mercy of our bombers. [...] I have ascertained from three independent sources that the bridgehead had been damaged by previous raids and that the Germans were forced to manhandle trucks across the damaged spans one by one in order to minimise the risk of total collapse of the bridge [...] many Germans and Italians were also injured in the bombing and they as well as Allied PWs received treatment in the Orvieto hospital.[23]

Given the military situation in Italy, the Germans were eager to get as many POWs out as soon as possible. The cattle-trucks were overloaded – in Wally Wolhuter's case, he counted 50 men in his truck. This overcrowding prevented the men from sitting down and from using the bucket that was supposed to serve as a toilet. Ever resourceful, the men made a plan:

> We discovered that by stretching up we could see through a small grille near the roof of the truck. Those whose needs were urgent used this opening to urinate through, a couple of men lifting another until he could reach to put his 'personal equipment' through the grille before letting go. It was hilarious, with advice being offered from all parts of the truck as to the best way to go about it [...] for anyone who happened to look at the train as it passed this must have been a strange and amusing sight![24]

While Wally managed to keep his sense of humour in this testing situation, he was also a keen observer, noticing how some of the guards were not exactly cheerful about their totalitarian duties. As they neared the German border, a deal was made between guards and captives. The guards were desperate to supplement their cigarette rations as they were only issued with three per day. The POWs promised them a supply from their Red Cross parcels if the guards allowed them time to pick apples and grapes in the fields. Later on, at Bolzano, a German officer reprimanded local civilians and threatened to imprison them because they were speaking to the *'verdammte Englander'*. The officer ordered the guards to arrest the next civilian who spoke to the POWs, but as soon as the officer turned his back, the guards 'all laughed and said, *"Dass ist Scheisse"*.' It was also at Bolzano that Wally spoke to a German soldier who had fought at Tobruk, and instead of blaming the man for his captivity, Wally was happy to find someone who had shared in the desert experience. The men chatted happily while waiting for the railway bridge in Bolzano to be repaired, comparing their views on Tobruk.

However, Wally was not completely ingenuous, and he held the view that the Nazis would be responsible for the downfall of Germany.

When their guards were replaced by older men who had served in World War I, Wally found that many of them shared his views. From his conversations with the older guards, he remembered how they

> had no sympathy with the Nazis and told us they were fed up with it all. When certain that they could not be overheard, they admitted that the war had turned into mass murder and expressed their conviction that Germany could not win [...] the guards had the habit of first looking warily over their shoulders before speaking or replying to questions and we noted that the *'Deutsche Blick'* (German look or glance) was something fairly general, particularly when Germans spoke to prisoners-of-war in a way that might be regarded by others as being too familiar.[25]

For HL Wood and others transported from Laterina the journey took on an entirely different mood. They seemed almost to enjoy their untroubled trip, seeing it as a form of war tourism as they 'lived and laughed [their] way to Europe's citadel of culture'. For Wood, the national differences between Italy and Germany could be spotted in the natural environment, as 'the Teuton's love of symmetry was shown in his unconscious regimentation of the countryside – no bushes or trees dared dot the green fields.'[26]

Wood's experience, however, was the exception. As in North Africa and in the transit camps of Italy, poor hygiene conditions on the trains caused new outbreaks of dysentery. In some cases, men were locked into trains for several days with little more than a small bread ration, stale drinking water and a latrine bucket.[27] Fred Geldenhuis believed that 'it was normal to transport POWs in cattle trucks, but is below human dignity when it lasts for a few days. The toilet bucket is placed in the truck and not cleaned out at all. You can well imagine what it was like.'[28]

Disastrous results on general conditions

The German *Oberkommando der Wehrmacht* (OKW) was responsible for the system of prison camps. All POWs were first sent to large transit camps, also known as *Durchgangslager* or *Dulag*, before they were sent to smaller work camps, known as *Arbeitskommandos*. *Stammlagers*, also known as *Stalags*, were permanent camps used to house non-commissioned officers and privates. Those who were unwell or injured remained behind in Stalags when the rest of the rank and file were sent to labour camps. Fred van Alphen Stahl was one of those declared unfit for labour, and he spent the rest of the war in Stalag VIIIB near Lamsdorf. Officers were accommodated in an officer's camp, known as *Offizierlager* or *Oflag*, while British and American airmen were held in *Stalag Luft* camps. Separate camps for naval and merchant marine POWs were also set up.[29] While transit camps such as Stalag IVB at Mühlberg could accommodate as many as 7 000 prisoners at one time, work camps, which fell in the same administrative area, could consist of fewer than 100 prisoners, depending on the specific work they were sent to do.[30]

For many, the arrival in Germany, along with being 'processed in a brutally efficient manner', was a shock to the system. Giving name, rank, and army number, they were then issued with identity tags. All POWs were also photographed holding up boards which displayed their names and numbers. Wally Wolhuter remembered that they were searched, fumigated, inoculated and then had their hair shaved. He was impressed by the 'efficient German supervision and the good organization'.[31] For David Brokensha, however, the process was an especially harrowing experience. He was able to tolerate the barbers who sheared their heads with sheep clippers, and he could also stand being deloused 'by a Russian prisoner [who] sat in front of a bucket smelling of creosote [and who] applied the mixture with a mop on our armpits and on the groin area.' However, when David realised that they were going to be inoculated as well it all became too much for him. By the time he reached the inoculation queue it was three in the morning, and he fainted twice while waiting. He fainted a third time as a doctor struggled to inject him with a blunt needle, leaving him with a life-long fear of injections.[32]

At no point were POWs informed of what was to happen to them, being simply herded along from one thing to the next. But there were

David Brokensha. COURTESY DAVID BROKENSHA

also small acts of subversive resistance. For those at Stalag VIIA, POW registration was grasped as an opportunity to disrupt the German 'preoccupation with bureaucratic record keeping' by swapping names with friends while being photographed. Unfortunately, this backfired as POWs then found themselves receiving each other's letters once they were settled in permanent camps. Meanwhile, at Stalag VIIIA, at Gorlitz in Lower Silesia, Aussie Hammond and his friends made the most of manipulating the registration procedure when some decided to promote themselves, having heard that NCOs could not be forced to participate in work camps.

When questioned about civilian occupations, some, like Aussie Hammond himself, claimed to be farmers, possibly hoping for easier placement in rural labour. To mock the recording process, others gave occupations such as 'pickpocket', 'lion tamer', and 'acrobat'. These were evidently recorded and, in one apocryphal account, when a POW declared himself to have been a 'sorter', his interrogator wanted more details. The answer was, 'I used to work in a grocery store, sorting fly shit out of pepper.' The answer failed to amuse the interrogator.[33]

It did not take long for the Allied POWs to realise that they were in a much better position than the Soviet POWs. While in Stalag IVB, Dick Dickinson made a note in his diary that 'the Russians have a hard time', but he did not elaborate on this statement.[34] In the same camp, Wally Wolhuter noticed that the Russians were held in a separate section, but that the rest of the camp was a mixture of many nationalities.[35] In Stalag VIIIA, Aussie Hammond noticed how 'pathetically skinny and harmless' the Soviet POWs appeared. He was told by Belgian POWs that Germans regularly approached the Russians to form a volunteer corps to join the German Army. Apparently this recruitment method among the Soviets was very successful as they were promised food and uniforms. Aussie's surprise at the ease at which the Russians were able to switch sides was explained by his Belgian friend: the Russians 'die like flies [in the camp], so who can blame them if they are tempted?' According to the Belgian POW, the Russian dead were buried immediately as instances of cannibalism in the Russian compound had been reported.[36]

The difficult conditions had evidently by this time created a sense of camaraderie among POWs of different nationalities, and this extended towards the Soviets. In the Moosburg transit camp a Russian captive escaped from the Soviet compound and joined the South Africans. To help him to blend in, he was given an alias, 'Jan van der Walt', and taught to say *'Ek praat net Afrikaans'*. From Moosburg he was transported with his fictive countrymen to Stalag VIIIB, where he avoided an encounter with a female interrogator by leaving UDF POWs to claim that he could only speak Afrikaans.[37]

Records suggest that the tale of the Soviet POW may have been semi-legendary, for there is more than one version. Ike Rosmarin's memoirs supply a different camp number[38] and give the alias as 'Johannes van der Merwe'.[39] Another Stalag VIIA inmate recalled that a Russian POW entered their hut following a failed escape attempt in which he had been seriously beaten by his captors. By concealing him under the floorboards, the Union soldiers were able to help him to recover, thereafter adopting a 'bogus British identification to pass muster if any questions were asked'.[40] The discrepancies over the Russian's language, identity, and injury may point to a POW myth, but it does show that these men were united against their captors, something that would become increasingly important in the second half of the war.

Once they were registered, the newly arrived POWs had to adapt to their new circumstances. This was not an easy task however, because, just like the much criticised American newcomers in Italy a year before, the arrivals from Italy now had to adapt to an already established routine that had been set by those who had been there for much longer. By August 1943, the POW camps in Germany were crowded with Allied soldiers. However, when Italy surrendered, space had to be found for thousands more. In October 1942, for instance, the number of POWs in Stalag VIIIB was about 18 000. A year later, that number had increased to 30 000.[41] When Italy surrendered, the OKW was faced with 600 000 Italian POWs and 50 000 Allied POWs, all of whom had to be accommodated, forcing the hurried construction of additional camps as captives streamed in.[42]

As in North Africa and Italy, early experiences in German transit camps were grim. The bunk beds were packed to capacity, with some men having to share beds. David Brokensha and Wally Wolhuter both remember that they had to sleep on the floor.[43] Protecting Power and Red Cross inspections again produced numerous reports on conditions experienced by POWs, although the ratings used by inspectors were often inconsistent and open to differing interpretations, depending on what circumstances made up 'excellent', 'satisfactory' or 'wholly inadequate'. In their reports, some inspectors also seemed to have taken into consideration the effects of the general deterioration in Germany as a result of the war, and judged camp conditions at uneven or lower standards. In effect, some specific conditions may have been described as 'unsatisfactory' early in the war and 'good' by 1945.[44]

If this suggests anything, it is that if conditions were seen generally as 'poor' during 1943 when most of the South Africans arrived in Germany, circumstances must have been trying. With inspectors despatched to each camp several times a year and copies of their reports sent to all the relevant countries, the result was a massive amount of camp documentation for analysis.[45] Around 130 Stalags accommodated British and American POWs, but South African POWs were housed in a relatively small number of them.[46]

A report by the ICRC in November 1943 described Stalag IVB as a 'poor camp' and while its hygiene arrangements were described as 'satisfactory', the medical attention to POWs was deemed 'no longer adequate'.[47] Dick Dickinson and the two Brokensha brothers found themselves here, while the memoirs of Jack Mortlock and Dennis Mugglestone indicate that they too were sent to this camp on arrival in Germany. By February 1944, Stalag IVB was still accommodating many different nationalities who were not segregated into different compounds as was the case with most other Stalags. Camp authority also allowed POWs of different ranks to remain together, although officers informed the Red Cross inspector that they expected to be moved to officers' camps, while enlisted men were under the impression that they would be sent to work camps. NCOs viewed Stalag IVB as a permanent camp and expected to remain there for the duration of the war.[48] In that sense, opinions of the camp seemed to differ by rank.

Wessel Oosthuizen was among the over 11 000 POWs sent to Stalag XVIIIA in Wolfsberg, where conditions were described mostly as 'adequate' by an ICRC inspector in November 1943, although on clothing his report observed that, 'except for the men from Italy the clothing position is satisfactory'. The main inspection criticism was that the medical officer cleared men for work when they were obviously unfit for labour.[49] Although representations were made, it was not until April 1944 that camp medical officers were instructed to 'grade prisoners of war according to the work they are able to perform by taking into consideration the general state of health and the sickness established'.[50]

A delegate of the Protecting Power who visited Stalag VIIIA in October 1943 pointed out that it was 'badly overcrowded', with a severe shortage of beds and blankets. Other aspects of the camp were described as 'normal' (bathing and washing facilities), 'satisfactory' (toilet facilities), and 'rather poor' (food and cooking facilities).[51] When Aussie Hammond and AJ Cremer arrived with 695 other

South Africans in September that year, the camp contained 1 064 New Zealanders and 681 POWs from Britain, among other nationalities.⁵² Thereafter, by May 1944 the majority of POWs in Stalag VIIIA were confirmed as South Africans. An interrogation report on a repatriated POW noted the view that the South African camp leader, Regimental Sergeant Major Rossouw, showed favouritism towards South Africans and that British POWs 'suffer[ed] in consequence' by being overlooked. The cited reason for biased treatment was said to be the 'fact that many South Africans talk (sic) German [and this] results in the Camp leader obtaining support for his actions' from German command.⁵³

Although favouritism was not mentioned in 1944 camp inspection reports, with 'no complaints ... put to the Delegate of the Protecting Power', the influential role of Rossouw was noted. One report noted his effectiveness as camp leader in putting forward POW complaints over overcrowding in the discipline barracks, the wearing of clothing marked with red paint to indicate punishment, and the fact that men in punishment barracks were not allowed to participate in sports activities.⁵⁴ In March 1945, the Adjutant General, seemingly anxious to dispel any notion of special favouritism between South African POWs, quoted approvingly from the November 1944 Protecting Power report, stating that

> Conditions at this camp remain to be very good. The man of confidence, RSM Rossouw, indefatigably carries on with his fights for the betterment of the conditions of his fellow-prisoners both here at the camp and on the various working detachments and in all fairness it must be said, that he receives all support from German authorities.⁵⁵

Neither AJ Cremer nor Aussie Hammond was aware of tensions between British and South African POWs over preferential treatment. Indeed, for Aussie, he and other South Africans were 'British', minimising any Commonwealth national distinctions. However, friendship between South Africans and non-English-speaking Belgian prisoners, with whom conversations were usually conducted in Afrikaans, a language close to Flemish[56] may have led some British POWs to assume that they were speaking German, and that Rossouw had some Germanic affinity.

Conditions at Stalag VIIIB near Lamsdorf, were dismal when Fred van Alphen Stahl, Ike Rosmarin[57] and Peter Ogilvie arrived. Lamsdorf was the largest, holding over 30 000 POWs at its peak and controlling 235 work camps with 9 000 men. It was also the oldest POW camp, dating from World War I.[58] The South African authorities became aware of wretched conditions there as early as May 1943, before the arrival of the Sidi Rezegh and Tobruk prisoners, when a letter from a South African POW to his family reached the Adjutant General. Drawing on a familiar image of South African deprivation, the living conditions and food at Stalag VIIIB barracks were bitterly described as worse than those endured by South African mine workers.[59] By October 1943 the Protecting Power was emphasising that the large number of POWs from Italy had 'disastrous results on general conditions' in the camp and in the following month warned again of the effect that the Italian POW influx would have on all camps, the main concern being that of adequate food, clothing and accommodation.[60]

Confronted by such bleak accounts, AC Randall, acting on behalf of the Union's Adjutant General, informed Clara Urquhart of the local Red Cross that he was assuming 'that appropriate representations were submitted by the Protecting Power to the German High Command in July [1943]'.[61] While aware that conditions had deteriorated between March and June 1943, Randall still believed that prisoners in the work camps attached to Stalag VIIIB were experiencing better conditions than in the main camp. However, a November 1943 report from the Protecting Power revealed that circumstances in the work camps were little better, with food, hygiene, medical treatment and overcrowding the main concerns. In work camp E276, for instance, it was found that 'clothing conditions [were] bad especially of prisoners recently arrived from Italy', while in work camp E22 the quality of food was deteriorating and there was a 'poor' provision of medical supplies.[62]

Another aspect that caused great concern, at least for the South

African Red Cross, was news that Jewish POWs in Stalag VIIIB were being separated into Jewish labour camps. The Adjutant General, however, believed that the information was 'misleading' and that it referred to Palestinian POWs and not to British or Commonwealth POWs of the Jewish religion. He ascribed the separation of the Jews to Article 9 of the Geneva Convention which stated that 'Belligerents shall as far as possible avoid bringing together in the same camp prisoners of different races or nationalities.'[63] He emphasised that the Union would not take any action unless it received confirmation that South African Jews were being separated.[64]

Although Ike was 'scared stiff' when the Germans arrived at his Italian camp, he was not singled out as a Jew, nor was he sent to a Jewish labour camp when he arrived at Stalag VIIIB. In fact, Ike recalled an episode in which the German commander agreed to a request from Jewish prisoners that the tombstone of a Jewish grave be embellished with the Star of David.[65] Similarly, Fred van Alphen Stahl testified to the equitable treatment of a fellow POW who 'had sinus, which is not a killer, but they sent him across Germany with a guard to one of the clinics in the Alps, to have his sinuses attended to.' In at least these known cases, German camp command did not treat Jewish POWs differently from others. There were, however, cases of discrimination and maltreatment against POWs of Jewish origin, especially towards the end of the war. In Berga, for instance, Jewish-American POWs were put to work in a labour camp along with non-Jews. The circumstances in the camp did not meet the requirements of the standards of the Geneva Convention, and POWs were forced into slave labour, with many dying of starvation and illness.[66]

Officers were allowed to work according to the Geneva Convention, but little evidence exists to indicate that any of them actually volunteered for any working parties.[67] NCOs were permitted to undertake supervisory duties if they wished, while the rank and file had no real choice. While still in Italy, many POWs had, as already noted, worked on farms in accordance with the Geneva Convention stipulation that the work would not have any connection with military operations.

Of course, with the conflict having long assumed the nature of a

One of the German guards at Work Camp 1169.
COURTESY ANTHONY MORTLOCK

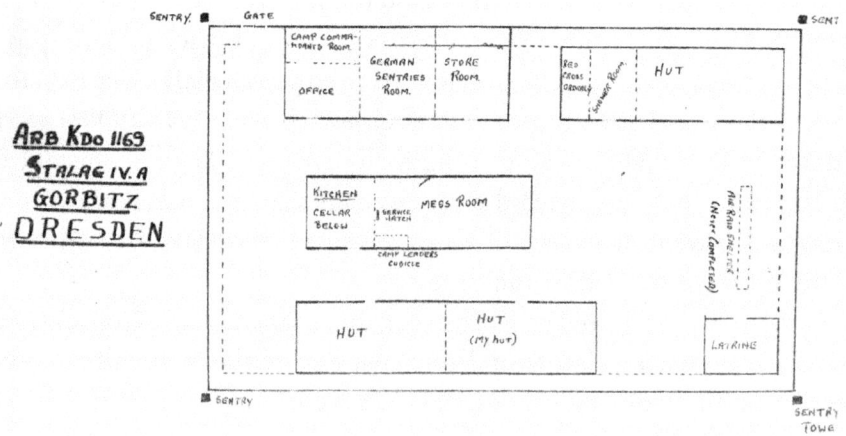

The layout of Work Camp 1169 near Dresden where among others, Jack and Harry Mortlock, David and Paul Brokensha tried to make themselves comfortable from 1943 to 1945. COURTESY ANTHONY MORTLOCK

South Africans in Work Camp 1169. Harry Mortlock is in the back row, 1st from left and his brother Jack is in the back row, 6th from left. COURTESY ANTHONY MORTLOCK

'total war', virtually any work, including agricultural work, was in aid of the war effort. The post-war 1949 revision of the Convention identified six categories in which POWs were allowed to work, these being agriculture, production or extraction of raw materials and manufacturing, but not metallurgical, machinery or chemical industries, public works and buildings, commercial business and arts and crafts, domestic service, and public utility services.[68] While many wartime captives had reservations about the type of work that they were required to do, in Germany most men appeared to welcome work as this was a means of dealing with long hours of boredom. Being part of a work camp also held other advantages, most of all the prospect of getting more food.

Fred van Alphen Stahl, Ike Rosmarin and Peter Ogilvie all remained in Stalag VIIIB until the end of the war. This camp became known as Stalag 344 in January 1944 when it was divided into two, with Stalag 344 being put in control of work camps to the west and Stalag VIIIB administering those to the east. It also seems that the camp division was to separate British POWs from American POWs.[69]

While Peter Ogilvie was not allocated to a work camp for some unknown reason, Fred van Alphen Stahl was continuously stricken with malaria, remaining in Stalag 344 as he was moved in and out of the camp hospital every three to four weeks. Although Ike Rosmarin spent most of his time in Stalag 344, he did get an opportunity to work as translator for a group who worked at a nearby training camp for German officers.[70] David and Paul Brokensha, together with Dick Dickinson, Jack Mortlock and possibly also Dennis Mugglestone, were all sent to work camp 1169 near Dresden where they worked in the post office. Mugglestone was transferred to Laussig near Leipzig to work in a cement factory in October 1943.[71]

Aussie Hammond, HL Wood, Cyril Crompton and Bernard Schwikkard all found themselves at different work camps in the vicinity of Breslau where they worked in sugar factories, with Bernard Schwikkard later being transferred to a coal mine near Waldenburg in Upper Silesia. Wood, registered at Stalag VIIIC at Sagan, also worked at a work camp in Poland, a coal mine in Fellhammer and a textile factory in Oberaltstadt.[72] Wessel Oosthuizen, registered at Stalag XVIIIA, initially worked on a wine farm on the border between Austria and Yugoslavia, but was later transferred to Graz in Austria where he joined other South Africans in a work party employed in filling in bomb craters. Fred Geldenhuis, chief of barracks 29–32 at Stalag VIIA, Moosburg, obtained the unique position of overseeing a group of black POWs in the camp's South Laager. This allowed him to move relatively freely between the different sections of the camp.[73] AJ Cremer remained in Stalag VIIIA until the end of the war, free of any labouring duties.[74]

In Italy, many POWs had come to realise that the provisions of the Geneva Convention did not mean adequate food. When it came to Germany, complaints from Allied POWs and from German soldiers regarding the quality and quantity of food were remarkably similar. Thus, in August 1943, German front-line troops complained of cabbage and potato soup that had a 'gluey' consistency, also described as 'nauseating but effective'.[75] Allied POWs also found the soup to have a consistency much like glue, and some even used it as glue to make model aeroplanes. Prisoners mixed their soup with sugar and corned

For a short but sublime time, bread and potatoes filled POWs' stomachs – until German infrastructure began to crumble before Allied advances. COURTESY DAVID BROKENSHA

beef to try to improve the taste, leaving barley bugs in the concoction in the belief that they contained vitamins.[76]

Dick Dickinson conceded that while the food in Germany was not always digestible, most men in his camp were putting on weight. Compared to the Italian bread, he considered the German bread to be inferior because it was made from potato flour and was 'pure hell' for anyone with a weak stomach. Though, to him, 'the only true answer [was] South Africa',[77] Dick and his friends had frequent debates on whether they would rather be in Italy or Germany.

The type and variety of food in work camps depended largely on the nature of the work done by the POWs, and in some cases they were actually fed very well. Unlike Dick Dickinson, Wally Wolhuter became particularly fond of potatoes, a staple in Germany. He remembered how they all

> developed a tremendous regard for the humble spud and learnt that one could survive on it alone for a very long time. Potatoes were, apart from bread, our favourite available food [...] a great deal of bartering took place in the potatoes that were brought in from outside the camp, principally by the French who worked on the farms and returned to camp in the evening. I was nearly always able to buy additional supplies with cigarettes and chocolate and [in] due course laid on a fairly regular source of supply.[78]

As the Geneva Convention had no conditions for food in work camps, merely stating that 'conditions governing labour detachments shall be similar to those of prisoners-of-war camps', it meant that POWs received Red Cross food parcels as well as extra food provided by the authorities in charge of the specific labour camp.[79]

Moreover, in most work camps, food from employers seemed to have been far more and of better quality than any of the rations provided in the main camps. Cyril Crompton and others who were assigned to a sugar beet farm in Breslau, received 'a big stew at midday, and in the morning a chunk of dry bread and ersatz jam which we would eat on the job'.[80] For his part, Aussie Hammond first became aware of the advantage of work camps when he met Belgian POWs who were labouring nearby the main camp. The Belgians would bring food with them and one night, they invited Aussie and others to join them in their compound. To the South Africans' delight, they washed down bread, potatoes and eggs with great quantities of Schnapps. Returning to their own compound later that night, the men were in a 'wonderful state of wellbeing [...] full of good farm food, more than we could comfortably hold. Loosening our belts, we lay back in our bunks feeling like lords of the earth. [A friend of Aussie] sighed contentedly, and with that he folded his hands neatly across his distended belly and gave vent to a tremendous burst of wind.' Inspired by the seemingly large quantities of food available to work parties, Aussie became the leader of work camp 4008, employed at a sugar factory, where he described the food as 'dull, but plentiful at last'.[81]

At the same time, the fact that POWs found conditions in work camps more congenial did not mean that they became complacent or passive. Once Aussie and his men were well established in the factory, they began stealing and trading in the sugar – as 'soldiers not factory workers'; and their German guards, also feeling the effects of food shortages, participated in this 'lucrative' black market.[82] Trading in sugar helped to augment POW food rations, something that became increasingly essential as German scarcities grew with the war entering its fourth year.

Bernard Schwikkard also worked in a Breslau sugar factory, where successful traders in sugar 'put it down their trouser legs in a stocking or whatever and take it into camp'. Endlessly creative, when they realised that the factory would not operate in summer, they started storing sugar in coal bags in order to continue with their trade. However, once the town's coal supplies began to dwindle, the factory's coal store became needed, leading to the discovery of sugar in coal bags. As punishment, Bernard and three others were sent almost 750 kilometres north-east to heavier labour at a coal mine in Oldenburg, far less appealing as a work camp than the sugar factory. Suffering from claustrophobia, Bernard had to find a way to get himself out of the mine. He started trading cigarettes for thermometers and got himself appointed as the labour party's medical officer. The thermometers were somehow tampered with to indicate a high temperature, and in this way Bernard was able to secure rest days for many fellow POWs who were considered '*krank*' and let off work for the day. Bernard also believed that a punitive element was at work, stating that 'Jews were sent to work in the coalmines because they were Jews.'

Bernard believed that it was during this period that he was able to acquit himself 'in a position of tremendous responsibility as a member of the camp staff [and] as medical orderly I was able to win the respect and trust of the other men [...] No one ever questioned the fairness of my decisions or complained about lack of attention to the sick.'[83]

Elsewhere, in work camp 1169 in Gorbitz, Dresden, beneficial trade was also taking place between POWs, guards and German civilians, which meant that Paul Brokensha could arrange for a birthday feast for his brother David. On 23 May 1944, David's twenty-first birthday, he

From left: Paul Brokensha, Jack Mortlock, David Brokensha, Harry Mortlock and Jake Jacobson in Work Camp 1169. COURTESY DAVID BROKENSHA

was treated to

> Breakfast: porridge, followed by fried sardines in tomato sauce with marmalade and white bread; Lunch: [...] a meat roll in batter; Afternoon tea: two real cakes, baked in the neighbouring bakery, made from: 2 heaped Klim tins of flour; ½ cocoa tin of sugar; ½ tin Klim; 1 packet of prunes, 1 packet of raisins; 1 tin egg powder; yeast; baking powder; the kernels of the prune pits; – plus extra ingredients for the icing.[84]

The Brokensha brothers and others with them in work camp 1169 were fortunate in that they worked in a post office where they soon realised that many of the parcels contained food. Dennis Mugglestone admitted that they supplemented their food by pilfering from parcels. On one occasion, for instance, POWs apparently found one that 'contained a roasted fowl and another parcel a set of dentures. The fowl was eaten on the spot and the dentures then wrapped up with the fowl bones and sent on its way.'[85] Food was not the only commodity, and the POWs in

UNEASY INERTIA

David and Paul Brokensha and Jake Jacobson braving the snow in Work Camp 1169.
COURTESY DAVID BROKENSHA

Dresden helped themselves to Leica cameras, pens and watches. Jack Mortlock remembered that they also found time to amuse themselves, at the same time doing their bit to make things difficult for the enemy, saying

> If we got landed with a truck that contained nothing to eat (as we very often did) then we indulged in the pastime of changing labels around. I remember a consignment of ladies' hats originally consigned to Berlin being re-consigned to the German Army at the Russian front. Very often Red Cross parcels used to pass through our hands. It was an unwritten law that no Red Cross parcel was to be tampered with but sent to its destination as soon as possible.[86]

Dick Dickinson's diary record, however, contains a version of a more serious incident, when a POW was caught stealing biscuits from a package. If caught, the consequences of theft from post office parcels were severe and sweeping:

> One of the English fellows was caught pinching biscuits today. There was a hell of a stink. Theft in Germany is, I should say, twice as bad as an offence as in any other country, and on top of it all, the theft was from a parcel to a German POW in America. The culprit is taken away and our camp commandant, a *Feldwebel*, takes it out on the rest of us. There were plenty of moans and squeals.[87]

As with numerous other aspects of captivity, South African POWs found that German medical treatment and repatriation matters were handled in a more effective and fair manner than had been the case with the Italians. The German camp system was better organised and its command was able to overcome organisational difficulties following the initial 1943 Armistice chaos. The Germans also appeared more cooperative than the Italians and even permitted a Berlin conference to be held where British medical officers in captivity were able to discuss medical issues in German camps. The fact that this took place in March 1945 may, however, be seen as a belated attempt to placate the advancing Allies. Still, it provided a window on medical issues in German camps.

Indeed, the concerns of the Berlin conference report were similar to those of the independent inspectorate which had been visiting camps regularly since the start of the war. That aside, its 1945 recommendations looked to be entirely unrealistic given German incapacity through a continuing loss of infrastructure and supplies. For instance, one recommendation was that the POW diet 'should be kept at a sufficiently high level to prevent epidemics', at a time when Berlin was barely able to feed its own. Other unfeasible recommendations included the building of new barracks in camps to alleviate overcrowding, allowing doctors communication with all camps in respective areas, and the conducting of a survey of all camp medical facilities, which 'would be most helpful to German and British medical liaison-officers'. One practical outcome was the appointment of a British medical liaison officer who would, among other things, 'have a small central store of valuable drugs for emergency distribution to British camps'.[88] This emerged at a crisis time when Aussie Hammond witnessed German soldiers being treated with bandages made of crêpe paper to treat horrific wounds sustained in fighting on the eastern front.[89]

While the other ranks were allocated to labour camps, those in officer camps had to find other ways to alleviate their boredom. The difference between Oflags and Stalags was evident not only in their living conditions and in the daily activities of men, but also in their average age, education and to some degree, attitudes towards their captors. Yet, there were also underlying commonalities, one of which was the tendency to allocate nicknames to German guards, and another the development of a distinctive POW jargon, although certain terms were different in Oflags and in Stalags. One example was the use of 'Goons' when referring to Germans.[90] Reverend James Chutter, a chaplain with the South African Second Division, and Jack Spencer,[91] both of them officers, used it in memoirs, whereas POWs interned in Stalags preferred to resort to 'Nazi'[92] or 'Jerry'.[93]

In December 1943, Chutter was sent from Stalag VIIA to Oflag VIIIF near Mährisch Trübau in the then Sudetenland. He described camp conditions as 'good'. POWs in this camp settled into their new environment with relative ease; they were able to initiate education programmes, sports and entertainment very soon after their arrival.[94] As officers were not required to work and could spend their hours as they wished, many devoted considerable time to devising plans for escape. The price of many failed attempts could be higher than just rigorous interrogation and punishment. In one case it was execution, when two men, 'whose escape had the nature of a special mission [were arrested and] shunted off to the Gestapo prison in Prague for questioning. Some months later [...] their remains, a "handful of grey ashes", in a most efficient-looking metal cylinder, were handed over for burial by our chaplains.'[95]

Being tasked with helping POWs to escape, MI9 devised various ways in which this could be achieved. Because MI9 also had the task of gathering information from escapees, most of their efforts went to officers' camps, as these men were considered to be in a better position to provide intelligence about the enemy. Various codes were developed which, when sent to POWs in letters from fictitious people, provided information about escape routes. MI9 also invented fictitious funds and societies from which parcels were sent. These packages contained escape material such as money, compasses, forged documents, maps, knives and chisels and even German uniforms, all of which were of use to escape committees in camps.

Two of MI9's most daring escape schemes were known as the Lancashire Penny Fund and the Hogmanay Scheme. The Lancashire Penny Fund was a fictitious organisation that sent Christmas crackers directly to German camp commanders along with letters asking the commanders to distribute the crackers to the POWs to 'brighten their Christmas Party'. Inside the crackers were money and maps. About half of these parcels got through to the POWs. The Hogmanay scheme was different in that it was aimed at labour camps. It took place in October 1943 and involved sticks of shaving soap that were sent to POWs in toilet parcels. The soaps contained maps and compasses along with money and a contact address for further aids. The success rate of this scheme was also about 50 per cent.[96]

The most well-known escape was of course from Stalag Luft III, masterminded by a South African, Roger Bushell. By digging tunnels, well equipped with lights and ventilation, the escape committee hoped to get 200 POWs out of the camp. Once out, the men could use their forged papers, compasses, maps, food rations, civilian clothing or German uniforms to secure their freedom as they moved across occupied land towards the Allies. Roger and some others even had train tickets with which they were to start their journey to freedom. However, things went wrong. A German guard noticed a man near the camp and realised that he was an escaped POW. Later the next day the Germans found the tunnel and after roll call 76 POWs were reported to have escaped. A furious Hitler ordered that the men were to be found and executed, but by this time Roger was on a train approaching Saarbrucken. Sadly for Roger and a fellow escapee, Bernard Scheidhauer, it seemed a stamp was missing from their forged papers and they were arrested at the French border. After interrogation, the two men were shot by Gestapo officers by the side of a road.[97]

After the war, MI9 issued the following account of the Stalag Luft III escape:

A mass escape from STALAG LUFT III in March, 1944, was a tragic climax to the history of escaping in Germany. There had been mass escapes before, but since the Spring of 1943, when the Germans adopted special measures for dealing with such outbreaks, most of the escapers concerned had been recaptured. The Escape Committee at STALAG LUFT III knew, therefore, that a mass break had less chance of success, but, on the other hand, the tunnel had taken a year to build, which seemed disproportionate effort if only seven or eight were to profit by it. The result of this mass escape is well known. Of the 74 who actually got out of the tunnel, only three reached England. The rest were caught by the Gestapo and SS Troops and 50 of them murdered. The rest were sent back to STALAG LUFT III and reported to the Escape Committee exactly what had occurred. They stated that everyone had strictly complied with the Geneva Convention and had given themselves up immediately they had been challenged, thereby carrying out the instruction laid down for all escapers. After this example of German ruthlessness P/W were discouraged from escaping in view of their ultimate certain liberation in the near future.[98]

CHAPTER SIX

THE ART OF BEING A POW

'*Alles verrückt*' – all mad – is how a German guard described a group of POWs entertaining themselves by pretending they were going on a day trip to Bournemouth in England. The POWs had formed a human train, complete with conductor, the passengers holding onto each other to mime wagons.[1] Boredom in many officers' camps led to the invention of fantasy games such as these; men who were not involved in labour had to rely on their imagination to keep themselves diverted. The other ranks in work camps had fewer empty hours to fill, but there too they had free time during which they had to find ways to amuse themselves. Free hours for them mostly involved rest, letter writing and the usual endless speculation about the end of the war. But many prisoners also became consumed by organised activities, such as sport, performing arts or attending lectures on a wide variety of topics.

German camps were generally better equipped than their Italian versions to provide for POW entertainment, sports and educational needs, not only because Germany seemed to adhere more closely to the terms of the Geneva Convention, but also because its camps were well-established prior to the arrival of most South African POWs. In 1943, for instance, while most of the Sidi Rezegh and Tobruk POWs were still in Italy, the Red Cross and the YMCA sent '10 000 soccer balls, 6 900 pairs of boxing gloves, 8 000 soft balls, 400 baseballs, 650 American footballs and 25 000 tennis balls' to various camps across Germany, while in Italy prisoners had to improvise and produce their own games and sports equipment.² However, although these camps were better equipped, to participate or not was still a decision each man made individually. The extent to which men joined in recreational activities was influenced largely by their personality, but in turn it also affected how they experienced their captivity.

George Tewkesbury was a member of the Black Watch captured during the Anzio landings in February 1944. His world view not only positively affected his captivity, but also influenced how he viewed every event in his life. George believed that without a sense of humour life in a POW camp would be unbearable. In Fallingbostel, Lower Saxony, where his camp, Stalag 357, was located, the temperature hovers around 0 degrees in winter. Apart from the cold, George remembered how the huts were infested with rats and lice. When they caught one POW stealing food from another, the man was ostracised, indicating that food was, as ever, a very important factor in POW life. To have maintained his sense of humour must have been very difficult for George, or perhaps he was the exception to the rule, because many other POWs did not take such an agreeable view of captivity.

A small city on a tiny piece of ground

Initially a transit facility, Stalag VIIIB at Lamsdorf became one of the largest camps in Germany, housing POWs from many different countries, including Australia, Belgium, Britain, Canada, France, Greece, New Zealand, The Netherlands, Poland, South Africa, the Soviet Union, Yugoslavia and the United States.³ Those not classified for work were accommodated in the large hospital complex, as were RAF officers who were unable to be accommodated in officers' camps. By 1944, the main camp held about 10 000 British prisoners, while in its 235 work camps there were a further 9 000 POWs – 'a small city on a tiny piece of ground', Ike Rosmarin called it.⁴ Because of its size, the camp was divided into two parts early in 1944, and became known as Stalag 344.⁵

Although Lamsdorf consisted of separate compounds, Ike remembered that POWs were able to move relatively freely between sections.

This was, therefore, a camp where prisoners were mixed across ranks and nationalities, requiring greater socialisation than in work camps. Because of its size and holding of men from many different walks of life, it also offered an immense range of sports, education or arts activities. While the degree of participation was a personal choice, many continued with activities they had followed in peace time. Others grasped new interests and opportunities, education being the most prominent. For many of working-class background, education in camps came as a bonus.

The more that POWs were able to alleviate boredom, the more they were able to sustain morale. For some, being a spectator was sufficient but for others, participation was vital and they took up pastimes that would never have been pursued in peace-time circumstances. Some were highly idiosyncratic, like Lieutenant-General Sir Philip Neame, a big-game hunter before the war, who became an expert at needlework.[6]

Just as in North Africa, camp newspapers served the purpose of boosting morale. These newspapers also provided a creative outlet, and a pastime, for the more creatively inclined among the POWs. One such humorous contribution, entitled 'Idle Ambitions', made light of the hardships men faced on a daily basis. The author described his ambitions and reasons why he would probably be unable to achieve them. His main ambition was to set fire to a racketeer, something he thought he would never achieve as racketeers were known to be 'notoriously fussy about things like that'. Another ambition was to push a pea uphill with his nose, but 'I sneeze and lose the pea, or get hungry and eat it'. Others included 'walk round with a bull on my shoulders [...] waggle my ears [...] or twiddle my thumbs'. Once he had achieved these ambitions, the author planned to 'settle down to a conventional existence on top of a pole'.[7]

Peter Ogilvie used his time more conservatively to develop his artistic ability and, as his memoirs show, was kept busy with illustrations of camp life. Unsurprisingly, artists were popular as many POWs wanted pencil sketches of themselves to send to their families. Peter, moreover, also used his creative talent to help the escape committee of Stalag 344 by falsifying rubber stamps and passports.[8] Fred van Alphen Stahl, also at Stalag 344, was very impressed by the work of the 'forgers and crooks and pickpockets' who used potatoes to create the stamps for those who needed fake documents.

German authorities were well aware of the continuous efforts of the escape committees, and they used both obvious and what they thought were less apparent ways with which to counter the plans of the escapers. Huts were searched on a regular basis and Alsatians were brought in to sniff out escape tunnels. The unfortunate dogs were, it seems, mostly outwitted by the POWs who sprinkled pepper on the floor, confusing the dogs. When the camp commander became aware of this trick, they confiscated all the pepper from the Red Cross parcels. By this time, however, a significant number of guards were entangled in trading schemes with the POWs, and pepper was simply traded for less important items.[9] For Peter Ogilvie, seemingly unaware of the pepper plot, the dogs were 'so savage that most prisoners would retreat before them to the highest bunks. But one day, after the French Canadians' bungalow was searched, five dead dogs were seen to be flung out of the windows into the snow.'[10] Although these men were known to be brutal, it is almost incomprehensible that the camp authorities would tolerate actions such as these against the dogs.

The escape committee, which operated almost like a secret organisation with its own intelligence division, seemed to have been involved in a plot far more serious than that of killing innocent dogs. Both Peter and Ike remembered a frozen body being discovered when the ice began to thaw in the early spring of 1944. Peter found it very 'strange, and sinister, that neither the Allied nor the German camp authorities had missed him'.[11] Both men assumed that this unfortunate man, dressed in a British uniform, must have been an informer whose task it was to supply the Germans with information about escape plans. Ike's assessment of the situation was that the man 'was a disguised Nazi and that our spy network had made short work of him'.[12]

In a desperate attempt to curb escapes, German authorities issued a declaration warning prisoners of 'death zones' where all unauthorised persons would be shot. These 'zones', according to the Germans, were the result of Britain's insistence on using 'gangster commandos, terror bandits and sabotage troops' to fight the war, something the writers of the declaration ironically considered to be against the principles of international law. The document was nailed to the doors of all the huts in the Stalags, but its effect on the POWs' determination to escape is unknown.[13]

Although Peter Ogilvie rendered an indispensable service to the escape committee at Stalag 344, the committee was so secretive that not even he was aware of its inner workings. Ike Rosmarin, on the other hand, seems to have been better informed. According to him, if a POW wished to escape, he would be evaluated by the committee and his name placed on a list. So great was the interest in escape that based on this list Ike's turn would come up in 1964!

Escaping was big business, not only for the sake of carrying out what many POWs thought was their duty, but also because it was something with which to fight boredom. Ike estimated that at any one time, at least four tunnels were being dug. For the construction of the underground shafts, the work and planning expertise of South African POWs from the Witwatersrand and other heavy industrial areas were at a premium, as escape organisers assembled 'engineers, carpenters, miners and artisans [to which the] South African coal and gold miners contributed' significantly. The large amounts of soil that resulted from these tunnels were used in the vegetable gardens; in turn, these vegetables were the result of seeds being sent to camps by the Red Cross. Regardless of this camp's highly organised escape committee, only a small number of men actually escaped successfully, most of them RAF men.[14] Ike recalled the escape of two of the rank and file but although they both reached England, they were recaptured at the Anzio landings in 1944 and ended up back in Stalag 344.[15]

Wally Wolhuter was a member of the escape committee in Stalag IVB. His duty was to obtain civilian clothing for those wishing to escape. According to Wally, tunnels were only used when large numbers of men escaped in groups. More common escape methods included simple strategies such as cutting wires, leaving the camp in disguises or hiding in wagons being taken out by work parties. It was considered easier to escape from labour camps, but as officers were not allowed

POWs at Potscherad near the Czechoslovakian border with Germany.
COURTESY ANTHONY MORTLOCK

to work, they often swapped identities with other ranks. The officers would then leave the main camp to join the labour camp, while their co-conspirators would remain behind in the main camp.[16]

Undoubtedly a number of South African POWs had mining experience, but this was not always a guarantee that their tunnels would be successful. From his work camp in Waldenburg where he worked in a coal mine, Bernard Schwikkard remembered how POWs became impatient with their tunnel duties and neglected the buttresses, leading to a collapse when a sentry walked across the area. The entire camp was called onto the parade ground and the German commandant reprimanded the men for trying to escape while it was clear that the war was almost at an end. The commandant was in turn chided by the camp leader who reminded him that it was a POW's duty to escape. Apparently the commandant 'apologised for his outburst'.[17]

The idea that some POWs considered it their duty to escape is based on a myth, which probably resulted from the orders given to RAF pilots, who were instructed to evade capture if shot down. Once they were captured, however, they were under no obligation

The Klim Orpheans Band entertaining POWs. COURTESY ANTHONY MORTLOCK

to escape. It is possible that pilots and officers came to regard escape as essential as they held more information which could have been useful to the enemy. Instructions regarding behaviour after capture included warnings that the enemy would attempt to obtain information from them, including the location of the base from where they launched their operation. However, that is as far as the instructions went. According to the Geneva Convention, escape attempts were to be expected from prisoners, but the Convention stated clearly that the 'greatest leniency' should be exercised when punishment was considered for offences 'in particular in appraising facts in connexion with escape or attempted escape'.[18]

For camp command, escapes were nonetheless a headache, and they encouraged POWs to participate in legitimate activities. These activities also provided guards with a control mechanism, enabling them to withdraw privileges if POWs were suspected of any unauthorised activity. Sport of all kinds was embraced, though rugby and cricket were especially popular with Commonwealth and British prisoners.[19] Thus, rugby 'test matches between Scotland, Wales, England, Ireland and the Royal Air Force were most popular'.[20] There were some unusual

THE ART OF BEING A POW

Playing the fool in Work Camp 1169, Paul Brokensha refereeing. COURTESY DAVID BROKENSHA

national contests, as Fred van Alphen Stahl remembered, when he 'even played hockey for South Africa in the camp, against the Indians ... which we won'.

The work camp in Laussig had a slightly different approach to the composition of its soccer teams. Here the men were divided into teams according to those who were married and those who were not. As in all camps, these matches were considered 'good killers of time', but here it seems participation in and support for the teams even enticed the guards, who took bets between them on the different teams. Even the camp commander became so drawn in that he 'threatened us with Sunday fatigues if we lost any match'.[21]

Apart from games like rugby and soccer, Ike Rosmarin recorded how POWs busied themselves on educational courses. In the Lamsdorf camp courses were presented by an Oxford University lecturer, but as David Brokensha recalled, they could be presented by anyone who had knowledge of a specific subject. In this way POWs were exposed to lectures on a very wide variety of topics.

Theatre groups were very popular, providing endless entertainment and even, it seems in the case of the Lamsdorf group, 'often toured other less-privileged prison camps'. Also in Lamsdorf, a military band provided music on a regular basis, and indoor games such as monopoly were popular during the winter months. The formation of a knitting group was one of the more unconventional ventures and these knitters 'unravelled anything they could find, re-wound the wool into skeins and then washed it to produce beautiful articles'. Ike evidently participated in almost all activities and 'was busy almost round the clock with welfare and entertainment committee duties which took a large slice of daylight hours'. Moreover, according to Ike, the Lamsdorf POWs also organised a hobbies fair in aid of the Red Cross, and at another time the camp's welfare committee sent clothing, soap, cigarettes and food to the concentration camp at Auschwitz.[22]

Not all camps were in the fortunate position of being able to send provisions to others. For Stalag IVB near Mühlberg, for instance, conditions were bad and overcrowding a contributing factor. It was only in January 1944 that the POWs there managed to establish their theatre, the Empire, where they performed the *Mühlberg Melody of 1944* to prisoners and their German captors. The site for the theatre was half of one of the barracks and the entrance fee was one cigarette.[23]

While numerous POWs seemed to have enjoyed Italian agricultural work, many more also found conditions in Germany so much better than those in North Africa and in Italy, that they went as far as to express positive sentiments about their captivity. Such emotions were not limited to the inmates of work camps or of larger transit camps, but depended heavily on how individual POWs reacted to their circumstances. Those who pushed to improve their conditions seem to have been more positive about their lot, while those who were inward-looking and more prone to dissension seem to have had a more bleak experience. For instance, the outgoing Ike Rosmarin, characterised by some of his fellow POWs as a racketeer, found that, 'strange as it may seem, I was getting a kick out of POW life!' By then, he had become involved in the escape committee at Stalag 344 at Lamsdorf, and had established a good relationship with the German officer in charge which allowed him a certain amount of freedom to explore the 'empty offices searching for things to steal'.²⁴

Dick Dickinson, on the other hand, had a more withdrawn response to being a POW and his diary is full of references to depression and homesickness. Yet, even for Dick, postal work at work camp 1169 – and the entire group's attempts to sabotage the German postal system – encouraged him to be somewhat less depressive about his captivity. 'Maybe Germany is not such a bad place after all,' he conceded.²⁵ In comparing the Italian experience with that of Germany, he reflected on how the 'Latin temperament' negatively affected the way POWs were treated, adding that, 'the Germans leave us in no doubt as to who is running the show and we know where we are. I think most of us prefer this.'²⁶

But you know, you needed to talk

Relationships between POWs, and between captors and captives, also influenced the way in which these men experienced their captivity. The most obvious way of making the best of prison life was to ensure convivial relationships between the men, and here it seems that the larger the camp, the more difficult this aspect became. In the larger Stalags men were more prone to experience discord, especially between servicemen of different nationalities or ranks, while in smaller work camps they were more able to form harmonious bonds.

In some instances, POWs were not immediately separated according to race and nationality following their arrival at big Stalags, exposing men to unfamiliar cultures and customs. Informal, easy-going segregationist practices would sometimes develop their own rhythms, maintaining sociability across hierarchies. At Stalag VIIA, for example, the Reverend James Chutter found himself in close contact with American and British airmen, black South Africans and Palestinian labourers all allocated the same hut, an episode which he described as 'a great experience of racial harmony. Natural courtesy was the outstanding feature. Without any conscious management, racial "toilet hours" observed,' and when forced to the toilets by dysentery, he was met with surprised

Jake Jacobson, David and Paul Brokensha, 'Len'.
COURTESY DAVID BROKENSHA

greetings of '"*hou umfundisi*" [from] my old flock from the Sunday afternoon gatherings in Tobruk'.[27]

In much smaller work camps, POWs could participate to a greater extent in their overall organisation, taking greater responsibility for their own well-being. As in Italy, highest rank POWs became camp leaders, while in places of more equal rank, leaders were elected democratically by fellow POWs. These men were responsible for communication with commanders, as well as for discipline and general organisational matters.[28] It was in Germany that camp leaders gained greater knowledge of the stipulations in the Geneva Convention through regular contact with Red Cross camp inspectors, and German authorities were also more conscientious in supplying copies of the Geneva Convention than were the Italians. David Brokensha, for instance, only became aware of the Convention when his brother Paul became leader at their German work camp in Gorbitz.

Paul Brokensha and Harry Mortlock with an unknown friend in the centre. COURTESY DAVID BROKENSHA

Paul Brokensha was a camp leader who was appointed on rank. Although he could have remained in an officers' camp, he chose to remain with his brother as they had promised their father that they would stay together throughout the war. Aussie Hammond, in work camp 4008, was another example of a South African camp leader chosen on rank.[29] As can be expected, there were always POWs who did not agree with the choice of camp leader, such as in cases where there were allegations of leaders abusing their positions. Dennis Mugglestone, for instance, was unhappy about the leader of his work camp, possibly work camp 1169 in Dresden, where Paul Brokensha was camp leader. Dennis regarded the leader as virtually a racketeer and felt that he was unfit: 'the WO who would be in charge of the postal staff, was the same one who was buried in clothing and footwear in Italy and he could not even say *"Ja"* or *"Nein"*.'[30] Jack Mortlock, on the other hand, was more accommodating, regarding Paul Brokensha as 'rather young and inexperienced for this unenviable task [of camp leader]. Perhaps an older man would have been better. As it was he was the only one who held the rank of sergeant, and on the whole he did not do too badly.'[31]

The reality of confinement was that most POWs were young men under stress, and who needed to curb more aggressive instincts. Burdens were made worse by food shortages, but were also relieved somewhat at the same time by the realisation by most POWs that they had to rely for basic comforts and support on a small friendly circle. It was also important to maintain a steady temperament, not being perturbed by personal crises. Following their capture and the sense of humiliation associated with it, it was especially important for POWs to maintain some dignity. In order to do this, it was often necessary to resort to a 'passive courage, [and] a stoic endurance'[32] which came to define soldiers' experience of fear, allowing them to cope in extreme situations and preventing them from being branded as cowards. Not expressing their fears and remaining unemotional in the face of hardship not only allowed POWs to cope psychologically, but also helped them fight against becoming helpless victims of their circumstances.[33]

Fred van Alphen Stahl's description of how POWs comforted one other in the hospital camp near Lamsdorf echoes much of what soldiers experienced in both the world wars. In the case of POWs and of fighting soldiers alike, the men distanced themselves emotionally in order to cope with grief:

> Well I'd think if you really felt, what would I say, sad, you couldn't show it, if you knew somebody lost his buddy, you wouldn't go moping and shake his hand, you'd just go up to him and say 'hi cocky' and probably give him a punch, you know you'd say 'now you're short of a bridge partner'.

Fred also recalled how one man's denial of reality actually provided other POWs with some comic relief. The man became known as Happy Harry and he used to entertain POWs by 'running around the field, amusing the crowds' at so-called 'international soccer [or] rugby matches'. Harry gained his 'happy' status when it became evident that he did not realise, or chose to ignore, the fact that his wife was expecting another man's child. Harry was oblivious to the obvious questions from puzzled fellow prisoners as he proudly showed off a letter from his wife informing him of the birth of their son, four or five years after his capture at Dunkirk. While it is impossible to guess at Harry's real state of mind and the reasons for his behaviour, he nevertheless provided a form of release to others, although inadvertently, by giving them a chance to project light-hearted bewilderment onto a 'happy' Harry.

In a more extreme example of denying reality and death, Samuel Hynes, an American airman, had the following to say about seeing the crashed plane of this friend:

> I felt I should do something; but I didn't know how a man grieves [...] I waited for my body to instruct me – to burst into tears, or a howl or a moan of misery – but it did nothing but fly the plane. Down there, under that wreckage, was the disintegrated body of a friend I had loved ...[34]

Despite the deliberate suppression of vulnerable emotions, some POWs had a need to communicate with someone on a deeper level and this could sometimes lead to confusion over sexuality. Dick Dickinson was often philosophically reflective over issues such as faith and virtue, especially during times of homesickness, depression and hunger. He was very careful not to make known his uncertainties about the nature of male friendship and homosexual attractions to his fellow POWs, although in hindsight he recalled a 'personal, personal friend, but I was friendly with half a dozen guys as a POW, you know, I was very fond of quite a few people there, but there was certainly no sexual attraction apart from this one Englishman. But you know, you needed to talk.'[35]

When a close friend left a 'small mascot teddy bear' on Dickinson's bed after transfer to another camp, his reaction to the loss revealed his feelings on friendship, on the need for some emotional closeness and awareness of how in a POW camp these impulses could be construed as homosexual in inclination:

> I keep my feelings to myself in case they are misconstrued, but in this all-male life that we lead there are times when feelings and emotions become gentle and soft. One wonders whether this can be regarded as 'normal'. It is normal to have women in one's life – not for sex, but for that deeper relationship and love and understanding that nourishes a little bit of femininity in a man and makes a better person of him. A life without women is certainly not normal. If I were to say that it is a queer life, the pun would be a bad joke and very much out of line.

In soldiering life, such close male friendships were, of course, not exclusive to POW experience, and ties had developed between some men while they were still undergoing training. As depicted by David Brokensha, these relationships were characterised by 'intense affection and occasional homoerotic undertones [and] such mates would be emotionally extremely close, and mutually dependent'.[36]

Another key aspect of camp friendships was that of differing nationality. Language played an obvious role in grouping POWs, especially those whose first language was not English. A British journalist in Oflag XIIB noted that the use of Afrikaans by South Africans irritated others unable to understand them, separating Union POWs from the rest, as the 'South African members of the camp certainly tended to stick together rather on their own in a way which the Australians and New Zealanders never did'.[37] Nonetheless, wider friendships did develop, though within the context of a POW camp, such friendships often started with ulterior practical motives, an example being Fred's friendship with two French POWs who became best friends.[38] Although a genuine relationship emerged, when he first befriended them it was because he recognised that their knowledge of camp life would assist him in his work as barrack leader.

Fred Geldenhuis only arrived in Stalag VIIA in October 1944, by which time its experienced French captives had established a strong routine and ran a well-organised camp system. With France having been invaded, the Germans assumed that French POWs would be less likely to attempt escape and thus allowed them more freedom than others, to the extent that they had set up a trading system with guards and civilians, Fred used them, also exploiting their contacts to procure parts for a radio that he was repairing.[39] Trading with guards depended naturally on easy relations, that being one of the reasons why beneficial links developed between captors and captives.

Conditions differed from camp to camp. In Stalag IVB near Mühlberg, a Red Cross inspector noted in November 1943 that 'discipline is rather difficult to maintain in this camp on account of the presence of prisoners of so many different nationalities'.[40] Here, Dick Dickinson's diary, among others, underlines the degree to which men continued to attach specific 'national' characteristics to their fellow prisoners. Accordingly, the Dutch were the 'most civil fellows' while the English 'squeal and cry quicker than us'.[41] For all that, memories mostly confirm that these differences were tolerable, and that organised sport was an outlet for group rivalries and antagonisms.

Outlets to relieve various pressures were, however, not always available. In Stalag IVB, for instance, conditions did not improve much and by July 1944 a Red Cross inspector was again reporting on overcapacity, while conceding that 'this is an assembly camp [and] conditions are normal'.[42] Crowded barracks invariably worsened POW relationships as it affected sleeping arrangements and food provision. As a result of Germany's decline towards the end of the war, the deteriorating situation in Stalag IVB became even more severe, 'due to influx of American prisoners following German Ardennes offensive causing excessive overcrowding'.[43]

Large camps, such as Lamsdorf and Mühlberg, which were used for registration and transit, were more prone to open conflict between guards and POWs, while smaller numbers of men in work camps meant that a larger percentage of prisoners came into direct contact with guards, in some cases leading to fraternisation. Whatever their location, the quality of POWs' daily life depended largely on their prison overseers, making it endurable or unbearable. In Stalag IVB, Dick Dickinson described a German sergeant as 'hard, harsh and uncooperative'; also, 'a guard struck one of our chaps with the butt of his rifle for no reason'.[44] Some tensions lay in German perceptions of

IN ENEMY HANDS

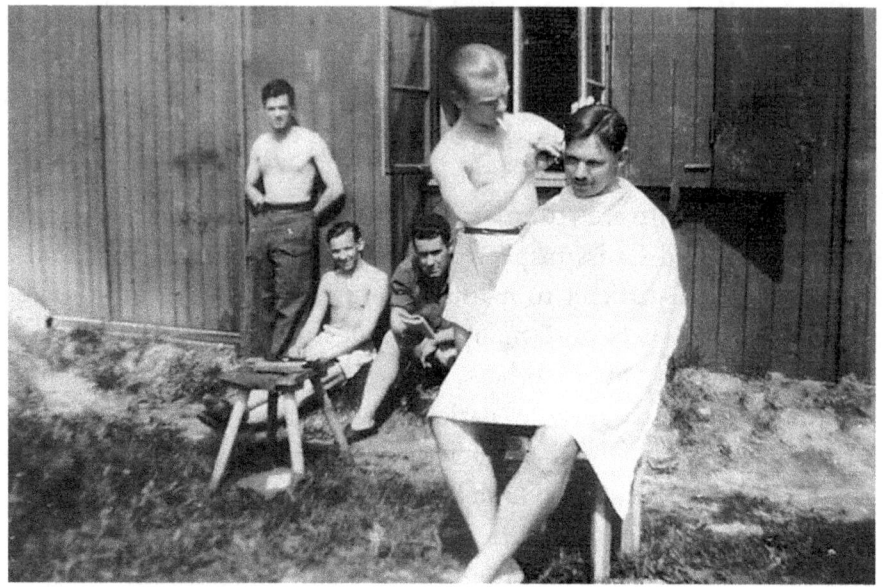

Carrying on with life in Work Camp 1169. Jock the barber plying his trade.
COURTESY DAVID BROKENSHA

insolence. As early as November 1943, a Red Cross report on this camp noted that British NCOs 'have not behaved respectfully to the German authorities' because they refused to salute their NCOs.[45] British NCOs insisted that they need not salute one another as they were of equal rank. The German view, however, was that Article 18 of the Geneva Convention stipulated that 'prisoners of war shall be required to salute all officers of the detaining Power [and] Officer prisoners of war shall be required to salute only officers of that Power who are their superiors or equals in rank'.[46] Excessive force from guards was likely to have had the consent of the camp commandant. The brittle situation at Stalag IVB improved, however, under a camp leader from Stalag IVA who understood the 'art of being a POW' – fluent in German and thus at negotiating, he tended to give orders rather than only take them from prison officers.[47]

When Dick arrived at the work camp in Dresden, he was surprised not only by its cleanliness but also by the friendly welcome from its commander, Horst Mainz. Because he had a POW son in the United

States, Horst apparently wanted to ensure that men in his camp would be treated as decently as his son was being treated in America.[48] On arrival at work camp 1169, Dick, the Brokensha brothers and Jack Mortlock all viewed Horst Mainz in a positive light, with David describing him as fair minded: 'even as early as October 1943, when we arrived at this camp, Horst was convinced that Germany would lose the war and he was concerned [...] that we were treated as well as possible'.[49] For a more reserved Jack, Mainz and his sentries were a 'decent lot'.[50]

As camp leader, Paul Brokensha had a close working relationship with the commandant and they seem to have agreed on a number of matters. In what was the most extraordinary example of cooperation between Paul and Horst, the matter of escape was discussed and decided on. David remembered how the commandant warned his brother of the consequences of escape, saying that 'if there's an escape, one thing you can be sure of is I will be banished and sent away, and the next commandant will be very tough'. Both men were aware that escape would result in punitive repercussions for everybody, but then again escape was something that was to be expected by both. By agreeing to convince the men not to escape, Paul ensured improved living conditions for them. Furthermore, his cooperation with Horst meant that the commandant was amenable to many reasonable requests, secure in the knowledge that he could rely on his prisoners.

Paul and Horst joined forces on more than just escape. The official capacity of the camp was 100 POWs, and Horst apparently asked Paul confidentially to see to the composition of the group – who stayed on and who was forwarded to another camp – 'so that all of us have as good a war as possible in the circumstances'. Although the Brokensha brothers duly selected mostly South Africans, they excluded some UDF servicemen for being 'troublemakers, given to quarrelling, or those whose morale was low'. Some British POWs also made it onto their list, but highly selectively, as David remained convinced that 'British POWs still harboured resentment against us as South Africans, whom they blamed for the fall of Tobruk'.[51] This selection appears to have been done in complete secrecy, as camp transfers occurred without reasons being provided. One such example was Dennis Mugglestone, who was moved to a camp near Leipzig to work in a cement factory. He could have been seen as a 'troublemaker' as he had made his feelings about the camp leader clear.[52] Even Jack Mortlock, who was a close friend of the Brokensha brothers, was ignorant of the stealthy selection procedure, and assumed that the Germans were responsible for moving 'all British soldiers and left only South Africans at 1169. Other South Africans were brought in to take their places. We were very sorry to see the "chums" go. We had made some good friends amongst them and a few of our countrymen that replaced them were below standard.'[53]

Relations elsewhere between POW work camp leaders and commandants were not as close as that between Paul Brokensha and Horst Mainz, but for the most part both parties agreed on some level of mutually beneficial cooperation. Aussie Hammond, camp leader at a sugar factory near Klettendorf, soon realised that he would have to act assertively if he wanted to get anywhere with claims for better treatment. The Germans, he gathered, respected rank, 'and I was not slow to play on this advantage whenever occasion arose'.[54] The fact that Aussie had by this time acquired a copy of the Geneva Convention helped him further to assert his terms. Aside from rank, he also discovered that the more junior sentries were vulnerable to pressure, for 'you could do almost anything with the German guards by threatening to make trouble, they were so dead-scared of being sent to the Russian front'.[55]

Aussie's relationships with guards and commandants were evidently based on a combination of veiled hostility and a precarious balance between controlled aggression and mocking humour. Antagonism towards their enemy captors was often disguised with humour and in Aussie's work group, men amused themselves by resorting to nicknames when referring to the German commandants, with Fish-Eyes and Snapperguts being the two most prominent. Fish-Eyes was described as 'blustering', but also as one who treated POWs with 'genuine kindness'. This, however, did not prevent prisoners from humiliating him when he attempted to master the English language. Aussie first heard about these language lessons when Fish-Eyes greeted him with, 'I kiss your arse.'[56] Snapperguts was the foreman at one of the factories where the POW work party regularly stole sugar. When it became clear that sugar was disappearing, guards were assigned to searches. However, 'the guards preferred to turn a blind eye, being just as keen to barter for stolen sugar as we were'. This left Snapperguts powerless to maintain control over the factory.[57]

Relationships between ordinary sentries and POWs also developed and in some cases even formed friendships that outlasted the war. Typically, when Ike Rosmarin became the translator for working parties employed to clean a sergeant's training facility near Stalag VIIIB, he realised that his position would provide opportunities to trade Red Cross chocolate, soap and cigarettes for potatoes and bread. He drew the sergeant in through their illicit trade and left him vulnerable as he was liable to be exposed for accepting contraband from a prisoner. The guard 'fell hook line and sinker' for Rosmarin's plan and they became great buddies. Ike did not stop there, and when he was assigned to assist an officer with his 'daily chores', he used the contents of a Red Cross parcel to involve the officer in a trading scheme. The German obviously believed that their friendship was genuine, and upon returning from leave, he presented Ike with a gift of a Swiss pocket knife – the last item any sensible guard would want a POW to have. Ike described the relationship as a unique association: the officer, who often expressed unhappiness with the Nazi regime, was 'a fine gentleman who restored my faith in human dignity and the German race'.[58]

To the west of Berlin, at a work camp near Laussig, the unfavourable nicknames Dennis Mugglestone and his fellow POWs gave their camp commander and two of the guards made their feelings clear. Glass-eye, Scarface, and Swine ranged from putting the 'fear of hell into all workers' to being 'a bully from A to Z and a pedigree Nazi'. Swine was in the unique position of being disliked even more by his own compatriots, who referred to him as '*Dikke Schwein*', as Bernard recorded it. Although Glass-eye was viewed with apprehension at first, he seems to have been a sympathetic camp commander, acting as Father Christmas during December 1943 and 1944. When Dennis was sent to help build a house near Leipzig, his perceptions about Germans in general were changed by the owner. Dennis found it hard to 'believe this man to be

Wolfgang, a guard and friend to David Brokensha.
COURTESY DAVID BROKENSHA

a German – more a pal to us and just the opposite' of the guards and camp commander.⁵⁹

Near Dresden, in work camp 1169, POWs also offered their guards goods, which, once accepted, put prisoners in what amounted to a powerful blackmailing position. One of the guards, known simply as Nelson, had accepted a new uniform from the POWs, who had put it together from various parcels they pilfered at the post office. Nelson also accepted stolen gramophone records. This left him 'completely in our power [...] he no longer carried much weight [...] if he tried to show his authority he was reminded that he had accepted stolen property'.⁶⁰ Ironically, at times this captor was also protected by his captives. When Nelson became romantically involved with a female worker at the Dresden station, he asked POWs to look out for officers while he and the woman enjoyed a tryst. When the officers arrived, Jack remembered how

> prisoners were hunting furtively all over the station for Nelson,

one even carrying Nelson's rifle. I have often wondered what that German officer would have thought had he seen a Mauser rifle being carried by a prisoner – fortunately it was a dark station. Nelson was eventually found, armed, and sent in the direction of the officer to report, and the girl sneaked back to her job on the belt.[61]

David Brokensha, perhaps more naïve and less calculating in forging friendships, formed an emotional relationship with a young guard who was sent to work camp 1169 late in 1944 after being wounded on the Russian front. His friendship with Wolfgang was evoked as love – 'yet there were no conscious homoerotic aspects', and 'there was no criticism from other POWs'. In that depiction, it seems as if Wolfgang was himself as innocently distracted as David.

As friendships developed, things became more relaxed between guards and prisoners, and this was especially the case in work camp 1169. On one occasion, while on their way to the tram in Dresden, a fellow POW took the guard's rifle, slung it over his shoulder and started shouting orders at prisoners in broken German while David and Wolfgang talked about what they would do after the war.[62]

Another instance of a personal relationship was that formed between AJ Cremer, an ordinary POW, and a German sergeant-major. AJ and a companion, Joe, played chess every evening and when Joe fell ill, the German officer, an older man who had been wounded on the Russian front, insisted on replacing him. Neither had sufficient linguistic skills to communicate properly with each other, but nevertheless a friendly understanding formed between them.[63] For others, friendship with Germans was never simple and relationships bore underlying tensions, not least as both captor and captive were always aware of possible adverse consequences should any regulations be broken. That awareness may even have motivated them towards mutuality and cooperation, and to overcome animosities arising from personal, cultural or ideological differences or disputes.

Such supportive cooperation was illustrated by an incident which occurred between Cyril Crompton and a guard as he was being escorted to a hospital to have his eyes tested. On the way, a group of

German officers stopped them and angrily enquired why Cyril had not saluted them. The guard salvaged the situation by lying, telling his officers that Cyril was blind; had he not done so, both Cyril and the guards would have been punished.[64] Like many others, Cyril's episode reveals that POWs and Germans had the capacity to create friendships despite being enemies, in situations which were complex and often delicate.

In many cases cooperation benefited both POWs and guards, but when things went wrong, POWs often managed to manipulate the situation so that it was ultimately the Germans who bore the brunt of the reprisals. Aussie Hammond, a classic opportunist, was an expert at displacing blame. His close relations with guards never weakened his practical commitment to the Allied cause. As camp leader, Aussie helped two POWs to escape from their work camp near Lamsdorf. When the Gestapo returned them two days later, the commandant was severely embarrassed and angered as it became clear that he had not been aware that the two men were missing. Attacking Aussie for not keeping a closer count on the POWs, he was met with a shrug and the nonchalant reply of 'You're the guard, not me!'[65]

A week at the holiday camp

In an overcrowded Lamsdorf camp, POWs suffered water shortages and inadequate toilet facilities, with Fred van Alphen Stahl recalling how all the windows in the washrooms were broken, meaning that the 'forty-seater' toilets were regularly covered in a layer of snow 'and you had to warm them up before you [could] sit down'. Despite these uneasy conditions, Fred also fondly remembered the camp's carnival acts, which he found especially entertaining, in particular one occasion when white servicemen from Natal 'blackened-up' in the familiar male group routine of Zulu mimicry. Having smeared their faces with black shoe polish, 'they were now Zulu warriors, and they screamed and danced and they made spears and shields and they were stomping and singing Zulu chants, and the Germans' eyes could have popped out of their heads when they saw this stuff'.

The Zulu theme was indeed a popular one, and in Stalag IVB, Wally Wolhuter participated in 'a display of Zulu warriors [...] which was the highlight of [Union] day.' It was especially the Zulu war dance that in Wally's view fascinated POWs from other nationalities. The Union Day celebrations also included a physical training show and a performance of *Sarie Marais* by a 'Dutch band'. The victory of the Springboks over the rest of the British Empire POWs in a rugby match (9-0), ended the day on a high note, with Wally reflecting that 'one could be proud of being a South African in the Stalag [...] we became intensely patriotic and South Africa never had any better ambassadors'.[66]

At the same time, not all kinds of recreational pastimes encouraged and overseen by the Germans were innocent horseplay. More ominously, Ike Rosmarin's memoirs also recalled an event in which 'mad sugar farmers were announced the winners of the coveted first prize, a week at the holiday "camp" at Gengshaven (sic).'[67] Situated near Berlin, Genshagen was in fact a camp for the recruitment of volunteers for the British Free Corps (BFC). The idea for a British corps initially came from John Amery, a dubious character whose father, Leo Amery, was a minister in the British parliament. Hitler found John Amery's suggestion interesting and gave permission for the formation of such a unit. It was made clear, however, that the aim of the BFC was to recruit 'quality' men who were committed fascists. A camp near Zehlendorf was set up for captive Allied officers, while the other ranks were sent to Genshagen.

In September 1943 this project became the responsibility of the *Schutzstaffeln* (SS). The propaganda message that portrayed these sites as 'holiday camps' seems absurd, and in the case of Zehlendorf, the project was a complete failure. Rank-and-file POWs also appear to have seen through the propaganda, but many nevertheless made full use of the opportunity to escape their dreary daily existence in their permanent camps. By far the majority of the POWs who visited Genshagen at some point during their captivity paid no attention whatsoever to the indoctrination attempts of the SS. Moreover, the camp leader at Genshagen, John Brown, was well versed in the secret MI9 code used to transmit coded messages through letters and apparently used his position to foil the SS by sending information to MI9 about British traitors.[68] By January 1944 the BFC had become part of the Waffen-SS and in May that year they renewed their recruitment campaign by sending a circular to camps informing POWs that the establishment of the BFC was a result of 'repeated applications from British subjects from all parts of the world wishing to take part in the common European struggle against Bolshevism'.[69]

The BFC initiative also, clearly, denounced the war against Germany, something that may have had some appeal for Afrikaans-speaking POWs, especially those with German ancestry, those who had joined up for jobs rather than for patriotic reasons, and those who still harboured resentment towards the British for the concentration camp excesses of the South African War. On the other hand, German propagandists were conveying a mixed message to any disaffected South African POWs. Declaring the post-1939 war to be a 'betrayal of the British people and British Imperial interests' clearly took no account of Afrikaner nationalism and of nationalist sentiment on independence from Britain.[70]

Upon arrival at Genshagen, prisoners were informed that the aim of the POW holiday camp was recuperation from physical and mental inactivity. However, for those who spent time there the real purpose of the camp was soon obvious. As George Oram of the 2nd Anti-Aircraft Regiment found, attempts were made to 'induce men to commit treason by joining the German army'.[71]

When a British soldier in a German uniform visited work camp 1169 in the summer of 1944, David Brokensha and others with him 'were enraged [...] especially by the sight of a small Union Jack neatly sewn next to the German eagle on his German uniform'. Nonetheless, when his camp was invited to send a group to the alleged holiday facility, David was tempted, as he was convinced that he would be able to withstand indoctrination. However, his brother Paul would not allow it as in his view mere attendance at Genshagen might be seen as disloyalty once the war was over.[72] Ike Rosmarin equated the idea of Genshagen with propaganda and in his memoirs he recalled captives being 'bombarded with thousands of anti-Semitic pamphlets', not without some

THE ART OF BEING A POW

Making the most of the warmer days in Germany. Paul Brokensha is on the extreme right.
COURTESY DAVID BROKENSHA

effect, as 'these blatant lies were swallowed by many POWs who vented their feelings on us'. For Ike, Genshagen was a 'super Nazi propaganda camp [where] the Nazis cleverly preyed on the feelings and emotions of the Kriegies'.[73]

It would seem that in some cases pro-BFC propaganda began in camps other than Genshagen. While at a work camp near Trautenau in the Czech Republic, AJ Cremer was convinced that the camp, which also boasted the best conditions he had come across during his time as a POW, was being used to promote the BFC. He recalled that they 'were encouraged to join the British Free Corps in what was termed the common European struggle against Bolshevism'.[74]

Only four of the group of 200 POWs who were with George Oram at Genshagen decided to join the BFC.[75] What the Nazis saw as crafty propaganda to recruit members to the BFC was viewed by their captives as a ridiculous notion. With less than 30 Allied members, the BFC failed miserably in its task.[76] Many years after the war, a number of former POWs cautiously alluded to BFC recruiters visiting camps, but very few of them acknowledged actual holiday camps, suggesting that the impact of the BFC recruitment drives was marginal. Even Wessel

Oosthuizen, who held the Germans in high regard, never considered the BFC; in fact, seeming totally unaware of its existence, he remained firm that it was in Germany that he experienced his worst times as a POW, saying 'that's where the hell started'.

'Ad absurdum'[77]

Over the course of the hostilities, there were many opportunities for Allied and Axis governments to accuse one another of not upholding the terms of the Geneva Convention in the treatment of POWs, as in Article 2 of the Convention which states that 'Measures of reprisal against them are forbidden.'[78] However, while the belligerents tried to outwit each other with threats of policy changes with regard to POW matters, the POWs themselves were only affected if the local camp authorities actually carried out any reprisal orders. Here, probably the most well-known single incident was the shackling of enemy prisoners following the Allied landing at Dieppe in August 1942. The hands of captured Germans were tied, it was claimed, to prevent escape. The British response to this touchy situation was poorly handled. At first, they tried to deny that such an order existed. Then it was asserted that the order had been issued without authority. And lastly, the position was that if an order had been given, it was to have been retracted immediately.[79]

The Oberkommando der Wehrmacht was infuriated by what it referred to as 'Wild West methods [which] will be immediately answered with the sharpest reprisals'. In the same document of 16 October 1942, the Germans listed other instances of the British contravening the Geneva Convention, including the tying up of German POWs following London's attack on occupied Sark in October 1942, and 'standing orders' during the Western Desert campaign in which German POWs were to have received neither 'food, sleep nor drink, nor any favour or comfort' until they had been interrogated. The tone and language of the OKW document was highly threatening and accusatory, denouncing the British as liars, whose use of 'barbaric methods' against captured Germans would be counteracted, so that 'British terrorists [would be] ruthlessly mown down wherever they appear'.⁸⁰

Most controversial of all was the concluding OKW hint that all Allied POWs would be treated in the same manner in which Germany had been treating Russian POWs unprotected by the Geneva Convention:

> Treatment contrary to the international law or inhumane treatment of German prisoners of war in any theatre of war, e.g. in Soviet Russia also, will thus from now onwards have to be atoned for by the totality of the prisoners taken by Germany without regard to their nationality.⁸¹

In London, the issue was taken very seriously and, for the first time, the War Cabinet became directly involved in POW affairs when Churchill intervened in response to these Nazi threats.⁸² Relying on his 'instinct', he had 'the strong impression that the original order for tying up prisoners came from Hitler and is a sign of his rage and fury and that it encountered a good deal of passive opposition not only from the German Foreign Office but from the German military authorities under whom the prison camps now fortunately are'.⁸³ Churchill was right.

Although the shackling of POWs started in 1942, the South African Red Cross only came to know about the measure by December 1943 when Clara Urquhart sent an urgent communication to the Prisoner of War Directorate in Pretoria, saying that distressed parents had brought in letters from their sons at Stalag VIIIB in which they mentioned that they were being tied up. Urquhart believed that 'apart from any physical handicap, the mental effect on the men must be very distressing'.⁸⁴ While the local Red Cross called for an urgent investigation, the POW Directorate had in fact been receiving all documentation relating to the shackling situation since it had begun, but had not informed the Red Cross in the Union.

By March 1943, discussions were held by the Swiss Minister in charge of British interests at which the German Army representative suggested that the shackling should be regarded as a 'symbolic act'⁸⁵ and no more. In addition, Swiss diplomacy reported that, according to the Senior British Medical Officers at Stalag 383 and at Eichstätt in

Bavaria,⁸⁶ the practice did not have a negative impact on the morale of POWs and that those who had been shackled were able to move about and were not isolated from the other prisoners.⁸⁷ Then, towards the end of that year, DD Forsyth, South Africa's Secretary for External Affairs, wrote to the Director of Information to confirm that he had been informed by the British government that shackling had ended in November. At the same time, Forsyth was also explicit that the press should not publish any reports on the issue as it was 'most important not to run the risk of shackling being re-imposed'.⁸⁸

By all accounts, POWs who experienced being shackled were not necessarily openly enraged by the practice, but also evidently understood that it was a matter to be handled with care, given their vulnerable circumstances. Thus, it was reported that while POWs had 'no complaints or demands [...] they asked the Swiss Legation officials to treat the matter with utmost discretion since their present condition was quite bearable and they feared that further steps and representations to German authorities might have an unfortunate effect'.⁸⁹

In reassuring letters, all of which were passed by censors, POWs calculatingly made light of their situation and wrote about it with humour, for instance, as with Frederick Lowe who wrote that 'it's a bit awkward to write with manacles [but] I'll be able to keep you laughing for hours when we are able to discuss all that's happened'. Another POW, Walter Robert Francis, insisted that he 'couldn't worry as [the chains] don't handicap me much, Big Joke, ha ha'. Oswald Hansen displayed the archetypal cunning and dead-pan sarcasm of the POW attitude when he declared that 'we are now with the world-famed chain gang, and we are issued with hardware every day but that does not worry us as the whole mechanism is very simple and is easily wangled as the *Ketang* remains *onder die kombers* all the time and is only displayed when required – life is a big joke here'.⁹⁰

Fred van Alphen Stahl, Ike Rosmarin and Peter Ogilvie were all at Lamsdorf, one of the prison camps where the shackling reprisal was carried out, yet they treated the episode humorously.⁹¹ Neither Peter nor Fred mentioned the shackling of prisoners, but for Ike and his friends, it became a game of comic resistance. Guards naturally had to tie and untie the shackles whenever POWs visited toilets, and 'as soon as their hands were tied the victims visited the toilets where a squad set about untying them – and back they went into the queue. The Germans could not understand why the queues never shortened!'⁹²

As most Union POWs arrived in Germany during 1943, those who experienced shackling only did so at a time when Britain and Canada had started to resolve the crisis. Moreover, as Germany became increasingly preoccupied with operational war matters, it paid less and less attention to on-going political and diplomatic arguments over conventions.⁹³ Notably, Red Cross reports on Stalag 344 indicated increasingly that the 'case today is a more symbolic one than a physical strain or pain [...] Camp authorities appear to shut an eye to the prisoners taking off their handcuffs and move about with the others'.⁹⁴

Leniency may have had something to do with many guards' growing doubts over Germany's chances of emerging victorious from the war. It may also have been a consequence of the humane bonds that had formed between some of them and POWs. On a more concrete level, the shackling of prisoners was an impractical arrangement for authorities who needed POW labour. In some cases, other ranks were freed from shackles, although their number was replaced by non-labouring officers being shackled. But even in Oflag 7B, officers had to be freed so that they could carry out so-called 'urgent camp duties'.⁹⁵

There is no doubt that the relationships between POWs and their guards were complex, but in cases where POWs came into contact with German civilians – while being transported on public trains or trams, or at work camps where some worked alongside or under the supervision of civilians – affinity or animosity were determined by myriad matters. Encounters with civilians were often genial, reminding both parties of their shared humanity, as with Aussie Hammond who witnessed a fellow POW handing out chocolates to two eager young girls at a train station: 'for a moment or two we were neither strangers nor enemies, but an ordinary group of people united by a bar of chocolate'. However, in this case guards soon intervened, ordering civilians out of the station's waiting room.⁹⁶

One feature of certain work camps was prolonged contact with

German citizens, which gave both sides an opportunity to experience a sense of normality as friendships developed over time. This was especially the case with camps such as 1169 and 10001 near Dresden and 4008 near Breslau where POWs worked together with civilians. According to strict OKW policy, relationships between POWs and German women were forbidden and both parties could face long periods of imprisonment or even the death penalty if they were found to be engaging in such relationships.[97] While POWs were generally aware of rules curbing associations with civilians, it seems that if relations between prisoners and guards were good, relationships with civilian women were often tolerated and, in some cases, even aided by guards.

Each POW approached this situation differently. Depending on their personal impulses and attitudes towards regulations, some risked liaisons with women while others restrained themselves, despite a deep emotional need for female companionship. One such example was Dick Dickinson in work camp 1169. He was not inclined to cultivate local female company as he had heard of a POW who had been detained for three months because of a suspected relationship with a German woman. Although the prisoner seemed to have escaped the harsher punishment of 10 years or death, the implicated woman was left 'disfigured for life'.[98] Although German authorities threatened punishment through the death penalty, there is no evidence that any POWs were sentenced to death for this offence.[99] The risk for German citizens was far greater than for POWs because they were putting themselves in danger of being ostracised from the *Volksgemeinschaft*, or community, who were expected to remain loyal to Hitler's ideals throughout the war.[100] Towards the end of the war many German citizens no longer had any faith in Hitler's ideology, but fear could still determine their actions to a large extent.

In his work camp near Gorlitz, Howard Bates was also careful about his contact with German civilians. Just like Aussie Hammond, his work group enjoyed handing out chocolates as a propaganda tool, but their surreptitious conversations with civilians were kept to a minimum because 'one never knew who was a Gestapo agent and punishment was severe for any collaboration'.[101]

On the other hand, relations were sometimes formed between POWs and those of other nationalities who found themselves in German-occupied territories as workers. At a Breslau work camp, for instance, Cyril Crompton and others formed friendships with Danish women whom they met mostly at the Breslau tram depots. These friendships were more easily and openly formed as they were not subject to regulations and sanctions, but it seems that they never took the form of 'personal relationships [as they] were never given any privacy with the girls'.[102]

At Mühlberg, Wally Wolhuter was astonished when a large group of women was led into the camp's *vorlager*, or temporary camp. Wally speculated that these women had participated in the Warsaw uprising, which took place just two months before. The uprising was brutally suppressed by German forces and when it ended, about 18 000 members of the so-called Home Army were sent to POW camps. Many others were sent from Warsaw to concentration or labour camps.[103] For Wally and many POWs in Stalag IVB, the sight of these women was a 'wonderful, stimulating experience'. Despite their own food shortages the men did not hesitate to provide the women with clothing and food by throwing it over the fences between the sections of the camp. In this case, however, establishing a relationship of any kind was especially difficult as both language differences and high fences prevented closer contact and communication. Nevertheless, the men 'spruced themselves up' before attempting to make eye contact with girls they found especially attractive. Love letters, tied to stones, flew across the fences at regular intervals, but three weeks after their arrival, the women were taken away.[104] Wally did not know where they were taken, but it is possible that these women were part of a group of about 1 700 female soldiers who refused to go to labour camps. Instead they were then sent to punishment camps.[105]

The gender imbalance in the camps and among the local population created unique social conditions. Just as the POWs had to do without female company, so German women on the home front experienced the absence of men. Dick Dickinson's diary, for example, reveals something of the desperation for emotional and physical closeness in Dresden and the extent to which civilians would virtually abandon themselves to obtain what they needed:

> We hear that a man can't walk down the main street of Dresden without being accosted by several women, and decent class women at that, including officers' wives. They will pay all expenses, including an apartment if one can get it. There is obviously a man shortage and women are finding things difficult [...] In Dresden and Breslau, the two main cities as yet unbombed, refugees from Berlin and other areas are compounding the problem [...] We have heard of a brothel in Strassburg (sic) where payment is required in food.[106]

This recollection is ambiguous, with women reportedly prepared to pay for male company, and then others whom men had to pay in food, yet it nevertheless illuminates the emotionally stressful effects and deprivations of war upon the civilian population. Dick himself never had sexual dealings with German women, but he found one, Brigitta, particularly engaging. She was a young German girl whom Dick estimated to have been about ten years old. He met her at the Dresden station and she became the lucky recipient of his Red Cross chocolates. In the mass bombing of Dresden, he speculates that she must have been killed as he did not see her again after February 1945 when the bombing of this city took place.

Dick's philosophical nature and his attempts at understanding his experiences and his observations regarding the effects of war on civilians helped him to feel that his original decision to volunteer had been justified, as in Germany he realised that National Socialism was a 'regime whose basic law is war', and that he had been right to volunteer, although at the time of volunteering he had not been motivated by these realities.[107]

On the other hand, there were POWs who entered into purely sexual relations and who had to make plans to secure privacy, at times at considerable risk. Aussie Hammond became involved in numerous relationships, both with German women and with foreign workers.

In an especially risky undertaking, he fell for a young Russian girl in the sugar factory at Klettendorf. Although the German guards treated Russian prisoners atrociously, this relationship seemed to have been tolerated to an extent. Although Snapperguts found Aussie's interest in this woman 'deplorable', he did not do anything to prevent the friendship from forming. The girl, known as Doushka, was very young, and Aussie never seemed to have had any sexual intentions in this specific instance. It was not only the message that had been made explicit to the POWs that 'Russians were heavily loaded with venereal disease [but also that] Russian girls had somehow retained a tender quality of youth and simplicity which appealed enormously to our restricted emotions'.[108]

In cases where POWs showed interest in German women, the state of their relations with guards or even a camp commandant determined to a large extent their ability to instigate relationships with women. Thus, at work camp 1169, Horst Mainz allowed Paul Brokensha to visit his German 'girlfriend' at night, something which his brother believed was the benefit of a 'good camp leader and camp commandant, so things were more relaxed'.

Similarly, the link between Aussie Hammond and Fish Eyes also enabled him to establish another relationship with a German woman. The optimistic POW saw an opportunity to befriend her when she shared with him how her husband had been killed in the North African campaign. When he found her stealing factory sugar, he manipulatively offered her more regular sugar in return for sexual favours. For a satisfied Aussie, she was 'a warm-blooded young woman who had evidently decided to make the best of the bargain'.[109] The adventurous Aussie's higher emotions seemed to intervene when he encountered Maria, the daughter of a shopkeeper in Weinberg. He apparently 'had no wish to take advantage of youth and innocence: in an otherwise alien and uncertain way of life it remained sufficient to know that the warm comfort of her affection was directed at me'.[110]

In Wessel Oosthuizen's case, the game was reversed when the supervisor of a group of German nurses fell for him. He was working on a wine farm near the Austrian border and recalls being unnerved by the stern position regarding German women. When Wessel injured his foot and was confined to barracks, the woman invitingly placed flowers at his door, but Wessel curbed his instincts, admitting decades later to still being regretful at the way he handled this episode. In the end, it seems, it was not so much the German regulations regarding relationships with local women, but the fact that he actually felt more attracted to her daughters, that determined his inaction. Her daughters were unfortunately, according to Wessel, 'taboo'.

A sort of twisted privilege

Most of the POW camps were near large cities or in areas where their labour was needed. Many of them were therefore also targets of the Allied strategic bombing campaign which commenced in the first quarter of 1943. The Americans directed their bombs at German infrastructure by day, followed by British bombing at night. Apart from destroying Germany's infrastructure, the aim was also to obliterate morale.[111] It was especially during the second half of 1944 that living conditions in urban areas and in POW camps worsened as the bombing campaign focused on Germany's transport infrastructure, leaving it unable to transport more than half of the goods needed on the front and in the cities.[112] By this time the majority of people under Nazi control no longer trusted their leaders or the messages they sent out.[113] It is estimated that 600 000 German citizens died as a result of the bombing campaign; however, the spin doctors continued to delude themselves that the people of Germany were resolutely withstanding the bombing onslaught.[114]

Heinrich Himmler, the head of the SS, continued to proclaim the prospect of German victory, seeking to counter declining public morale that could cause opposition to the Nazi Party.[115] POWs observed the increased use of fear in propaganda, with Dick Dickinson noting in his diary early in 1944 that posters of a 'furtive-looking individual' had appeared all over Dresden. German citizens were warned that the enemy was listening. Moreover, 'it was just then that the Hitler salute broke out afresh, and we suspected that the people had been warned to salute this way or else'.[116] After the June 1944 Allied Normandy landings, German military command was shaken up as Hitler tried to revive his war effort.[117] Thereafter, as Allied forces started to march on Germany itself, Nazi leadership created the *Volkssturm*, civilian forces that would be expected to defend the Reich in a noble battle.[118]

In September 1943 the Germans suggested that all camp locations should be made known to all belligerents 'in view of danger of bombing attacks'. Their concern seems to have been aimed only at their POWs in Allied hands, as no effort was made to move camps away from endangered areas in German territory.[119] In fact, it is clear from POW recollections and memoirs that captives were actually put to work clearing up damage following air raids. Near Lamsdorf, for instance, prisoners attached to work camps were forced to work among unexploded bombs and working hours were also increased as they were forced to work twelve hours under the supervision of heavily armed civilians.[120]

From Stalag XVIIIA, Wessel Oosthuizen was sent to a work camp near Graz where he and others had to fill up bomb craters so that rail lines could be restored. He found this work amidst unexploded bombs terrifying as they exploded without warning.[121] In fact, the Protecting Power reported in December 1944 that 28 POWs from work camp E793, near Stalag 344, had been killed as a result of incidents such as these.[122] The German response was that there was 'no ammunition dump which could endanger prisoners of war in the vicinity of Stalag 344'.[123] Such air raid deaths may be ascribed not only to the proximity of some camps to strategic bombing targets, but also to the American strategy of carpet bombing from 1943, as in the heavy raids on Bremen, Hamburg and Kiel.[124]

Despite the obvious dangers to POWs, the men were elated when they witnessed the bombing, their morale lifting as the strength of raids signalled increasing Allied supremacy. 'Excitement reigns,' wrote Dick Dickinson when he spotted his first American aircraft in April 1944.[125] In the work camp near Laussig, POWs counted 762 bombers, with Dennis Mugglestone describing it as 'a lovely sight and made us quite homesick to think the lads above would be home again in four hours'.[126] By April 1945, the Allies had dropped a total of 1.18 million tons of bombs on Germany.

It was especially the women on the German home front who bore the mental and physical brunt of these attacks. Many still had family members fighting in the disastrous campaign against Stalin's Red Army or in the north of Italy where the fascists were making their last stand.[127] Yet, it was from women that many POWs received kind treatment.[128]

It was not only the sight of Allied bombers that lifted POW spirits. Hundreds of secret camp radios broadcast the news of the D-Day landings. As Dick Dickinson observed four days after D-Day, 'we have a sort of twisted privilege of being witness to history from the inside. There appear to be as many Germans wishing the Allies success as there are not. They are speaking more openly, and the rise in morale of forced workers and prisoners-of-war is amazing.'[129] Although many Germans had had enough of war, others were driven by fear or by indoctrination to act against their fellow countrymen. Patriotic denunciations rose to almost 14 000 cases in 1944, with many of the victims executed by the People's Court.[130]

Morale among German fighting soldiers seemed less affected by events on the home front, and by the end of 1944 retreating soldiers were being used in propaganda efforts to raise civilian morale. The success of their efforts was difficult to determine.[131] As ever, POWs believed they had a part to play and they initiated their own informal propaganda crusade to illustrate to ordinary Germans that the Allies were coming out on top. Jack Mortlock, for instance, recorded that while at work camp 1169 they 'tried to keep ourselves as neat as possible, boots polished (the polish naturally came from the station) trousers pressed etc, as we felt that it was good propaganda for the Allied cause. We always marched smartly through the streets.'[132] In Stalag VIIA, the Reverend James Chutter saw black market trade between POWs and civilians as being of 'enormous' propaganda value, as items like soap, chocolate and coffee had become virtually unobtainable in Germany, while prisoners enjoyed supplies through the Red Cross. According to him, 'it made the Germans think'.[133]

Nazi intelligence had been aware since 1943 of the potentially demoralising effect of healthy and well-dressed POWs on German citizens.

An SS report commissioned on the subject found that the arrogant and superior attitude of British POWs was the result of Red Cross parcels that made it possible for them to maintain good personal hygiene and, especially towards the end of the war, to eat better than the German population.[134] Allied POWs were also a source of counter-information in the German propaganda machine. By 1944 POWs had a well-established information system supported by hidden radios and by news gathered from newly captured Allied soldiers. German soldiers, on the other hand, were fed strictly controlled information on the war's fortunes which by the end of 1944 had become totally unrealistic.[135] While German civilians were confronted with Nazi propaganda in the streets, they saw thousands of Allied bombers flying overhead on their way to their targets. In July 1944 the German security service, *Sicherheitsdienst*, took note of this and declared that daylight bombing raids were having a negative effect on morale.[136]

By September 1944 Dick Dickinson was noticing that the supply of Red Cross parcels to work camp 1169 was erratic. Although this was probably the result of the intensive bombing, he blamed the Germans. The POWs were forced to share parcels again – and, faced with another period of hunger and deprivation, Dick and a companion started to plan their escape. The plan was to hide in a truck transporting food parcels to German POWs in Sweden; however, nothing came of their scheme.[137]

For German citizens and guards at POW camps, the lack of food was worse. Hunger and desperation caused guards to help themselves to prison rations, and when POWs became aware of this, it inevitably led to conflict. Aussie Hammond first noticed diminishing food rations in January 1944, and after an investigation with Fish-Eyes, concluded that 'a fiddle was being worked, probably by someone in the quartermaster's stores'.[138] Dennis Mugglestone's experience was similar, starting with a declining bread ration and then the discovery that their camp commander, Swine, had been exchanging inferior swede jam for their Red Cross tinned jams. Enraged, POWs started to collect their food in bulk, instead of in individual portions, to curb Swine's meddling. In October 1944, Dennis and fellow POWs were ordered to consume food parcels by a set date, or face their confiscation. By Christmas, Red Cross consignments had dried up. The longer the delay, the more resentful the atmosphere between POWs and their guards became. When Red Cross supplies finally arrived again, guards 'came in full force and made a good mess of the parcels'.[139]

Another effect of bombing was its impact on relationships between POWs and civilians, including those that had developed before the start of mass air raids. For instance, the bombing of Dresden in February 1945 had a great effect on those in work camp 1169, which was located on the city's outskirts. Jack Mortlock felt that he had to avoid Annie, a German acquaintance, as he expected she would blame him for the death of her daughter. Yet she turned out to be fatalistically forgiving, acknowledging that 'war is that way'. On the other hand, the attitude of female civilian strangers was often violently hostile, turning on POWs as 'pigs and spitting at us. It was quite a relief to get back to camp.'[140] As Dick Dickinson's diary reveals, on occasion guards took action to protect their captives against enraged civilians. On one occasion, while walking back to their camp following an Allied attack, Dick saw a

> woman spit in Tom's face. Another woman asks them to excavate her husband, but the guard thinks that getting the chaps back to camp alive is a better option. Back in camp [the POWs] are prepared to go back and help, but the offer is turned down. After a few days the terror of war is forgotten and we receive our smiles again.[141]

Jack Mortlock recollected that during later raids, civilian deaths increased because air raid sirens were affected, 'due to the incendiary raid, lots of electric mains were disrupted; causing many sirens to short circuit and blow the "all clear". I remember one siren that continued for hours. It was largely due to these faulty sirens that lots of people were caught out in the open when the high explosive bombs arrived.'[142]

Allied POWs were used to help to excavate dead bodies trapped under rubble, which were then destroyed by SS 'extermination experts'.[143] In an exceptionally grisly part of his memoirs, Jack Mortlock recalled how he joined others in cleaning an air raid shelter which had been penetrated by a bomb:

> well, we had to scrape them off the walls with our spades. It was said that there were about twenty to thirty people in the shelter at the time. All we could find only filled half a wheel barrow. The largest portion that I saw was one solitary hand with a ring on one finger. Shoes had been completely blown off their feet. In some cases the shoes were still tightly laced.[144]

The fate of Dresden had a particularly painful outcome for David Brokensha's friendship with Wolfgang, as 'after the bombing in Dresden he wouldn't speak to me, and I was devastated, [...] I've heard his sister's flat had been bombed and she'd been killed so I can't blame him, but I remember.'

A six hundred mile hell march[145]

The POWs in the vicinity of Breslau, Poland, seem to have been spared the worst of the bombing, as Cyril Crompton could not recall any raids near his work camp at a tram depot on the fringe of the city.[146] Breslau was further east than most targets and out of range of the British and American bombers, but it was besieged by Soviet forces in early 1945. On 20 January that year, the city was evacuated as the Russians approached.[147] For Cyril and his fellow POWs, this meant the start of a long march that he referred to as a 'march with death'.[148]

Whatever Berlin's denials of Germany's deterioration, the evacuations of POW camps and of many German cities and towns were proof of an unstoppable Allied advance. As Soviet forces approached from the east and the British and Americans from the west, Nazi leadership became ever more obsessed with continuing the war and proclaimed selected sites as fortresses where the Wehrmacht and the Volkssturm were expected to fight to the bitter end.[149]

With all Northern Silesia declared a fortress, the POW camps in that area were now caught up in the conflict between Russian and German armies. Both, noted Bernard Schwikkard, 'knew the consequences of being taken POW. Hence both sides would rather fight to the death than be captured and taken prisoner.'[150] From as early as the beginning of 1944, camps in the east of German-occupied territories as distant as Lithuania were being evacuated, with POWs mostly required to walk to new camps within Germany. With the Russian advance the most imminent threat, Germany's evacuation of its POW camps in the east was a priority.[151]

The capital of Upper Silesia was Breslau, and it too had been declared a fortress. By December 1944, Cyril Crompton realised the depth of Russian penetration when he saw Germans preparing to blow up the bridge across the Oder: 'the Germans now admitted to us that the Russians were coming'. Scarcely a month later, Soviet troops had reached the Oder on both sides of Breslau and the city was evacuated.[152] At the camp near Waldenburg, Bernard Schwikkard could hear the artillery of the approaching Russians, increasing hopes of imminent liberation. But the arrival of the Russians was preceded by train-loads of wounded German troops and he was drafted in as a medical orderly. Despite having been 'simply … dumped in cattle trucks with or without water', the wounded soldiers were 'so fanatical and convinced of their superiority that some of them actually protested at being carried by us, their enemy, and referred to us as *"Swiner Honde"* (sic)' – pig dogs.[153]

Also at Breslau, Howard Bates was woken in the pre-dawn hours and marched to the station. On their way, the POWs were met by the 'vicious crackle of Tommy-guns and the blast of 20mm cannon burst' around them. As Howard took cover, he saw two Russian tanks with infantrymen continuously firing on the marching POWs. When the two tanks eventually moved away, the guards ordered them into a forest where they hid in a small cottage. Anxiety peaked again when the Soviet troops returned. A Polish guard, who according to Howard had been coerced into joining the German Army, explained in Polish that the group were POWs. The Soviet troops accepted this, but they remained 'totally hostile'.[154]

It was only at the end of that day that Howard and others were allowed to attend to the POWs who had been shot in the initial attack. Howard counted a number of his friends among the dead. The next day the Germans attempted a counter-attack, which led to the two sides shooting at each other across the village where the POWs were taking cover. Eventually, the fighting ended with the capture of the Germans. To celebrate this victory, the Russian soldiers made themselves at home in the POWs' barracks and started drinking vodka. Ironically, they also

> insisted on us joining in and poured out liberal tots in our mugs. Their Vodka was a very raw, strong drink which, at the first gulp, burned its way down into one's stomach and then the impact shot back and almost blew the top of one's head off. Between gulps there was constant singing and we had to keep toasting 'Churchill, Stalin, Roosevelt'!!![155]

Later that night, the Russians, for a reason that remained a mystery to Howard, returned to the barracks and, following a search among the refugees, dragged one man out and executed him in the nearby woods. Following this harrowing experience, Howard and the other POWs took matters into their own hands and started making their way west. Along the way they were joined by Jewish refugees who had fled from a concentration camp. When they arrived at Oels, they were told to leave the refugees behind and wait until there was a sufficient number of British POWs before they could be sent on their journey to Odessa, from where they would be transported to Naples and then to Bari. From this Italian repatriation camp they went to Cairo and only then, eventually, back to South Africa.[156]

In some instances, German guards warned POWs against the brutality of Russian soldiers, even convincing some of them not to wait for liberation by Soviet forces but to march westwards to be freed by American or British troops. Consequently, many POWs chose to march with their German captors in a shared attempt to avoid the Russians. Nonetheless, it has been estimated that five per cent of all POWs managed to escape while on the march. This was despite the threats that they would be shot if caught or that five POWs would be shot for every one who escaped.¹⁵⁷

But, as Peter Ogilvie discovered, such threats were not always real. Trying to conserve energy along the way, he discarded his possessions, including his diary. Behind him, Staff Sergeant O'Neill was struggling to keep up, and finally collapsed as he reached for Peter's diary, which he mistook for a Bible. When a German guard approached, both men expected O'Neill to be shot, as they had heard shots being fired at the back of the column since the start of the evacuation march. Instead, he was helped onto a wagon, joining a group of others who had been presumed shot. According to Peter, the Germans were threatening to shoot those who could not keep up, so that only the utterly exhausted would fall behind. Each time such a man was picked up, guards fired two shots, driving on the marchers and at the same time signalling to the wagon to collect another POW.¹⁵⁸

Perhaps shaken by previous experiences of being transported, some POWs were panicked to hear that their camps were to be evacuated. Ike Rosmarin, for instance, 'felt sick with worry and was sweating profusely in spite of wintry weather'.¹⁵⁹ He managed to evade the first evacuation from Stalag 344 by pretending to be ill, delaying his departure. On hearing rumours that the camp was to be evacuated a second time, Ike and a few others escaped and hid out in a nearby forest, waiting for liberation. When news came that the Americans were very close, they returned to their camp. Meanwhile, shortly after the liberation of the Lamsdorf camp, many other POWs returned from nearby hiding places.¹⁶⁰ Others, like Aussie Hammond, hoped to escape the march entirely by taking matters into their own hands. Granted, not all agreed with him, as some 'thought it would be better to go west with the Germans rather to wait for the Russians, who to most represented a fearful, unknown quantity'.¹⁶¹ Aussie and 18 others, however, had no desire to go on a march into the unknown. They managed to hide within the camp enclosure as the majority of the POWs left.

Following the evacuation, Aussie grew impatient and decided to set out alone in search of the Russians. Following a few days of liberty, he was discovered by German soldiers while hiding in a hut with Polish refugees. By now, circumstances for both sides had altered quite dramatically. An exhausted German NCO was concerned with the state of young soldiers under his command, and had no plans to take prisoners. Aussie also made no effort to hide his identity, declaring calmly, 'I'm British.' The enemy warned him that seeking out the Russians was unwise as they would 'shoot without waiting for you to speak first'. Although sceptical of anti-Russian sentiment, Aussie was persuaded to join the Germans on their move westwards. He got as far as Weiden, remaining a 'part-time prisoner' until the camp was liberated by Americans.[162]

Just as in North Africa, numerous POWs narrowly missed being liberated as they were evacuated just before the Russians arrived. Again, too, circumstances were not dissimilar to pre-Armistice Italy, as poorly nourished POWs were unprepared for the deprivations that they faced on their journey. To add to this, most men commenced marching in unusually cold January or February winter months, marked by severe snow storms.[163] As with previous transportation experiences, prisoners were again at risk of being attacked, this time by Allied fighters who were strafing columns of men whom they mistook for German forces.[164] A terrified Cyril Crompton, marching from Breslau, was among those strafed by American fighters, with friends dying in numerous attacks. The strength of his determination to survive became evident one day as he dived for cover while clutching a piece of bread, thinking that he was 'going to eat this whether I die or not'.[165] News of these inadvertent air attacks on POW columns containing their troops only reached South African authorities well into 1945 through a Red Cross distribution list.[166]

The threat of air attacks compelled POW columns to continue marches at night, placing an even heavier burden on their already exhausted bodies. Cyril estimated that they marched about 900 kilometres between January and April 1945, and that only some 30 or 40 of the original 140 who had left his work camp survived the trip due to strafing, exhaustion and starvation.[167]

Meanwhile, the Brokensha brothers, Jack Mortlock and Dick Dickinson were still on postal work near Dresden, only later joining the thousands of mobile evacuees. However, their experiences while on the march were no less harrowing. On the way to Czechoslovakia, David's group was abandoned by its German guards, which was a relief as they had heard rumours that Hitler was planning to hold back POWs as hostages.

Such rumours were not unfounded. As the Nazis became more desperate in the final months of the war, they began to openly break the terms of the Convention. Early in 1945, Josef Goebbels, Hitler's propaganda minister, suggested that revenge be taken for the bombing of Dresden in February of that year, with one Allied POW to be shot for every German citizen who had died there. If this order was carried out, it would have resulted in the deaths of 100 000 POWs. However, men like Colonel-General Alfred Jodl, OKW chief of operations staff, had by this time realised that Hitler's orders were, at times, unrealistic and impracticable. Jodl was able to delay or completely do away with such orders by focusing on trivial matters such as 'exact wording'.[168]

However, the group was now left to fend for itself. It was during this time that David and five or six others were strafed by Russian or German fighters. David recalled that this was when he received his war wound:

> not a very glamorous one, the Germans were strafing us from above, from airplanes and there were some trees and we all made a dive for … it doesn't give much cover, but automatically I was clinging onto a tree and then I felt this … and I put my hand up and it was covered with blood, and I thought 'oh no', I'd heard Churchill on the radio […] the day before saying the war was over, and I thought now the war is over and I'm going to die.

David did not die, but the wandering POWs came across heavily inebriated Russian soldiers who were firing into the air. One of the POWs compared them to his 'farm labourers on a Saturday night: they were all getting drunk'. Although they appeared friendly, dressing David's wound, David was shocked to see how pitiless they were towards refugees. The small group of POWs decided to move on in search of the Allies, as at this point of their journey they felt far from liberated. Their trip towards the Allies was not all doom and gloom though, and the group of POWs took some time to enjoy a 'jolly party' at an abandoned mansion in Chemnitz, sharing gin cigars with French and Belgian girls who had recently found their way out of Nazi labour camps. It was from this house that David collected his only souvenirs of the war, a pair of blue birds of Meissen china. Becoming impatient with their situation, Paul convinced David that they should take bicycles from civilians to speed up their journey. This act remained with David until long after the war as 'one of those bad memories that most of us accumulate'.[169] Nevertheless, it brought them to an American military base, where, ironically, they met with suspicion. After David identified himself as South African, 'a sergeant was asked, "There's a guy here who says he's a South African, whose side is he on?" His response to the soldier was "You dope, haven't you heard of Jan Christian Smuts? Let him through" ... so that's the day [of liberation], lovely words.'

Naturally, the further west the Stalag, the closer the Allied forces. For Dennis Mugglestone, for instance, the march lasted only ten days, but it was not without incident. When one of the German guards fired at passing Allied planes, one pilot turned around and machine-gunned a nearby German and his horse. Dennis remembered how the horse was cooked by 'ravenous POWs' seconds after it was killed. Some time later, he and fellow POWs were alarmed by the state of their accompanying guards, as they 'were panic stricken [and] we decided to take matters into our own hands and bade *au revoir* to them'. When they reached a narrow bridge, there was such a concentration of refugees that they slowed down to almost a standstill. It was then that Dennis realised that their ranks had been joined by their former guards, hoping to avoid capture. The tables were turned, however, because on the other side of the bridge were American soldiers sorting out Allied POWs from Germans.[170]

Not all Union prisoners were freed through camp evacuations and movement in the direction of friendly forces. In cases such as Stalag VIIA and Stalag VIIB, POWs waited to be liberated by incoming Allied forces, as camps were handed over in the presence of representatives of the Protecting Power. At Stalag VIIB, the surrendering commander complained of the Americans who, following the take-over, 'made their way enthusiastically to the town, where they behaved in a fairly undisciplined manner'. Many deprived POWs needed no encouragement to follow suit, heading for nearby towns to procure food and any other goods they deemed necessary or valuable.[171]

In Weiden, Aussie Hammond was placed in charge of the town until American infantry arrived in full. Aussie's natural aptitude for leadership became apparent when he saw large-scale looting taking place. While Aussie shouted *'Raus! Los!'* and waving a gun, his friend fired a few shots from a Tommy-gun. With threats that they would be shot if caught looting, most returned to the camp, but a few German women approached him 'crying and saying they would be without food if we did not allow them to loot. I felt sorry for them, but this was no time to relax discipline, and I ordered them away in harsh tones.' Once the civilians were sorted out, Aussie liberated Nazi and Gestapo insignia from the town hall to keep as war souvenirs.[172]

For most POWs, liberation was marked by uncontrolled personal emotions, and many could not hold back tears. For others, the news of the formal signing of peace came as an anti-climax. For Dick Dickinson, 'things [had] gone on too long and too slowly'.[173] The plain fact was that liberation was mostly simply a matter of being handed over to Allied control. For many UDF captives, true freedom would only become a reality when they reached South Africa again. For the time being, they remained dependent on others, even for basic needs such as the provision of food and shelter.

CHAPTER SEVEN

ANXIOUS ANNIES

Letter writing was a popular pastime with which soldiers filled up the gaps of empty time between battles or digging defensive lines – or in POW camp. While at Tobruk, Michael de Lisle dutifully wrote a letter to his mother each week. When he was captured this stopped, and there was no way in which he could let her know what had happened to him. The shock of capture, the lack of food and water during the early days in the temporary camps of North Africa, was made worse by his 'great anxiety' for his mother who he knew would be worried when she received no news from him. Communication between POWs and their friends and families now became part of a huge bureaucratic machine, one which Michael had no control over.

Following battles, families who did not receive letters from those who had survived the fighting were informed that their sons or husbands had either perished or were missing. On 15 July 1942, three weeks after his capture, Howard Bates's family received a telegram informing them that their son was 'reported missing believed prisoner of war'. This telegram was then followed by a registered letter from Defence Headquarters in Pretoria confirming the news and giving the information that the South African Red Cross Society was in charge of enquiries and would send further information immediately it became available.

These telegrams and letters caused great uncertainties for families. In Howard's case, his concerned brother had written to him on 6 July, asking why they had not heard from him for almost a month. Just two

When they received this telegram from the Red Cross, Howard Bates's parents knew that he was no longer simply listed as 'missing'. COURTESY ENID BATES

days earlier, in the Benghazi POW camp, Howard had been handed a pre-printed postcard from the Italians which was meant to inform his family of his captivity. The first sentence on the card read 'I am alright (I have not been wounded (or) I have been slightly wounded. I am a prisoner of the Italians and I am being treated well.' The POW would scratch out the relevant sentence.

It is not known when Howard's card reached his parents' home, but on 23 September, the family received another telegram which stated that the International Red Cross had confirmed that Howard was now a POW in Italian hands. This was followed by a 'greetings and good news' telegram from the Red Cross saying that they were pleased to inform the family that Howard was a prisoner.

In many other cases, distressed families in the Union waited months for confirmation that sons or husbands were accounted for as prisoners,

```
                              WRC/7/79/22769/W/P.
REGISTERED.

                                Officer-in-Charge
                                   War Records,
                                Defence Headquarters,
                                        Pretoria.
Dear Mr. Bates,

                                        30 JUL 1942
              It is with great regret that I have to
confirm my telegram informing you that your son
L/Bdr. Howard John Bates

was reported ''missing, believed prisoner of war,'' on the
20th June, 1942.
              It will be helpful to you to know that in
all cases where men are reported missing, I inform the South
African Red Cross Society, which immediately transmits cabled
enquiries through the International Red Cross Committee at
Geneva. If, therefore, it is confirmed that he is a prisoner
of war, you will receive information either from me, or from
the Red Cross Society immediately conclusive news is obtained.

              In that regard it will be unnecessary to
add that because of the almost universal extent of the war,
and the large number of enquiries reaching Geneva, some
exercise of patience, whilst admittedly difficult, is necessary.
But you may be assured that everything possible is being and
will be done to relieve your anxiety as soon as it is humanly
possible to do so.

              It will be of interest, and probably you
are already aware, that broadcasts from Rome and the Vatican
City frequently contain information relating to prisoners of
war. My office has accordingly arranged for copies of these
broadcasts to be supplied to it, and any relevant information
which may result will be passed to you at once.




                                            In the/
```

The registered letter: confirmation of Howard Bates's captivity. COURTESY ENID BATES

and were no longer listed simply as missing. Many POWs only received these pre-printed postcards once they reached permanent camps in Italy, three or four months after they were captured.

At the outbreak of hostilities, there was no clear policy arrangement

> **4-7-1942** (post mark date)
>
> My dear, DAD & ALL
>
> I am alright (I have not been wounded (or) ~~have been slightly wounded~~). I am a prisoner of the Italians and I am being treated well.
>
> Shortly I shall be transferred to a prisoner's camp and I will let you have my new address. Only then I will be able to receive letters from you and to reply.
>
> With love
>
> (signature) H.J.Bates
>
> Written at Benghazi. Howard.

Howard Bates's first communication after capture, words courtesy of the Italian authorities.
COURTESY ENID BATES

in place for communication with POWs, but as the war progressed and increasing numbers of Allied soldiers were taken prisoner, responsibility for the handling of POW affairs was passed from the War Office to the Directorate of Prisoners of War. In the provision of any official confirmation to relatives, the Directorate was still dependent on information from enemy countries which, especially while POWs were still in transit camps, could take months to materialise.

Official information came as belligerent governments made name lists available to the Protecting Power, who would then make these available to the relevant POW Information Bureau of the British Foreign Office.[1] The whole procedure was both cumbersome and often imprecise. Notification of POW status by enemy governments was frequently slow and name lists then had to be analysed by London authorities to determine POW nationalities. On top of the regular omission of nationality, there was the further complication of language difficulties between POWs and captors which often led to names being misspelt.

Incomplete lists despatched to London also failed to include regimental numbers, again making personal verification difficult.[2] Where POWs were seriously ill or wounded and unable to provide adequate details, the process was even further delayed.

Establishing a clearly agreed inter-governmental position on communication in this sphere of the war was a complicated matter. An important example of this was the issue of telegraphic payment for informing families of the deaths of prisoners. While unable to establish the overall basis of financial arrangements between enemy governments and the ICRC, Britain stuck to paying a fixed sum to the ICRC for telegram costs. As such paper agreements were supposedly reciprocal, there was squabbling over the equitable sharing of the costs of communication, complicated by the financial strains of the changing fortunes of war for various belligerents.[3]

London channelled information and oversaw all reciprocal agreements with enemy authorities, but even in Britain, many POW families became so frustrated with the slow process that they turned to informal sources. For those in a far-distant South Africa, efforts to gain accurate information were even more frustrating. Although Britain readily took the initiative, there were frequent delays as Whitehall had to wait for the agreement of Dominion governments before action could be taken on any decision. One such instance was the delay in ratifying an Anglo-Italian agreement on notification of POW deaths and serious injuries, because Pretoria was slow to confirm their acceptance of the arrangement.[4]

Further communication misunderstandings also hampered contact between prisoners and their families. With no direct wartime communication between Rome and Pretoria, it was agreed that information on camp deaths would be relayed between respective Red Cross societies. This, however, encouraged the assumption that the Red Cross would take responsibility for other reciprocities, something which the local body was unwilling to do.[5] By April 1943, subcommittee A and the London War Office were still considering unresolved questions around communication between the POW information bureaux and enemy governments, including, for instance, that of 'the extent to which, as regards to nationals of the governments represented on the subcommittee, there is evidence of reciprocity by the enemy pwibs [prisoner of war information bureaux].' The committee was also requested to consider

> whether the proposal of the IRCC [also ICRC] for direct telegraphing between British Commonwealth PWIBs and Geneva of the names of dead prisoners should be approved; and if so whether such direct telegraphing should be confined to notifications of those dying in captivity or cover all notifications of names, dead and alive.[6]

Without a doubt, the enormous number of prisoners taken at Tobruk presented a crisis for official communications as well as for the ICRC. Figures available to it showed that by the end of August 1942, the total missing or believed prisoner-of-war casualties amounted to 15 731, of which only 4 550 were confirmed POW by the ICRC. Those counted as wounded, killed or returned to their unit amounted to 1 372, leaving 9 809 still missing. By 10 October 1942, the ICRC was able to confirm a further 3 911 as POW, but that still left 5 898 unaccounted for.[7]

Not surprisingly, while government bureaucracies continued to busy themselves with procedural points, many Union POW families relied more and more on unofficial sources, as did their counterparts in Britain. With the ICRC inundated with queries about the missing, families turned to the service provided by the Vatican radio. The Catholic channel seems to have been the main source of news about Italian-held POWs for their South African families, with the local Red Cross approaching the Catholic Archbishop of Bloemfontein for Church liaison assistance in obtaining information on missing soldiers. An already established communication channel from Lisbon via Lourenço Marques helped to facilitate this.[8]

After months of silence on her son's fate, Michael de Lisle's mother eventually heard that he had been captured when the Catholic Church in South Africa distributed a list of names which they received from a Vatican radio broadcast. For Fred Geldenhuis's father, confirmation of

> All Saints' Rectory.
> Booysens.
> Johannesburg.
> 12/9/42.
>
> Dear Mrs Geldenhuis,
>
> In case you have not already heard : this is to let you know that the following name and address was given in a list of Prisoners of War, broadcast from Berlin, to-night.
>
> Sergeant F.* Geldenhuis, — Mr W. J. W. Geldenhuis, Box 102 Cullinan, Transvaal
>
> Yours sincerely,
> (Rev.) Noel Roberts
>
> (* or S ?)
>
> N.B. The list of names and addresses was read very quickly, and the German pronunciation of words, in some cases, was difficult to follow, but if this address is correct, the information given should enable you to identify the name: so I am sending it as I received it.

A broadcast from Berlin confirmed Fred Geldenhuis's capture. COURTESY ILSE GELDENHUIS

his captivity also came via the Vatican short-wave external radio service,[9] though he had first heard that Fred was missing and 'probably' taken prisoner three months earlier when he received a telegram from the South African authorities in June 1942.

When Fred van Alphen Stahl's mother received news that her son had gone missing, the loyalist minister of the local Afrikaans church in the small rural town of Malmesbury tried to comfort her by tactlessly suggesting that her son would be better off dead than a prisoner of the Germans. This soldier's mother had to wait upon the Red Cross for notification, which only came months after his capture.[10] While waiting for official information, families in the Union also occasionally gained information about those 'missing' from stories brought back by men who had been able to escape early in the war.[11]

Correspondence between POWs and their families involved restrictions. Letters from POWs to South Africa were limited to two letter cards and four postcards per month. When they were transferred from transit to permanent Italian camps, POWs received postcards on which they could fill in simple information on their health and provide a return address. By the time they reached Germany, prisoners had to

> (Mr) E.H. Stephan,
> "Louvain"
> Bell Road,
> Claremont. C.P.
> September 12, 1942.
>
> Mr. W.J. Geldenhuys,
> P.O. Box 102, Cullanan, Tvl.
>
> Dear Mr Geldenhuys,
> In a Broadcast message picked up from Zeesen that this evening it was announced that Sergeant F.W. Geldenhuys was a Prisoner of War in Axis Hands. This was all the message said. There was no mention of his Regimental number or where he was at the moment.
> As I listen in to Vatican Radio regularly do you want me to advise of any further information I may pick up, should his name be called. It will be advisable when writing to me to let me have his regimental number.
> Sincerely Yours,
> E H Stephan

This is how Fred Geldenhuis's father came to know of his son's capture by enemy forces.
COURTESY ILSE GELDENHUIS

pay a quarter-mark of the camp currency, *lagergeld*, per letter or card.[12]

The fragmentary way in which news could be relayed to families is illustrated well in the case of the Brokensha brothers. Both Paul and David were captured at Tobruk and stayed together throughout the war, but news of each one's capture reached their parents three months apart. David Brokensha's mother was informed of his POW status in August 1942, the same month in which the eldest brother, Guy, was reported killed in action. News of Paul's captivity was only confirmed in November of that year, when the two of them reached Italy. In another more extreme case, Stanley Smollan's parents heard nothing about their son from the time of his capture in June 1942 until he arrived in Cairo in February 1944, following his escape to Anzio from a POW camp after the Italian Armistice.[13]

In response to Tobruk and to Red Cross organisational difficulties, the South African Prisoner-of-War Relatives and Friends Association (POWRFA) was established in July 1942. Its aim was to work with the Red Cross, to assist in the dissemination of information to families, and to help to improve conditions for South African POWs through the supply of food, clothing and other necessities to Italian and German prison camps. In a poignant appointment, David and Paul Brokensha's father, Rae, was elected chairman of the Relatives Association one month after the fall of Tobruk. Its proclaimed role was that of rehabilitation, concerning itself with the 'physical and mental welfare of prisoners of war and to facilitate their re-establishment in civilian life' upon their return.[14]

In September 1942, the Red Cross agreed to collaborate with the Association and in the following month it organised its first event in support of POW families – a day of prayer to be held on 23 November, the first anniversary of the Battle of Sidi Rezegh and six months since the fall of Tobruk.[15] Throughout the war, the Association published pamphlets which informed relatives of POWs on relevant issues. These included information on camp locations and descriptions of the surrounding environment. Some pamphlets provided instructions to family and friends on how to address letters and parcels to POWs, and what could and could not be included in parcels. In some cases the

The censor's stamp appeared on all letters. COURTESY ENID BATES

instructions seemed arbitrary, such as the one that stipulated that no more than six words were allowed on the back of photographs, or that clothing may be sent, but that corduroy items were not allowed. Pyjamas were allowed, but only if they were striped.[16]

From the start, unlike its British counterpart, POWRFA had a strained relationship with the War Office and with the Foreign Office, though the local Association interacted smoothly with officialdom and with other bodies concerned with POW interests.[17] Throughout the hostilities, it coordinated with the Red Cross, the Union Defence Force Prisoners-of-War Welfare Committee and the South African Gifts and Comforts Organisation.

With support organisations based mostly in Johannesburg, families in more remote smaller towns were often beyond their reach and unable to make use of their services,[18] but this did not stop relatives in smaller settlements from organising their own support groups. The 'Anxious Annies' was one such group. They were the mothers, wives and girlfriends of POWs from the Second Anti-Aircraft Regiment, popularly known as the Ack Ack Regiment, most of whom were captured at Tobruk. Fred van Alphen Stahl's mother was a member of the Malmesbury branch of this informal society.

Following the 1943 Armistice, most of those men who escaped successfully from Italian camps and reached Allied lines were repatriated to South Africa. The majority of South African POWs, however, had to wait until Germany finally accepted defeat in May 1945 before going home became a realistic option for them. For many, the liberation they experienced when Allied forces arrived at their POW camps, or when their forced marches finally came to an end, did not signify real freedom. They were still not in control of their own lives, and the decisions they made and the actions they took at this time were often the result of a needs must situation.

For a number of men the first leg of their journey as free men was curiously similar to some of the journeys they experienced while they were still in captivity. Before they reached Britain, most of them were deloused yet again, by this time a familiar POW experience. With hunger being the most pressing need for many during their captivity, liberation did not mean instant and abundant food. For AJ Cremer at least, the sudden access to food handed out by American soldiers at the hospital camp where he was recovering from dysentery almost brought his captivity to a tragic end. Several of his fellow POWs died during the first night of their freedom as a result of too much food after months of living on very little sustenance.[19]

In Britain, each of the Dominions had a separate camp for demobilisation and the white South Africans were accommodated in a camp in Brighton before being repatriated to South Africa. Soldiers of the Non European Army Services Corps were sent to different camps across Britain, where they were provided with clean clothes, food and comfortable accommodation. Gunner Maurice Edwards of the Cape Corps described his demobilising experiences as 'everything to amuse the mind and nothing to worry over'. Maurice was one of those who recognised Rae Brokensha's paternal role in helping returning POWs, saying that 'Mr Justice Brokensha took over where [the Red Cross] left off.'[20]

As chairman of POWRFA, Rae Brokensha went to Brighton to assist POWs with their passage home. Some soldiers spent up to four months in England waiting to return to the Union, being treated to a 'royal life'[21] which included 28 days' leave with the benefit of free railway passes.[22] The stay included organised tours to Parliament in Westminster and to South Africa House. But there was also an overwhelming impulse simply to return home as soon as they could, whatever their enjoyment of new-found British freedom. For Mrs AS Ogilvie of the POW Information Bureau at South Africa's High Commission, it was clear that these footloose demobbed men were finding it difficult to function in a civilian environment, preferring to 'just wander about and not having to do anything'.[23] Typical of these were the two Brokensha brothers. For most of the war unaware of their father's welfare activities, in an extraordinary moment they came across him by chance in a telephone booth in the camp at Brighton. Rae knew that his sons were due to arrive in Brighton, but had been unsure of the exact date. He was in the telephone booth trying to get this information when David and Paul spotted him. Paul greeted his Dad with 'Ok, Pop, no need to waste your pennies, here we are!'[24]

No cheers and no tears

The joy and happiness of finally arriving home was for many a short-lived experience as they suffered from what became known as 'barbed-wire disease'. While in captivity, many had spent hours fantasising about returning home, but these daydreams were often not realised. Meanwhile, for those who returned to homes in Britain, the experience was undoubtedly even more demoralising. The daily burdens and deprivations that the country had endured left some citizens even regarding POWs as having been fortunate in escaping many of the conflict's grimmer realities.[25]

Those on the South African home front had been largely unaffected by the war, and this caused families and friends of returning POWs and soldiers to be especially uninformed of the deep impact it had had on the men. On the other hand, because the country was left relatively unscathed, returning servicemen found their re-adaptation to civilian life made easier, though only if they were able to set aside their feelings of not being understood. When the POWs returned home, it was often in an atmosphere of disenchantment, as it seemed that the local population did not fully appreciate what they had done or experienced.

This disregard for their contribution to the war was also detected in the press, as on 30 April 1945, the *Star* reported simply that the arrival of several POWs at the Johannesburg station was a 'quiet but happy welcome [and] there was no exuberance of emotion – no cheers and no tears'.[26] The low-key manner in which returning POWs were welcomed in the Union was in stark contrast to the way in which they were received at the temporary base in Brighton, where they were thanked for their contribution to the war effort by Lord Croft, Under-Secretary for War. The *Star*, reporting on the same issue, included comments by Heaton Nicholls, High Commissioner for the Union, on Smuts's contribution to the post-war peace process and the information that he was trying 'to lay the foundations of the edifice for which you have been fighting'.[27]

Officially, returning soldiers and POWs were thanked for their contribution at various points along their journey. For instance, when they boarded ships on their way to Britain, some received 'welcoming notes' from the ship's Master and the Officer Commanding.[28] The Red Cross also handed out cards that wished the men a 'happy return home'.[29] The South African POWs each received a letter from the Prime Minister's wife, Isie Smuts, in which she acknowledged that they had endured a 'hard time & faced many dangers & made great sacrifices in order that we might live in peace & security & enjoy our accustomed freedom'.[30] In October 1945, all demobilised soldiers, including former POWs, received cards from JC Smuts in his capacity as Minister of Defence. In this correspondence, Smuts admitted that readjustment to civilian life might be problematic, but he tried to encourage the men by adding that 'patience and tolerance will be needed and the demands upon your courage and spirit of service will remain as great as ever'.[31] Because many former POWs expressed feelings of guilt and shame as a result of their captivity and because they felt they did not contribute towards the war effort in the usual way, many of them may have viewed Smuts's words with some cynicism.

Once in South Africa, most POWs decided to focus on their personal dreams and ambitions instead of entering into another war, even if an ideological war to be fought at home. It seemed as if the assumption by Major DL Charters of the Royal Army Medical Corps, himself a former POW, was somewhat misplaced, at least in the South African context, when he stated in the *Sunday Times* in January 1945 that POWs

> have gained in tolerance, understanding, patience, forbearance and courage. They have acquired a bigger concept of comradeship and the community of life. They more fully recognise the need for the individual to pull his weight in the interests of the group. The average prisoner has demonstrated a high standard of adaptability, and will do so again when he returns home to the post-war world.

The heading of this article was 'Prisoners of War will not present peace problem' and someone at military headquarters obviously found it interesting, because the section quoted above, now in the military archives in Pretoria, was marked by hand-drawn lines.[32] While it is true that POWs became more resilient and resourceful during their captivity, their exposure to various ideologies and general aversion to unfairness meant that their voices were less likely to be heard conspicuously for or against any political party. After years in POW camps, few of them were inclined to fight battles for others.

However, there were notable exceptions, as was the case with Sir De Villiers Graaff, who was captured at Tobruk in 1942. This mishap put a temporary halt on his political career as he was nominated by the United Party for the Hottentots-Holland district in the same year. He returned to South Africa to become a Member of Parliament in 1948 and later leader of the United Party, the official Opposition until 1977. Already during his time as POW at the Modena officers' camp, Graaff had participated in a group that regularly discussed ideas regarding post-war scenarios for South Africa. His contribution concerned mainly constitutional matters, although he also presented lectures on Friesian cattle. Still, though he made a significant contribution towards opposition politics throughout his career, it cannot be said that his POW experiences motivated him to enter into this sphere.

In fact, it is clear from his memoirs that had it not been for the United Party's persistence he would have preferred to spend more time on his farm and concentrate on expanding his legal firm after the war.[33]

In Britain, POWs received far more support than their comrades in the Union. The establishment of the Civil Resettlement Units helped returning POWs to adapt to post-war life and to bear the trauma with which many were left as a consequence of lengthy captivity. By 1946, up to 15 000 men had taken part in this voluntary scheme.[34] The Union of South Africa did not develop any similar organisations. Indeed, in many ways, South African POWs had little choice but to bottle up their emotions, frustrations and personal discontents and carry on with life. The South African political climate was beginning to show signs of change and war veterans were not its priority.

During the war, and with Smuts's support, a decision was made to record the country's role in the war. It was the task of Captain JAI Agar-Hamilton to collect relevant data and to see to it that the information was preserved in an official historical account. When the war came to an end, this project became known as the Union War Histories. However, Agar-Hamilton experienced problems from the start, not only with the lack of trained military historians, but also with a growing lack of interest from those in power. When Smuts lost the election in 1948, Agar-Hamilton faced an uphill battle as the National Party started to withdraw resources from the project. By 1961 he and his colleagues had produced three volumes, but by this time Dr Hendrik Verwoerd was Prime Minister and the government had become engrossed in ideologies of race. Participation in the war caused divisions among the citizens of the country, but the obstinacy of the NP now resulted in the sacrifice of a large and significant part of the country's history.[35]

After the war, the National Party was especially concerned about perceived 'communist' tendencies among returning soldiers and kept a close eye on their activities. Nor were they alone. As early as May 1943 official concerns about the ideological direction of the Springbok Legion, formed in 1941 to fight for the rights of soldiers, were raised about the 'Communist-inspired organisation which is hoping to cash in on discontented elements in the UDF'. According to an Information

Officer, those in the UDF who were leaning towards communism had 'decided not to worry about placating the Government and have openly become Communist'. Another officer stated that the communists among the veterans were 'organising a society for disbanded soldiers after the style of MOTH so if the present Government does not carry out its promises to the exservicemen (sic) SA will once again become a merry maze of politics and gangs'. What would have been in mind was the example of a non-commissioned officer so dissatisfied with the domestic political situation that he went as far as to conclude:

> our leaders here today shall be our leaders when things are normal again and not the ticks who have been living on the fat of the land at the expense of our blood. There is no such person in the army as English and Afrikaans, we're all one, 'South Africans', in other words 'Afrikaaners' [sic] and we've no intention of selling our country to any other bastard, as a big section of parasites are trying to do just now, for the present we've a job on our hands so we cannot pay 100% attention to other things, but when its [sic] over its going to be 100%.[36]

In an effort to protect the position of white war veterans in the labour market against the perceived competitive threat of black workers, the Smuts administration formed a Soldiers' Charter. One of its aims was to assist war veterans to find their feet and to ensure that all volunteers would be included in state recognition of its responsibility towards exsoldiers.[37] For most white POWs the post-war government aid schemes for returning veterans made employment and economic security a viable possibility because the Directorate of Demobilisation provided sheltered labour opportunities, gratuities and even clothing grants.[38] However, for female and black veterans, the situation was different. Women could only request demobilisation based on 'compassionate reasons', and if granted, they would lose all benefits.[39] Black volunteers, on the other hand, were compensated with a khaki suit and £2. Those who found jobs after the war were also given bicycles, not so much for compensation purposes, but so that they could get to work on time.[40]

Union authorities made no distinction in status between former POWs and former soldiers, the only exception being a March 1945 amendment when the Smuts government altered the terms of the Military Service Bill so that no former POW would 'be compelled to render at any place beyond the said territorial limits any military service whatsoever'. The previous wording had included, 'without his consent'.[41] As the war was over by this time, this change in the Service Bill made little if any difference to those who had volunteered four or five years earlier. Most veterans held the Soldiers' Charter in low regard and felt disappointed at what they considered to be the Smuts government's 'ungratefulness' for their contribution to the war.

Former POWs were not treated any differently from other veterans after the war. A number of them had to deal with feelings of guilt and cowardice, with David Brokensha even wanting to volunteer for service in the Far East to make up for what he thought was his lack of contribution to the war effort while he was a captive.[42] Ike Rosmarin had similar feelings of what he considered his 'hands-upping to the enemy without any real resistance', something that continued to trouble him for many years.[43] Guilt even found Michael de Lisle, who had escaped in Italy and fought with the partisans for a time. When he learnt about the UDF's role in the Italian Campaign, he felt that he was 'second best [and] trying to save my own life while they had been fighting for the cause'.

Dick Dickinson's last diary entry reveals his state of mind upon reaching Britain on 15 May 1945:

> We land at Guildford in Surrey and are back on 'Home Territory.' It is a few weeks short of four years since we left South African soil. It is also that time since I had a hot bath. Could Winston Churchill have gone four years without his hot bath? I doubt it. But if Churchill and I were to be compared, there would be a thousand-and-one differences. Not least of which would be the fact that I never won this war. Churchill (and some others) did. I only kept a diary.[44]

Dick Dickinson made full use of his time in Britain following his liberation. He toured the British Isles and even participated in a recording of Afrikaans songs for the BBC in July 1945. Dick arrived home in Queenstown on 12 September 1945, but ten days later he was on his way back to the University of the Witwatersrand to resume his studies, which he completed in 1946.[45] He then worked in Johannesburg and in 1948 started a career as a soil consultation officer in the Bethlehem area of the Orange Free State, eventually buying a farm near Harrismith. His response to the outcome of the 1948 election was, 'very disappointed obviously [...] I couldn't understand how these intellectual people could believe that [apartheid] could work'.

Regret was also part of Fred van Alphen Stahl's post-war experience. He would have liked to have been in the 'final push', but instead he had been

> pushing my luck, you know, [...] you regret that you never went through the final push, because that would have been your aim and ambition when you joined up, to be on the winning side physically, so that is a regret [...] All things considered, you can count your blessings, there's people who went into prisoner-of-war camps who didn't come out whole mentally, physically, so that's war, that's life. [...] You do have regrets that you weren't in at the end on the winning side as it were, doing your bit, not on the bench, you would have liked to have been in the scrum at that time.

Fred returned to his pre-war occupation and became a junior prosecutor in Cape Town. In later decades, he returned to military life when the Border War of South West Africa/Namibia commenced, but had no interest in career promotion and was content to remain a lieutenant in the rear while serving in the army's risk management and loss control divisions. When a young lieutenant jokingly referred to him as the oldest lieutenant in the army, he became known in this affectionate way among the younger and junior recruits.[46] For his part, Fred also met and befriended senior members of the National Party government, one of whom was JJ (Jim) Fouché, who became Minister of Defence in

1959. At the eightieth anniversary of the Bloemfontein Race Club in the Orange Free State, when Fred congratulated Fouché on his appointment he was apparently informed by the new minister that he had been reluctant to accept the position. In a supreme irony for an Afrikaner Nationalist, Fouché admitted to having been reading Churchill's volumes on World War II to prepare for his military responsibilities.

When Michael de Lisle returned to the Union in 1944 following his escape in Italy, he secured a 'modest pension' from the authorities by manipulating his medical board tests. His response to being examined for mobility was, 'in captivity I had lots of time to teach my knee not to jerk when it was tapped'. Soon afterwards, he was able to resume his education at the University of Cape Town, where he found that the university had credited him with his first academic year 'on the strength of six months' study in the first half of 1940'.[47] The period following his return was exceptionally busy, as he was studying towards his BA degree, 'leading a rock climb every Sunday, [...] I was running a night school for coloured children in Woodstock; I was on the mountain club committee at the university and on the ex-service committee; I was busy.' At the same time, he found it hard to return to his life in his mother's house: she did not understand that he had matured into a man while he had been away, and small things like being instructed to switch off his bedroom lights by 9.30 caused immense frustration.

Michael found it difficult to discuss his POW experience after the war because, as he said, 'people talked, but they just didn't understand'. In 1946, he went to Britain to further his education and was away when the National Party won the 1948 election. It left him shocked, but also 'very out of touch with South African feelings'. However, he believed that had he stayed on in South Africa he would have joined the Torch Commando, which grew out of the Springbok Legion in 1951, and supported the United Party in the 1953 election. Michael believed the Torch Commando stood for constitutionalism and civil rights, a 'principle which was being betrayed by an apartheid government'. Inspired by teaching Italian to fellow POWs, Michael decided to continue with a teaching career when the war ended and not to follow the theological route of becoming a minister, as his family had expected he would do. He married in 1955, a time in which he was still 'talking Italian and crying out in [his] sleep'. In the 1980s Michael was ordained an Anglican priest.[48]

When Clive Luyt volunteered he was working as an articled clerk at an accountancy firm, and when he returned he completed his examinations to become a chartered accountant. As an older man after the war, he found it hard to enter the labour market on a junior level, while others much younger were already in more senior positions because they had not volunteered for the UDF at the outbreak of hostilities. He viewed these non-volunteers as unpatriotic *'bangbroeke'* who had been selfish enough to put themselves before their country. Clive's involvement in rugby after the war led to a delightful coincidence: following a match during the All Blacks tour in 1949, a fellow former POW brought him his missing watch strap, which a friend had repaired in POW camp. The strap remained on the watch which he used for the remainder of his life. Clive Luyt became an Honorary Life Member of the SACS Old Boys' Union, his former high school.

Following his successful escape and joining up with the Allies at Anzio early in 1944, Stanley Smollan was first evacuated to Cairo and from there flown back to South Africa with a small group of escaped POWs who were given the publicity of an 'official welcome' at the Waterkloof airfield in the Transvaal. This was followed by three months' leave. Stanley believed that his POW experiences gave him 'proper perspective on values, you know what a loaf of bread meant, what a small meal meant, those things which you take for granted'. On the liberal side of the post-war political clashes between the Torch Commando and Ossewabrandwag sympathisers, for Stanley 'it got a bit ugly at times'. He entered into a family business and went on to enjoy a successful working career in finance. When Stanley visited Italy in later years, he met Tammaso de Lellis, the Italian POW whose repatriation he had tried to secure shortly after the war.

When the war in the Far East came to an end, so did David Brokensha's ambitions to rejoin the army. Awarded a scholarship to study at Cambridge, he obtained a degree in Anthropology. However, he believed that the scholarship selection committee pitied him when it heard that he had been a POW, and he could not help wondering if this was the reason why he was awarded the scholarship. When the Nationalists came to power, David, as a liberal English-speaking individual, was unable to secure a sought-after government position at the Department of Native Affairs, and ended up working in Tanganyika, where he met his life partner. In 1986, his brother Paul died and this prompted David to write his autobiography.

Throughout his captivity, Bernard Schwikkard had dreams of arriving home on a Sunday, with the roast on the table and his family sitting there waiting for him. In those recollected dreams he would ignore his family and head straight for the food. When he was finally liberated he and a few companions immediately ordered German women to cook them a meal – 'a wonderful meal, we gorged ourselves'. Bernard was one of the first South African POWs to arrive at the Brighton compound and pleaded to be sent home at the earliest available opportunity. He flew back crammed into a Dakota with a group of POWs to an air force base where they were welcomed by the Women's Auxiliary, who were very kind: 'they put me on a train and gave me sort of bedding and something to eat and I phoned my mother – this was a tremendous emotional time for me [...] I was the first of the family to get back' – and he got his Sunday roast.

Rand Mines, Bernard's employer before he volunteered, had been paying him throughout the war. When he returned to his employment he received an increase which, combined with an education grant from the military, enabled him to complete his courses in mining and to marry in 1948.

Bill Hindshaw remembers arriving back in the Union on April Fool's Day – earlier than most, because of his successful escape in Italy. Once in South Africa, he considered returning to Italy for some time, as he 'would have married there [...] but that's all water under the bridge'. Before the war, Bill had worked as an apprentice bricklayer and after his return was offered a position at a training college for master builders where he eventually became principal.

Following three months in England, in 1945 Fred Geldenhuis returned to South Africa on a Union Castle mail liner that had been converted into a troop ship. He did not enjoy the voyage, for it reminded him of POW camp, 'where the fellows every evening used to walk around in groups, partly to keep in motion, partly to pass the time'.⁴⁹ He also spent much time wondering about his welcome, as before the war he and his stepmother had not enjoyed a good relationship. Moreover, he was also acutely aware that his father's neighbours were members of the Ossewabrandwag. His ship arrived in Cape Town in August 1945, and he reached Pretoria after a three-day train journey. Not recognising anyone on the platform as there to welcome him, he was heading for a bus station when he heard a girl's voice:

> 'Hello Frikkie' [...] Well, I took her and kissed her and said, 'who are you' and she said she's Annatjie. I could not recall an Annatjie so kissed her again. Just then the other person came up to us and I recognised her as Kotie de Waal, Annatjie's sister, whom I knew from school days, and particularly our friendship. So I kissed her too.⁵⁰

During his three months' army leave, he visited friends in Natal as an escape from a tense domestic atmosphere. That leave was cut short when Fred was told that he was needed to help with the mounted escort at the opening of Parliament in 1946. He continued his soldiering life as Regimental Sergeant Major of the Prince Alfred's Guard, retiring finally at the age of 69. In his eightieth year he visited Italy and met some of those who had helped him during his short-lived period of freedom following the Armistice.

Like Bernard Schwikkard, Wessel Oosthuizen used to fantasise about enjoying a Sunday roast, specifically a leg of lamb with gravy and peas. Like Bernard Schwikkard, he confessed to having been more fixated upon the fantasy meal than on embracing his family.⁵¹ Wessel's parents were unaware that he had returned to South Africa and he was taken to the family farm by a cousin who met him by chance near the train station in Johannesburg. Reflecting upon his POW experiences, Wessel believed that they made him a better person. His feelings towards the German nation reflected the complexities of mixing theoretical political ideologies and real-life personal experiences. Wessel compared the Nazi actions towards Jews to British concentration camps during the South African War, but he also remembered that the intensely passionate nature of white politics before the war started to dissipate after the 1948 accession of the Nationalists. Thereafter, he believed, most people became more tolerant. Long comfortable in uniform, Wessel continued with his career in the police force and eventually retired to the Southern Cape coast.

When Mathys Beukes returned home he was permitted to write his outstanding university examinations – most universities made allowances for returning soldiers, as they had done before 1939 when students had volunteered for service in the UDF. Having escaped from Italian captivity he had returned to South Africa before the war was over. He had no intention of staying on in the military, especially when he was obliged to write a report on how his psychological state had been affected by his experience as a POW. By this time Mathys was thoroughly fed up with military bureaucracy, and when an officer asked him what his reason was for getting out of the war early, he lost control, verbally attacking the officer and asking him confrontationally, 'who said I want to get out of the war, is there anything else you want to know, are there any more oaths that you want me to sign?'

Mathys resumed his judicial career as a prosecutor, but first had to get past the commanding Nationalist network in the Department of Justice, which was in a position to dictate his location of work. By circumventing the system and threatening to go to Jan Smuts himself with copies of key paperwork, Mathys eventually managed to get sent to Cape Town, just where he wanted to be, leaving him 'very satisfied with the outcome of events'.[52]

JC Smuts and the 'end of an era'

In some ways, Smuts's declining popularity through the 1940s and his weakened position in white politics after the war might be compared to the ways in which returning POWs perceived their country's political and social situation after 1945. The Union's POWs had

Fred Geldenhuis accompanying Jan Smuts at a parade in 1948. COURTESY ILSE GELDENHUIS

been exposed to profound events in Europe which influenced their consciousness and sense of the world, and left many thinking differently about their place in their own country. Moreover, weary of conflict and war, they simply wanted to enjoy the notion of a 'normal' life. Smuts, too, experienced shattering world events and participated centrally in global movements, encompassing the work of the Imperial War Cabinet, Commonwealth policies, and the direction of the League of Nations as well as the post-war formation of the United Nations. Yet Smuts the internationalist was unable to realise his vision in South Africa. The United Party's reliance on the soldiers' vote and its misjudgement of the support among certain of its constituencies during the 1943 election indicated that his interpretation of the South

African situation was skewed. Although he won the 1943 election, it is widely considered that the electoral victory was an 'illusion' as a result of the effect of the progress of the war on the soldiers' vote, and that the polls were not a realistic indication of their true political feeling.[53] Later, like most of those POWs who had fallen in behind him as Smuts men, he gravely underestimated the influence and determination of the Nationalists.

When Jan Smuts lost the election in 1948, the lukewarm or unappreciative stance of the war-time government was supplanted by emphatically more discriminatory Nationalist actions and a blatant disregard for veterans' loyal service during the war.[54] Some POWs felt more acutely frustrated, having a particular sense of entitlement because of their special wartime circumstances. In a few cases, ex-POWs attempted to create public awareness about their needs. In one instance, a former POW wrote an open letter to the *Rand Daily Mail*, explaining that delays caused by 'endless questions and red tape' were preventing POWs from returning to jobs and were subjecting them to 'even more anxiety and worry'. The letter went on to say that POWs were unwilling to tell civilians or authorities about their prison experiences 'because they learnt not to indulge in self-pity', but without fair treatment, the 'waste of human material [...] will undoubtedly cause much resentment'.[55] Still, when considering the decisions that POWs made following their return, it becomes evident that most became preoccupied with personal needs and objectives. Turning inward, they seemed to have had enough of organising for resistance, let alone conflict.

When Jan Smuts died in 1950 it was, as one leading South African historian has concluded, the 'end of an era in the history of South Africa'.[56] For POWs, too, in a modest yet also meaningful way, it was the closing of a small door of some recognition for their wartime sacrifices, and while many of them simply wanted to get on with their lives, it did not mean that they all approved of what was happening in the country. A note left by Dennis Mugglestone in his memoirs most aptly summarises the feelings of discontent with the new post-war political direction:

I wore these two tabs right through the war & survived POW life, so that you & your extremist comrades & rebels may enjoy the freedom you have to-day. May all the sane & right thinking South Africans pester you so much during the rest of your Nazi domineering rule, that you see nothing else but RED, tabs & all.

STERKSTROOM AND DISTRICT CONSOLIDATED WAR FUND.
W.F. NO. 322.

Returned Soldiers Fund.

Board of
Trustees :
H. D. de Wet,
Chairman.
W. A. Currie,
Vice-Chairman.
Committee.
D. A. J. Fourie
S. W. Smart,
Mrs. Ray Hartley,
J H. Goosen,
(Hon Liason Officer)
Mrs. M. J. de Wet.
(Red Cross)
Mrs. W. A. Currie
(S.A.W.A.S.)
Hon. Secretary :
H. P. Fuller.
Hon. Auditor :
Mrs. M. Maartens.

Sterkstroom, C.P.

2/2/46 194

Dear *Mr. Mortlock*,

At the beginning of the War our committee decided to open a fund to assist men and women of the armed forces on their return to civilian life. The Government, through the establishment of the Demobilisation Committee, made ample provision for all contingencies, and it was then decided to devote our funds and efforts to a measure of appreciation to those who had served their country in time of trouble.

The enclosed cheque for £ *9 : 9 :* therefore comes to you from your fellow citizens of Sterkstroom, who have had your welfare deeply at heart while you were serving in the armed forces, in sincere appreciation of the service you have rendered South Africa.

Please do not regard this cheque as a charitable contribution in any way—it is not. Most of the fund was built up by generous public support, for the specific purpose of indicating, in a small way, our gratitude for what you have sacrificed to maintain the honour and prestige of our Country.

An amount of £100 has been set aside to provide for a suitable memorial for those of your comrades who did not return. The form that this memorial will take has still to be decided upon.

We are pleased you have returned to us, rich in experience and sound in body and mind, and we sincerely trust that you will soon settle down in your civilian occupation, and play your part in the great constructive tasks that still lie ahead.

Thank you.

Yours sincerely,

[signature] Chairman.
[signature] Secretary.

Good news from the Returned Soldiers Fund. COURTESY ANTHONY MORTLOCK

Afterword: 'Laugh at life'

When George Tewkesbury was 17 he volunteered and joined his mother's Scottish regiment, the Black Watch. He was captured on 4 February 1944 during the Allied landings at Anzio. George spent most of his captivity in Stalag 357, near Fallingbostel in Germany, and endured his POW experiences with an unrestrained sense of humour. It was during his confinement, he believed, that he learnt to 'laugh at life, because if you don't laugh at life there's nothing'. The camp commandant was an infamous man who seemed to enjoy setting his Alsatian on POWs for even the smallest of transgressions. George also remembered how a POW was shot while trying to climb the camp fence. On the commandant's orders, the dead man was left hanging on the fence as a lesson to the others.

On 16 April 1945, George and his fellow POWs woke up to find that all of the German guards had disappeared during the night. While most of the POWs ransacked the food stores, George decided to go to the officers' hut to see what he could 'nick'. He found the camp commandant's uniform and a flag, but decided against taking these lest he be mistaken for a Nazi sympathiser. He did, however, take the commandant's medals and a small knife, which he found in the uniform pockets. Following the war, George met his wife while on a trip to South Africa and settled in Cape Town.

Some years later, George went to a pet shop in Newlands and found that the owner, Willy, had also been a POW in Stalag 357. The two of them became firm friends. Not long after that Willy phoned George with extraordinary news. The German commandant of Stalag 357 had visited the shop that morning to buy food for his dog. The astounded Willy apparently could not stop swearing at the German, whereupon the former commandant announced that 'the war is over and I'm happy here in South Africa, I am living in Camps Bay'. ('It had to be a camp,' Willy added wryly.) Nevertheless, Willy told him in no uncertain terms to leave the shop at once.

George started to experience pangs of guilt. Should he return the medals to the commandant? Seeking advice from his church, he was told to return the medals. Not completely satisfied with the answer,

George approached a military man about the situation, and was told that the medals were 'captured property' and rightfully belonged to George. Secondly, he was told that 'the war is over and thirdly [that it] is nobody's bloody business'. Although George was tempted to write an article for the Camps Bay newspaper about his loot, he did not. He did, however, keep the medals.

NOTES

CHAPTER ONE

1. Kochavi, A.J. 2005. *Confronting Captivity: Britain and the United States and their POWs in Nazi Germany*: 53–54.
2. Geldenhuis, FJW. nd. *A Soldier's Scrapbook*: 17–43.
3. Wessel Oosthuizen interview: 4 December 2010: 'Hulle het my soort van oorrompel [...] toe het ek maar die eed gevat maar hulle het eintlik valse voorwendsels [gehad] toe sê hulle 'jy werk vir die staat dit is net 'n bewys dat jy getrou is aan die staat se eed' dan kry jy 'n rooi lussie toe het hul my nou daar vasgetrek.'
4. Fred Geldenhuis interview: 9 July 2010, Pretoria. 'Toe het ons vrywillig, baie vrywillig ander nie vrywillig.'
5. National Archives of South Africa (hereafter NASA) SAP.1/146/40/A. Commissioner of the South African Police to the Minister of Justice in Cape Town. 14 January 1950. Unfortunately no further archival evidence on this issue was found.
6. Shearing, T & D (eds). 2010. *From Jo'burg to Dresden. A World War II Diary by EB Dickinson*: 5.
7. Bates, HJ. 1992. *Lest We Forget*: 7–9.
8. Evans, RJ. 2008. *The Third Reich at War*: 112.
9. Wessels, A. 2000. 'The first two years of war: The development of the Union Defence Forces (UDF) September 1939 to September 1941.' *Military History Journal* 11(5): online at http://samilitaryhistory.org/vol115aw.html.
10. Ogilvie, P & N Robinson. 1975. *In the Bag*: 14.
11. Du Toit, BM. 1991. 'The far right in current South African politics.' *The Journal of Modern African Studies*, 29(4): 632.
12. Lowry, D. 2000. *The South African War Reappraised*: 215–216.
13. Pakenham, T. 1982. *The Boer War*: 166, 171.
14. Churchill, WS. 1973. *The Collected Works of Sir Winston Churchill, Vol I. My Early Life: My African Journey*: 273.
15. Marks, S. *Oxford Dictionary of National Biography*, Smuts, Jan Christiaan (1870–1950). Available at http://www.oxforddnb.com/view/article/36171?docPos=1. Accessed 1 November 2011.

NOTES

16 Pretorius, F. 2000. *Life on Commando During the Anglo-Boer War 1899–1902*: 43, 69.
17 Du Toit, BM. 1991. 'The far right in current South African politics.' *Journal of Modern African Studies*, 29(4): 629.
18 Wessels, A. 2011. 'Boer guerrilla and British counter-guerrilla operations in South Africa, 1899–1902.' *Scientia Militaria, South African Journal of Military Studies*, 39(2): 14.
19 Surridge, K. 2012. 'An example to be followed or a warning to be avoided? The British, Boers, and guerrilla warfare, 1900–1902.' *Small Wars & Insurgencies*, 23(4–5): 616.
20 Van Heyningen, E. 2008. 'Costly mythologies: The concentration camps of the South African War in Afrikaner historiography.' *Journal of Southern African Studies* 34(3): 508–509.
21 Pakenham, *The Boer War*: 560–569.
22 Giliomee, H. 2003. *The Afrikaners. Biography of a People*: 268–273.
23 Thompson, L. 1995. *A History of South Africa*: 159.
24 Grundlingh, A & S Swart. 2009. *Radelose Rebellie? Dinamika van die 1914–1915 Afrikanerrebellie*: 15–21.
25 Nasson, B. 1995. 'War opinion in South Africa, 1914.' *The Journal of Imperial and Commonwealth History* 23(2): 248–276.
26 Grundlingh, A & S Swart. *Radelose Rebellie?*: 121.
27 Thompson, *A History of South Africa*: 160.
28 Whatley, CA. *Scottish Society, 1707–1830: Beyond Jacobitism, Towards Industrialisation*: 50.
29 Smuts, JC. 1942. *Plans for a Better World: Speeches of Field-Marshal the Right Honourable JC Smuts, PC, CH, KC, DTD*. The Challenge to Freedom: Speech at St Andrews University on 17 October 1934: 86 & 99.
30 Giliomee, *The Afrikaners*: 442.
31 Kienzle, K. 1979. 'German-South African Trade Relations in the Nazi Era.' *African Affairs*, 78(310): 83–88.
32 McCormack, 'Man with a mission': 544.
33 Weale, A. 2010. *The SS: A New History*: 227.
34 Ibid: 965–967.
35 This was Chief of General Staff Pierre van Ryneveld's opinion of those South Africans who seemingly supported the Nazi cause at the start of the war. Fedorowich, K. 2005. 'German espionage and British counter-intelligence in South Africa and Mozambique, 1939–1944.' *The Historical Journal*, 48(1): 213.
36 Matin, HJ & N Orpen. 1979. *South Africa at War. Preparations and Operations On The Home Front*: 27.
37 Wessels, 'The first two years of war'.
38 Added to the number of dead were 587 000 Polish soldiers who were taken prisoner and about 133 700 who were wounded. The German casualties amounted to 16 000 dead and 32 000 wounded. Zaloga, SJ & H Gerrard. 2002. *Poland 1939: The Birth of Blitzkrieg*: 86.
39 Wessels, 'The first two years of war'.
40 McCormack, RL. 1979. 'Man with a mission: Oswald Pirow and South African Airways, 1933–1939.' *Journal of African History* 20(4): 544, 556.
41 Fedorowich, K. 2005. 'German espionage and British counter-intelligence in South Africa and Mozambique, 1939 – 1944.' *The Historical Journal*, 48(1): 222–223.
42 Nasson, B. *South Africa at War 1939–1945*: 5, 23–24, 55.
43 Grundlingh, AM. 1999. 'The King's Afrikaners?: Enlistment and ethnic identity in the Union of South Africa's Defence Force during the Second World War, 1939–45.' *Journal of African History*, 40: 11.; Roos, N. 2005. *Ordinary Springboks: White Servicemen and Social Justice in South Africa 1939–1961*: 33.
44 Marx, C. 1994. 'The Ossewabrandwag as a mass movement, 1939–1941.' *Journal of Southern African Studies* 20(2): online at EBSCO Host Academic Search Premier.
45 Grundlingh, 'The King's Afrikaners?': 351–365.

CHAPTER TWO

1. De Lisle, M. nd. *Over the Hills and Far Away: My Twenties in the Forties*: 5.
2. Schwikkard, BE. 1999. *My Life Briefly Told*: 20.
3. Crompton, C & P Johnson. 2010. *Luck's Favours: Two South African Second World War Memoirs*: 8–18.
4. Corjava, S. 2008. *Hitler and Mussolini: The Secret Meetings*: 35–48.
5. Tarr, R. 2009. 'The foreign policies of Hitler and Mussolini', *History Today*. Available at http://www.historytoday.com/russel-tarr/foreign-policies-hitler-and-mussolini. Accessed 20 October 2014.
6. Corjava, *Hitler and Mussolini*: 35–48.
7. Sadkovich, JJ. 1989. 'Understanding defeat: Reappraising Italy's role in World War II.' *Journal of Contemporary History* 24(1): 29–33.
8. Corjava, *Hitler and Mussolini*: 56.
9. Mussolini made this statement in a letter to Churchill two weeks before he declared war on the Allies. Brown, JA. 1990. *The War of a Hundred Days: Springboks in Somalia and Abyssinia 1940–41*: 47.
10. Bourhill, J. 2011. *Come Back to Portofino: Through Italy with the 6th South African Armoured Division*: 47.
11. De Lisle, *Over the Hills and Far Away*: 5.
12. Ibid: 11.
13. Crompton & Johnson, *Luck's Favours*: 20.
14. Schwikkard, *My Life Briefly Told*: 22
15. Bentz, G. 2012. 'From El Wak to Sidi Rezegh: The Union Defence Force's first experience of battle in East and North Africa, 1940–1941.' *Scientia Militaria* 40(3): 179.
16. Agar-Hamilton, JAI & LCF Turner. 1957. *The Sidi Rezegh Battles 1941*: 73–74.
17. Crompton & Johnson, *Luck's Favours*: 26–27.
18. Schwikkard, *My Life Briefly Told*: 24.
19. Sir Alan Gordon Cunningham, Commander of the Eighth Army. Strawson, J. *Oxford Dictionary of National Biography*; Cunningham, Sir Alan Gordon (1887–1983). Available at http://www.oxforddnb.com/view/article/30991?docPos=7. Accessed 3 November 2011.
20. Brown, JA. 1991. *Retreat to Victory: A Springbok's Diary in North Africa: Gazala to El Alamein 1942*: 36.
21. Schwikkard, *My Life Briefly Told*: 25.
22. Crompton, C & P Johnson, *Luck's Favours*: 32–33, 37.
23. Schwikkard, *My Life Briefly Told*: 25.
24. Somerville, C. 1998. *Our War: How the British Commonwealth Fought the Second World War*: 94.
25. Ogilvie, P & N Robinson. 1975. *In the Bag*: 12.
26. Herbert Hammond was born in Salisbury but was known as Aussie because he had lived in Australia for most of his childhood. He returned to South Africa in 1938 and volunteered when war started in 1939.
27. Chambers, J. 1967. *For You the War is Over. The Story of HR (Aussie) Hammond*: 7.
28. Ogilvie & Robinson, *In the Bag*: 12.
29. Ibid: 12–13.
30. Ibid: 14.
31. Chambers, *For You the War is Over*: 7–8.
32. DOD Narep/ME/3. *Account of the adventures of the fellows taken at Sidi Rezegh.*

NOTES

Statement by repatriated POW, 'Mr W'.
33 DOD UWH Narep/Me/1. *Baden's letter to Joe after the Battle at Sidi Rezegh, 13.12.1941.*
34 DOD UWH Narep ME 1. *An episode at Sidi Rezegh by Johannes of 5 Bde.* A note accompanying this document states that the extract concerning Johannes was cut from the official Brigade diary on the instructions of Major General Brink.
35 Grundy, KW. 1983. *Soldiers without Politics: Blacks in the South African Armed Forces:* 67–68.
36 Van Heyningen, C. 1966. *Uys Krige:* 37.
37 Krige, U. 1960. *Sout van die Aarde:* 31.
38 Holland, J. 2006. *Together We Stand: Turning the Tide in the West: North Africa 1942–1943:* lxxiv; Klein, H. 1965. *Springboks in Armour. The South African Armoured Cars in World War II:* 171.
39 Norrie became Major General of the Royal Armoured Corps in 1943. Howell, PA. Australian Dictionary of Biography; Sir Charles Willoughby Moke Norrie (1893–1977). Available at http: //adb.anu.edu.au/biography/norrie-sir-charles-willoughby-moke-11254. Accessed 3 November 2011.
40 Agar-Hamilton & Turner, *The Sidi Rezegh Battles 1941:* 271.
41 Brown, *Retreat to Victory:* 34–36.
42 Shearing, T & D (eds). 2010. *From Jo'burg to Dresden. A World War II Diary by EB Dickinson:* 45.
43 Ibid: 65.
44 Barnett, C. 1960. *The Desert Generals:* 117–165.
45 Fennell, J. 2013. 'Courage and cowardice in the North African campaign: The Eighth Army and defeat in the summer of 1942'. *War in History,* 20/1: 100.
46 Barnett, C. 1960. *The Desert Generals:* 175.
47 Mortlock, J. 1956. *The Endless Years: Reminiscences of the 2nd World War:* 6–7.
48 Brokensha, D. 2007. *Brokie's Way: An Anthropologist's Story. Love and Work in Three Continents:* 64–70.
49 Somerville, *Our War:* 138. The Benghazi Handicap took place in April 1941 and the Gazala Gallop in June 1942, just before the fall of Tobruk. In both cases the Allied forces were moving towards Egypt, away from the Germans in the West.
50 Klein, H (ed). 1946. *Springbok Record:* 182 & 186.
51 Shearing, T & D (eds). *From Jo'burg to Dresden:* 40–41 & 61.
52 Orpen, N. 1971.*War in the Desert:* 182–183.
53 TNA, WO 32/10160/360, *Auchinleck Despatch on Operations in the Middle East,* 1 November 1941 to 15 August 1942.
54 Barnett, C. 1960. *The Desert Generals:* 152–153.
55 Ibid: 117–165.
56 De Lisle, *Over the Hills and Far Away:* 19.
57 Cremer, AJ. nd. *Oorlogsherinneringe:* 16.
58 Holland, *Together We Stand:* 38–39.
59 Reuter. 'Frontier Escarpment in Allied hands'. *The Times,* 20 June 1942. News. 4.
60 Orpen, N. 1971. *War in the Desert:* 302–303.
61 Pimlott, J (ed). 1994. *Rommel in his Own Words:* 89.
62 DOD UWH Narep ME 13. Notes on interview on 18 Nov 1946 with Capt DG Fannin ex-int offr 4 SA INF BDE.
63 DOD UWH Narep ME 3. Statement by 196202(V) PTE. Gert Daniel van Zyl of C COY, 1 SAP. '*Ons was soos 'n klomp skape sonder 'n herder.*'
64 DOD UWH Narep ME 13. Notes on interview on 18 Nov 1946 with Capt DG Fannin.
65 Ibid.
66 DOD UWH Narep ME 13. Report of Interview – General HB Klopper DSO – Major LCF Turner – Chief Narrator (Land) 6 May 1946.

67 DOD UWH Narep ME 13. Notes on interview on 23 Nov 46 with Col W Mc A Richards CRA 2 SA DIV in Tobruk.
68 DOD UWH Narep ME 13. Report of Interview – General HB Klopper DSO – Major LCF Turner – Chief Narrator (Land) 6 May 1946.
69 DOD UWH Narep ME 13. Notes on interview on 18 Nov 1946 with Capt DG Fannin ex-int offr 4 SA INF BDE.
70 DOD UWH Narep ME 13. Notes on interview on 20 Nov 46 with Maj Wessels 2/c South Africa 2 LAA REGT in Tobruk.
71 DOD UWH Narep ME 13. Notes on interview on 23 Nov 46 with Col W Mc A Richards CRA 2 SA DIV in Tobruk.
72 Mortlock, *The Endless Years*: 28.
73 Ibid: 25.
74 Wood, HL. n.d. *Memoirs of a Prisoner of War:* 1; Mugglestone, DIH. nd. *Destination Unknown:* 20.
75 Cremer, A.J. nd. *Oorlogsherinneringe:* 17.
76 Rosmarin, I. 1999. *Inside Story:* 11.
77 Somerville, C. 1998. *Our War:* 139.
78 Wood, HL. n.d. *Memoirs of a Prisoner of War:* 1.
79 DOD UWH Narep ME 1. *Western Desert Campaign Statement by Col Du Plessis on the fall of Tobruk.*
80 DOD UWH Narep ME 1. *Tobruk. Account by Lt AN Goldman, DCM and Sgt CH Spear, MM.*
81 Brokensha, *Brokie's Way:* 72.
82 Mortlock, *The Endless Years:* 30.
83 De Lisle, *Over the Hills and Far Away:* 19.
84 Bates, HJ. 1992. *Lest we Forget:* 69–72.
85 DOD UWH Narep ME 3. Statement by 196202 (V) PTE Gert Daniel van Zyl of C COY, 1 SAP.
86 DOD UWH Narep ME 1. *Tobruk. Account by Lt AN Goldman, DCM and Sgt CH Spear, MM.*
87 DOD UWH Narep ME 1. *Western Desert Campaigns: A letter by John Davidson 5399 7 Field BTY 3rd Regt (25 VI 42) to his family re fall of Tobruk.*
88 Tungay, WR. 1948. *The Fighting Third:* 205–221.
89 Shearing, T & D (eds). *From Jo'burg to Dresden:* 67–77.
90 Pimlott, J (ed). 1994. *Rommel:* 113.
91 Stewart, A. 2006. '"The Klopper Affair": Anglo-South African Relations and the Surrender of the Tobruk Garrison.' *Twentieth Century British History*, 17(4): 517.
92 Van der Waag, I. '"The Thin Edge of the Wedge": Anglo-South African relations, dominion nationalism and the formation of the Seaward Defence Force in 1939–1940', *Contemporary British History* 24, 4, 2010: 429.
93 Stewart, A. 2008. 'The British government and the South African neutrality crisis, 1938–39.' *English Historical Review* CXXIII (503): 947–972.
94 Stewart, A. 2008. 'The "atomic" despatch: Field Marshal Auchinleck, the fall of the Tobruk garrison and post-war Anglo-South African relations.' *Scientia Militaria: South African Journal of Military History*, 36(1): 78.
95 NASA BTS 1/54/12.
96 Rosmarin, *Inside Story:* 17.
97 Summerfield, P. 'Dunkirk and the popular memory of Britain at War, 1940–1958'. *Journal of Contemporary History* 45/4. 2010. 788; Gilbert, A. 2006. *POW Allied Prisoners in Europe, 1939–1945:* 128.
98 Roos, N. 2005. *Ordinary Springboks: White Servicemen and Social Justice in South Africa 1939–1961:* 34.

NOTES

99 NASA BTS 1/54/12.
100 *Rand Daily Mail:* 17 July 1942.
101 Schwikkard, BE. 1999. *My Life Briefly Told:* 25.
102 Mortlock, *The Endless Years:* 19.
103 Rosmarin, *Inside Story:* 8.
104 Battistelli, PP. 2010. *Erwin Rommel: The Background, Strategies, Tactics and Battlefield Experiences of the Greatest Commanders of History:* 55–56.
105 Holland, J. 2006. *Together We Stand: Turning the Tide in the West: North Africa 1942–1943:* 37.
106 Rosmarin, *Inside Story:* v; Flederman, A. 2005. *And Direction Was Given:* xv.
107 Wolhuter, SG. nd. *The Melancholy State:* 19.
108 Cremer, AJ. nd. *Oorlogsherinneringe:* 18.
109 Mugglestone, DIH. n.d. *Destination Unknown:* 23.
110 Wolhuter, *The Melancholy State:* 31.
111 Fedorowich, K. 2005. 'German espionage and British counter-intelligence in South Africa and Mozambique, 1939–1944.' *The Historical Journal*, 48(1): 211–222.
112 Furlong, P. 2005. 'Allies at War? Britain and the "Southern African Front" in the Second World War.' *South African Historical Journal*, 54(1): 18, 26.
113 Shearing, T & D (eds). *From Jo'burg to Dresden:* 69.
114 These distances are by road, the exact routes taken by POWs is not known. Google Maps. Available at https://www.google.co.za/maps/dir/Benghazi,+Libya/Tubruq,+Libya/. Accessed on 21 August 2014.
115 Ogilvie & Robinson, *In the Bag:* 21.
116 Ibid, 22–23.
117 De Lisle, *Over the Hills and Far Away:* 25.
118 Leigh, M. 1992. *Captives Courageous. South African Prisoners of War World War II:* 24.
119 MMH, File B472: Memoirs of GH Collet.
120 MMH, File B472: Memoirs of LG Tupper.
121 Rosmarin, *Inside Story:* 16.
122 Mortlock, *The Endless Years:* 31.
123 DOD UWH Narep/Me/1. Baden's letter to Joe after the Battle at Sidi Rezegh, 13.12.1941.
124 Cremer, *Oorlogsherinneringe:* 20.
125 Ogilvie & Robinson, *In the Bag:* 25–26.
126 Cremer, *Oorlogsherinneringe:* 19.
127 NASA BTS 9/55/1 Vol 2: South Africa House, London, to Secretary of External Affairs, Pretoria. 8 October 1942.
128 Brokensha, *Brokie's Way:* 75.
129 Ibid: 75.
130 Kannemeyer, JC. 2002. *Die Goue Seun: Die Lewe en Werk van Uys Krige:* 334.
131 De Lisle, *Over the Hills and Far Away:* 19.
132 Absalom, R. 1995. 'Hiding History: The Allies, the Resistance and the Others in Occupied Italy 1943 – 1945.' *The Historical Journal*, 38(1): 120.
133 Gilbert, A. 2006. *POW Allied Prisoners in Europe, 1939–1945:* 207–208.
134 Bennet, A. 2005. *The Geneva Convention: The Hidden Origins of the Red Cross:* 212.
135 Gilbert, *POW:* 208.
136 Mugglestone, *Destination Unknown:* 22.
137 NASA BTS 9/55/1 Vol 2: South Africa House, London, to Secretary of External Affairs, Pretoria. 8 October 1942.
138 DOD UWH Narep ME 4. Axis cruelty to native prisoners.
139 Knoetze, JC. 1994. 'Historical survey of the Non-European Army Services outside of the Union of South Africa (part II).' *Scientia Militaria, South African Journal of Military Studies* 24(2): 36–37.

140 Cremer, *Oorlogsherinneringe*: 18. 'Ek kon maar net lag.'
141 Crwys-Williams, J. 1992. *A Country at War 1939–1945: The Mood of a Nation*: 384.
142 Friedman, G. 2003. *The Piano War*: 158.
143 DOD UWH Narep ME 2. Statement by No 4448 L/CPL Job Maseko alleging to have sunk a boat in Tobruk harbour about 21 July '42.
144 Ibid.
145 Knoetze, JC. 1994. 'Historical Survey of the Non-European Army Services Outside of the Union of South Africa (part II).' *Scientia Militaria, South African Journal of Military Studies* 24(2): 37.
146 De Lisle, *Over the Hills and Far Away*: 30.
147 Ditsong National Museum of Military History (hereafter MMH) B.472. *Instructions to all European Ranks if taken prisoner-of-war*.
148 DOD Narep/ME/3. *Account of the adventures of the fellows taken at Sidi Rezegh. Statement by repatriated POW, 'Mr W'*.
149 Leigh, *Captives Courageous*: 14–31.
150 Wolhuter, SG. nd. *The Melancholy State*: 36.
151 DOD UWH Narep Me 2. Statement by Rev Maj Patrick J Nolan.
152 DOD UWH Narep ME 4. Enemy treatment of prisoners in Cyrenaica after Sidi Rezegh, extracts from a report by a SA officer, Major HW Boardman, 1 SA Irish.
153 MMH, File B472: Memoirs of GH Collet.
154 De Lisle, *Over the Hills and Far Away*: 33.
155 Langley, L. *National Geographic: Weird and Wild*. Available at http://newswatch.nationalgeographic.com/. Accessed 26 August 2014. The Desert Rats Association. Available at http://www.desertrats.org.uk/assoc/. Accessed 26 August 2014.
156 Shearing, T & D (eds). *From Jo'burg to Dresden*: 69.
157 Brokensha, *Brokie's Way*: 76.
158 Shearing, T & D (eds), *From Jo'burg to Dresden*: 69.
159 De Lisle, *Over the Hills and Far Away*: 29–30.
160 Brokensha, *Brokie's Way*: 77.
161 De Lisle, *Over the Hills and Far Away*: 21.
162 Shearing, T & D (eds), *From Jo'burg to Dresden*: 60–61.
163 Ibid: 69.
164 Rosmarin, *Inside Story*: 14.
165 DOD UWH Narep ME 4. Enemy treatment of prisoners in Cyrenaica after Sidi Rezegh, extracts from a report by a SA officer, Major HW Boardman, 1 SA Irish.
166 Friedman, *The Piano War*: 200.
167 MMH, Pam B472 PRI: *Reproductions from Prisoners of War Newspapers, The Benghazi Forum & Tuturano Times*.
168 De Lisle, *Over the Hills and Far Away*: 29.
169 Friedman, *The Piano War*: 200.
170 Leigh, *Captives Courageous*: 29.
171 De Lisle, *Over the Hills and Far Away*: 27.
172 MMH. Pam B472 BAI: *Escape from Tobruk by Lieut LH Bailie*.
173 DOD UWH Narep ME 2. *Western Desert Campaign. Statement by no 14051 Reuben Maloyi escaped POW from Mersa Matruh*.
174 Friedman, *The Piano War*: 226.
175 Ibid: 185, 190–192, 208–209, 240, 247.
176 MMH, Pam B472 PRI: *Reproductions from Prisoners of War Newspapers, The Benghazi Forum & Tuturano Times*; Hurst, E. 19 March 1943. Capt Hermer.

NOTES

CHAPTER THREE

1. Gilbert, M. 1986. *Road to Victory: Winston S Churchill 1941–1945*: 145.
2. Holland, J. 2006. *Together We Stand: Turning the Tide in the West: North Africa 1942–1943*: 165, 180.
3. MMH, File B.472: Memoirs of LG Tupper.
4. Saks, D. 2009. 'Long Journey to Anzio.' *Military History Journal* 14(5): 191.
5. Mortlock, J. 1956. *The Endless Years: Reminiscences of the 2nd World War*: 34.
6. Leigh, M. 1992. *Captives Courageous. South African Prisoners of War World War II*: 29.
7. MMH, File B.472: Memoirs of LG Tupper.
8. Wood, H.L. n.d. *Memoirs of a Prisoner of War*: 7.
9. Fennell, J. 2011. *Combat and Morale in the North African Campaign: The Eighth Army and the Path to El Alamein*: 282–286.
10. Knoetze, JC. 1994. 'Historical survey of the Non-European Army Services outside of the Union of South Africa (part II).' *Scientia Militaria, South African Journal of Military Studies* 24(2): 37.
11. Crompton, C & P Johnson. 2010. *Luck's Favours: Two South African Second World War Memoirs*: 41.
12. Shearing, T & D (eds). 2010. *From Jo'burg to Dresden. A World War II Diary by EB Dickinson*: 70.
13. Gilbert, A. 2006. *POW Allied Prisoners in Europe, 1939–1945*: 48.
14. Crompton & Johnson, *Luck's Favours*: 41.
15. Leigh, *Captives Courageous*: 36–37.
16. Mugglestone, DIH. nd. *Destination Unknown*: 25.
17. Rosmarin, I. 1999. *Inside Story*: 19.
18. Mugglestone, *Destination Unknown*: 30.
19. Brokensha, *Brokie's Way*: 82.
20. Ibid: 81–82.
21. Chambers, J. 1967. *For You the War is Over. The Story of Herbert Rhodes (Aussie) Hammond*: 17.
22. The ship, originally known as the *Jason*, was also referred to as the *Sebastian Venier* and the *Bastiano Veneri*. See Leigh, M. 1992. *Captives Courageous*: 39; and DOD UWH Narep ME 3. Mr Whittaker Sidi Rezegh and captivity afterwards (Greece and Italy) related to Mrs GR de Wit by Mr Whittaker.
23. Leigh, *Captives Courageous*: 39. The details regarding number of those on board and those who died do not correspond between different sources. Leigh states that 2 200 men boarded, while Whittaker stated the number as 2 100. Bernard Schwikkard, one of the POWs onboard, estimated the number of prisoners at 2 500, while Crwys-Williams put the number at 'over two thousand'. In August 1942, the *Nino Bixio*, also packed with POWs, was torpedoed by *HMS Turbulent* and 432 men lost their lives in the blast, after which the ship was steered to Navarino on the Greek coast. Gilbert, *POW*: 51.
24. Ogilvie, P & N Robinson. 1975. *In the Bag*: 31–37; Crwys-Williams, J. 1992. *A Country at War 1939–1945*: 194–199; Crompton & Johnson, *Luck's Favours*: 43–46; Chambers, *For You the War is Over*: 17–21; DOD UWH Narep ME 3. Mr Whittaker Sidi Rezegh and captivity afterwards (Greece and Italy) related to Mrs GR de Wit by Mr Whittaker.
25. Schwikkard, BE. 1999. *My Life Briefly Told*: 26; DOD UWH Narep ME 3. Mr Whittaker Sidi Rezegh and captivity afterwards (Greece and Italy) related to Mrs GR de Wit by Mr Whittaker. Gilbert, *POW*: 49. Mason, WW. 1954. *Prisoners of War Official History*

Prisoners of War New Zealand in the Second World War 1939–45: 111.
26 Chambers, *For You the War is Over:* 16 & 18.
27 Ogilvie & Robinson, *In the Bag:* 31; DOD UWH Narep ME 3. Mr Whittaker Sidi Rezegh and captivity afterwards (Greece and Italy) related to Mrs GR de Wit by Mr Whittaker.
28 Ogilvie & Robinson, *In the Bag:* 31.
29 Crompton & Johnson, *Luck's Favours:* 44.
30 Ogilvie & Robinson, *In the Bag:* 33.
31 Ibid: 34
32 Crwys-Williams, *A Country at War 1939–1945:* 198.
33 DOD UWH Narep ME 3. Mr Whittaker Sidi Rezegh and captivity afterwards (Greece and Italy) related to Mrs GR de Wit by Mr Whittaker.
34 Gilbert, *POW:* 49.
35 Crompton & Johnson, *Luck's Favours:* 45.
36 Schwikkard, *My Life Briefly Told:* 27.
37 http://www.jocks.co.za/. Accessed 27 April 2011.
38 Crompton & Johnson, *Luck's Favours:* 3, 45.
39 Chambers, *For You the War is Over:* 19.
40 Ibid.
41 DOD UWH Narep ME 3. Mr Whittaker Sidi Rezegh and captivity afterwards (Greece and Italy) related to Mrs GR de Wit by Mr Whittaker.
42 Ogilvie & Robinson, *In the Bag:* 36; DOD CE 4/15. Union of South Africa Censorship. Correspondence suspected to require special attention; Mason, WW. 1954. *Prisoners of War Official History: Prisoners of War New Zealand in the Second World.*
43 Ibid.
44 Crwys-Williams, *A Country at War:* 199.
45 DOD UWH Narep ME 3. Mr Whittaker Sidi Rezegh and captivity afterwards (Greece and Italy) related to Mrs GR de Wit by Mr Whittaker.
46 Ogilvie & Robinson, *In the Bag:* 32.
47 Crwys-Williams, *A Country at War:* 199.
48 DOD UWH Narep ME 3. Mr Whittaker Sidi Rezegh and captivity afterwards (Greece and Italy) related to Mrs GR de Wit by Mr Whittaker; Schwikkard, *My Life Briefly Told:* 28.
49 Ogilvie & Robinson, *In the Bag:* 38.
50 Schwikkard, *My Life Briefly Told:* 28.
51 Ibid: 29.
52 Ibid.
53 Geldenhuis, FJW. nd. *A Soldier's Scrap Book:* 102.
54 Ibid.
55 Ibid: 111.
56 Ibid.
57 Mason, *Prisoners of War:* 228.
58 Chambers, *For You the War is Over:* 49.
59 Ogilvie & Robinson, *In the Bag:* 48.
60 Wolhuter, SG. nd. *The Melancholy State:* 38.
61 Ogilvie & Robinson, *In the Bag:* 48.
62 Beaumont, J. 'Protecting Prisoners of War 1939–45,' in Fedorowich, K & B Moore. 1996. *Prisoners of War and their Captors in World War Two:* 278–279.
63 Schamberger, P. 2001. *Interlude in Switzerland: The Story of the South African Refugee-Soldiers in the Alps during the Second World War:* 1.
64 Beaumont, 'Protecting Prisoners of War': 279.
65 Leigh, M. 1992. *Captives Courageous:* 60.
66 Mortlock, *The Endless Years:* 37.
67 Mugglestone, *Destination Unknown:* 27.

68 Ibid: 27.
69 Cremer, AJ. nd. *Oorlogsherinneringe:* 22. '... hier het ek tot die besef gekom dat die land en al sy mense seker met vlieë boer.'
70 Mortlock, *The Endless Years*: 43.
71 Brokensha, *Brokie's Way*: 89. Chambers, *For You the War is Over*: 43.
72 Mortlock, *The Endless Years*: 43.
73 Shearing, T & D (eds), *From Jo'burg to Dresden*: 85.
74 Cremer, *Oorlogsherinneringe*: 22–23.
75 DOD AG (POW) 1527/85. UDF POW. Italian POW Camp No 85. Report by Rudolph I Iselin on Camp No 85. 8 March 1943.
76 Mortlock, *The Endless Years*: 38.
77 Geldenhuis, *A Soldier's Scrap Book*: 100–101.
78 Hindshaw, W. nd. *An Account of my Experience as a Prisoner-of-War and Escapee in the Italian Alps during the Second World War*: 20.
79 DOD AG (POW) 1504B/6 Vol I. UDF PW. Camp locations by areas (Italy) including strengths.
80 DOD AG (POW) 1527/85. UDF POW. Italian POW Camp No 85. Report by Rudolph I Iselin on Camp No 85. 8 March 1943.
81 NASA BTS 9/55/1 C Vol I. Correspondence from Secretary for External Affairs to High Commissioner, London. 1 March 1943.
82 Brokensha, *Brokie's Way*: 83.
83 Mugglestone, *Destination Unknown:* 30. Mugglestone was moved to a bungalow on 19 January 1943.
84 Hindshaw, *An Account of my Experience*: 22–23.
85 DOD AG (POW) 1537 Vol I. Correspondence from Director General of Medical Services to Adjutant-General. 4 December 1942.
86 DOD AG (POW) 1537 Vol I. UDF PW. Rations. Report by Italian Red Cross Delegation. July 1943.
87 DOD AG (POW) 1582 Vol I. Correspondence from South African Red Cross Society to the Secretary for External Affairs. 7 April 1943.
88 DOD AG (POW) 1537 Vol I. Food Parcels for South African prisoners-of-war in Italy and Germany. 26 January 1943.
89 DOD AG (POW) Vol I. Telegram from Secretary for External Affairs, Cape Town to High Commissioner, London. 22 March 1943.
90 DOD AG (POW) 1537 Vol I. Correspondence Secretary for External Affairs to the Adjutant-General. 18 February 1943.
91 Hindshaw, *An Account of my Experience*: 14–15.
92 Mugglestone, *Destination Unknown*: 28, 31.
93 Geldenhuis, *A Soldier's Scrapbook*: 111.
94 Ibid.
95 Chambers, *For You the War is Over*: 61.
96 Ibid: 62.
97 Ogilvie & Robinson, *In the Bag*: 56.
98 Deakin, FW. 1966. *The Brutal Friendship: Mussolini, Hitler, and the Fall of Italian Fascism*: 249 & 293.
99 Cremer, *Oorlogsherinneringe*: 23.
100 Ogilvie & Robinson, *In the Bag*: 53.
101 Ibid: 51–58.
102 Shearing, T & D (eds), *From Jo'burg to Dresden*: 77.
103 NASA BTS 9/55/1 C Vol I. Correspondence from Secretary for External Affairs to High Commissioner, London. 1 March 1943.
104 BTS 9/55/1 C Vol I. Correspondence from Secretary for External Affairs to High

Commissioner, London. 1 March 1943.
105 ICRC International Humanitarian Law, Treaties and Documents. Convention relative to the treatment of Prisoners-of-War, Geneva, 27 July 1929. Available at http: //www.icrc.org.
106 Mugglestone, *Destination Unknown*: 28.
107 Mortlock, *The Endless Years*: 40.
108 Chambers, *For You the War is Over*: 52–53.
109 Shearing, T & D (eds), *From Jo'burg to Dresden*: 76.
110 DOD AG (POW) 1537 Vol I. Food Parcels for South African prisoners-of-war in Italy and Germany. Cigarettes and tobacco for South African prisoner of war. Note by Squadron Leader Keeling, British Red Cross Society. 26 January 1943.
111 Chambers, *For You the War is Over*: 36–37.
112 Rolnick, AJ & WE Weber. 1986. 'Gresham's Law or Gresham's Fallacy?' *Journal of Political Economy*, 94(1): 185.
113 Mortlock, *The Endless Years*: 40.
114 Gilbert, *POW*: 160–161.
115 Hindshaw, *An Account of my Experience*: 21.
116 DOD AG (POW) 1527/85. UDF POW. Italian POW Camp No 85. Report by Rudolph I Iselin on Camp No 85. 8 March 1943.
117 National Museum of Military History, Pam B472 PRI: *Reproductions from Prisoners of War Newspapers, The Benghazi Forum & Tuturano Times*.
118 DOD AG (POW) 1527/82. UDF POW. Italian POW Camp No 82. Report No.3 on Prisoner of War camp No 82 and the hospital at Arezzo visited on 24 and 25 February 1943 by Captain L Trippi.
119 National Museum of Military History, Pam B472 PRI: *Reproductions from Prisoners of War Newspapers, The Benghazi Forum & Tuturano Times*. 2 July 1943.
120 Chambers, *For You the War is Over*: 49.
121 DOD AG (POW) 1527/122. Report on prisoners of war camp no. 122 visited on October 2, 1942 by Captain L Trippi.
122 DOD AG (POW) 1527/122. Prisoners of war camp no 122 visited by Dr de Salis on the 11th April 1943.
123 MI9 Historical Report, Appendix A. *Secret Conduct of Work no. 48. MI9*. Available at http: //www.arcre.com/archive/mi9/mi9appa. Accessed 18 September 2014.
124 Dean, C & M Dean. 2009. 'Games and pastimes helped POWs escape.' *Krygshistoriese Tydskrif*, 14(5): 194–195.
125 DOD AG (POW) 1527/122. Prisoners of war camp no 122 visited the 14th October 1942 by Dr de Salis. At the time the Italian censors did not allow books in isiZulu, most probably because they did not yet have censors who were educated in the language.
126 Spitz, HH. 1978. 'The universal nature of human intelligence: Evidence from games.' *Intelligence* 2(4): 377.
127 DOD AG (POW) 1527/75. Report on Camp 75, date of visit: 4th March 1943. DOD AG (POW) 1527/75. Copy of Telegram 0103/4023/PW2. 25 June 1943.
128 The rules of the game, in English referred to as Bucca Bucca, are described in Brewster, PG. 1944. 'Some African variants of Bucca Bucca.' *The Classical Journal*, 39(5): 293–296.
129 Brokensha, *Brokie's Way*: 89.
130 Shearing, T & D (eds), *From Jo'burg to Dresden*: 77.
131 De Lisle, *Over the Hills and Far Away*: 47.
132 International Humanitarian Law – Treaties and Documents. Convention relative to the Treatment of Prisoners of War. Geneva, 27 July 1929. Available at http: //www.icrc.org Accessed 30 May 2011.
133 ANCAZ POW Freemen in Europe. nd. http: //www.anzacpow.com.
134 DOD AG (POW) 1527 Vol 1. Copy of letter received from South African Red Cross

Society. Undated.
135 DOD AG (POW) 1527 Vol 1. PSM Report. 23 July 1943.
136 DOD AG (POW) 1527 Vol 1. Copy of letter received from South African Red Cross Society. Undated.
137 De Lisle, *Over the Hills and Far Away*: 42.
138 Ibid: 43.
139 United States Army 1943–1945. 15th Air Force. Available at http: //www.2ndbombgroup.org/15thAirForce.htm. Accessed 28 August 2014.
140 International Humanitarian Law – Treaties and Documents. Convention relative to the Treatment of Prisoners of War. Geneva, 27 July 1929. Available at http: //www.icrc.org. Accessed 30 May 2011.
141 DOD CE 4/15. Union of South Africa Censorship. Correspondence suspected to require special attention.
142 DOD CE 8/5/1. Directorate of Prisoners of War Monthly Directorate Letter. October 1942.
143 Article 69 of the Geneva Convention states: 'These [medical] commissions shall consist of three members, two of whom shall belong to a neutral country and one appointed by the detaining Power; one of the medical officers of the neutral country shall preside. These mixed medical commissions shall proceed to the examination of sick or wounded prisoners and shall make all appropriate decisions with regard to them. The decisions of these commissions shall be decided by majority and shall be carried into effect as soon as possible.' International Humanitarian Law – Treaties and Documents. Convention relative to the Treatment of Prisoners of War. Geneva, 27 July 1929. Available at http: //www.icrc.org. Accessed 30 May 2011.
144 The report on the Military Hospital at Perugia states that it was visited on 25 May and then again on 4 September 1943. DOD AG (POW) 1527/Misc. Report No 2. On British prisoners of war undergoing treatment at the Military Hospital, Perugia.
145 Ibid.
146 DOD AG (POW) 1527/Misc Report No. 2. On hospital Celio in Rome visited on January 21, 1944.
147 International Humanitarian Law – Treaties and Documents. Convention relative to the Treatment of Prisoners of War. Geneva, 27 July 1929. Available at http: //www.icrc.org. Accessed 30 May 2011.
148 DOD AG (POW) 1527 Vol 1. Report by Lt Col JS Alexander on return from POW hospital for British at Piacenza, Italy on the subject of medical commission for repatriation of the disabled: International Red Cross.
149 Ibid.
150 Shearing, T & D (eds), *From Jo'burg to Dresden*: 70.
151 NASA BTS 9/55/1/B Vol 1: Copy of correspondence between British Foreign Office and United States Embassy during March 1941 on the subject of application of the Prisoners-of-war Convention, 1929. 7 April 1941.
152 Gilbert, *POW*: 219.
153 Mathys Beukes interview: 'hy het my moed ingepraat, en die eerste ding wat hy vir my sê is – hy praat Afrikaans – en hy sê "wanneer is die oorlog oor?" ek sê "more", hy sê "dis 'n bietjie optimisties", ek sê vir hom "kaptein, waar ons laas in sekondes gelewe het, hierso leef ons net vir 'n dag, as jy die dag oorleef het dan het jy goed gedoen."'
154 Chambers, *For You the War is Over*: 59–60.
155 Leigh, *Captives Courageous*: 88–89.
156 Roos, N. 2010. 'The Springbok and the Skunk: War Veterans and the Politics of Whiteness in South Africa during the 1940s and 1950s.' *Journal of Southern African Studies* 35(3): 654.
157 Shearing, T & D (eds), *From Jo'burg to Dresden*: 120.

158 Hindshaw, *An Account of My Experience:* 21.
159 Ogilvie & Robinson, *In the Bag*: 56.
160 Bates, HJ. 1992. *Lest We Forget:* 81.
161 DOD AG (POW)1527 Vol 1. Correspondence between Defence Headquarters and Adjutant-General, Pretoria. 11 May 1943.
162 Ibid.
163 Wolhuter, *The Melancholy State:* 43–45.
164 Bates, *Lest We Forget:* 85–89.
165 DOD AG (POW) 1527 Vol 1. An airgraph received from the London Committee of the South African Red Cross Society. 9 June 1943.

CHAPTER FOUR

1 Brokensha, D. 2007. *Brokie's Way:* 89; William Hindshaw interview: 19 March 2010, Johannesburg.
2 Frankl, VE. 1962. *Man's Search for Meaning: An Introduction to Logotherapy from Death-camp to Existentialism:* 6.
3 Ibid: 21.
4 Ibid: 92.
5 Liddle, POW & I Whitehead. nd. 'Not the image but reality: British POW experiences in Italian and German camps.' *The Second World War Experience Centre*. http://www.war-experience.org/history/keyaspects/captivity/default.asp. Accessed on 22 October 2010.
6 Chambers, *For You the War is Over: The Story of HR (Aussie) Hammond*: 60.
7 Shearing, T & D (eds). 2010. *From Jo'burg to Dresden:* 76.
8 Chambers, *For You the War is Over:* 60.
9 Ursano, RJ. 2003. 'Prisoners-of-war: long-term health outcomes.' *The Lancet Extreme Medicine* 362: 22–23.
10 Shearing, T & D (eds), *From Jo'burg to Dresden*: 82.
11 National Museum of Military History, Pam B.472 PRI: *Reproductions from Prisoners of War Newspapers, The Benghazi Forum & Tuturano Times.*
12 Gilbert, A. 2006. *POW Allied Prisoners in Europe, 1939–1945*: 122–123.
13 Mugglestone, DIH. nd. *Destination Unknown:* 28.
14 De Lisle, M. nd. *Over the Hills and Far Away*: 50.
15 Wolhuter, SG. nd. *The Melancholy State*: 41.
16 Chambers, *For You the War is Over*: 53–54.
17 Gilbert, *POW:* 200.
18 Wolhuter, *The Melancholy State*: 107.
19 Cremer, *Oorlogsherinneringe:* 27.
20 Chambers, *For You the War is Over*: 41.
21 Shearing, T & D (eds), *From Jo'burg to Dresden:* 79–80.
22 DOD AG (POW) 1527/85. UDF POW. Italian POW Camp No 85. Report by Rudolph I Iselin on Camp No 85. 8 March 1943.
23 Bates, HJ. 1992. *Lest We Forget:* 103.
24 Ogilvie, P & N Robinson. 1975. *In the Bag*: 62.
25 Rosmarin, I. 1999. *Inside Story*: 17.
26 Mugglestone, *Destination Unknown:* 29.

NOTES

27 Ibid.
28 International Humanitarian Law – Treaties and Documents. Convention relative to the Treatment of Prisoners of War. Geneva, 27 July 1929. Available at http: //www.icrc.org. Accessed 30 May 2011.
29 Killingray, D. 'Africans and African Americans in Enemy Hands,' in Fedorowich, K & B Moore. 1996. *Prisoners of War and their Captors in World War Two*: 191.
30 DOD CE8/5/1. Directorate of Prisoners of War Monthly Directorate Letter. December 1942.
31 DOD AG (POW) 1527/82. UDF POW. Report No 1. On the camp for British prisoners of war in Italian hands No. 82. 8 October 1942. The man in question was the South African Private Samuel Maclan; 7125.
32 DOD AG (POW) 1527/85. UDF POW. Italian POW Camp No 85. R. Jones (Political Secretary) to Secretary for External Affairs, Pretoria. 12 October 1943.
33 Ibid.
34 DOD CE8/5/1. Directorate of Prisoners of War Monthly Directorate Letter. February 1943.
35 Killingray, 'Africans and African Americans in Enemy Hands': 195 & 199.
36 Bates, *Lest We Forget:* 106.
37 DOD AG (POW) 1527/85. UDF POW. Italian POW Camp No 85. CE 15/8/150. Extract from letter by No. 11711 Pte. Andrews Dlamini sent to Adjutant-General, Pretoria from Deputy Chief of Staff, Defence Headquarters.
38 Crwys-Williams, J. 1992. *A Country at War 1939–1945: The Mood of a Nation*: 384–387.
39 DOD CE 4/15. Union of South Africa Censorship. Correspondence suspected to require special attention.
40 DOD AG (POW) 1527 Vol 1. DCS (DMI) Defence Headquarters to DAG (POW), Pretoria. 27 May 1943.
41 Ibid.
42 Ibid.
43 Wolhuter, *The Melancholy State*: 45.
44 Shearing, T & D (eds), *From Jo'burg to Dresden*: 93.
45 Bosworth, RJB. 2005. *Mussolini's Italy: Life under the Dictatorship 1915–1945*: 5.
46 Mortlock, *The Endless Years*: 39.
47 Chambers, *For You the War is Over*: 57.
48 NASA BTS 9/55/1A Vol I. Correspondence from DD Forsyth [Secretary for External Affairs] to South African Red Cross. 28 September 1942.
49 Gilbert, *POW*: 224.
50 NASA BTS 9/55/1 D Vol I. Directorate of Prisoners of War. 2 January 1942.
51 NASA BTS 9/55/1 D Vol I. Letter from Adjutant General to Secretary for External Affairs regarding repatriation proposals by the International Red Cross Committee.
52 NASA BTS 9/55/1 D Vol I. Correspondence; Swiss Legation. 5 January 1944.
53 Ogilvie & Robinson, *In the Bag*: 74.
54 Vance, JF. 1993. 'The war behind the wire: the battle to escape from a German prison camp.' *Journal of Contemporary History*, 28(4): 677.
55 Gilbert, *POW*: 280–282.
56 DOD CE 4/15. Union of South Africa Censorship. Correspondence suspected to require special attention.
57 Ogilvie & Robinson, *In the Bag*: 72.
58 Ibid: 73.
59 Hindshaw, W. nd. *An Account of my Experience as a Prisoner-of-War and Escapee in the Italian Alps during the Second World War*: 18.
60 Geldenhuis, FJW. nd. *A Soldier's Scrap Book*: 112–113.
61 Shearing, T & D (eds), *From Jo'burg to Dresden*: 75.
62 Gilbert, *POW*: 284.

63 Ogilvie & Robinson, *In the Bag*: 72.
64 Brokensha, *Brokie's Way*: 83–89.
65 Shearing, T & D (eds), *From Jo'burg to Dresden*: 86–88.
66 Crompton & Johnson, *Luck's Favours*: 52.
67 Leigh, M. 1992. *Captives Courageous. South African Prisoners of War World War II*: 217–218.
68 Crompton & Johnson, *Luck's Favours*: 153.
69 Ibid.
70 Schamberger, P. 2001. *Interlude in Switzerland. The Story of the South African Refugee-Soldiers in the Alps during the Second World War*: 11.
71 DOD AG (POW) 1527 Vol 1. Adjutant-General to General Secretary C Urquhart. 18 August 1943.
72 DOD AG (POW) 1527 Vol 1. Political Secretary to Secretary for External Affairs, Pretoria. 30 August 1943.
73 Crompton & Johnson, *Luck's Favours*: 167.
74 Ibid: 167–169.
75 Lamb, R. 1993. *War in Italy 1943 – 1945: A Brutal Story*: 162.
76 Schamberger, *Interlude in Switzerland*: 11.
77 Crompton & Johnson, *Luck's Favours*: 175–179.
78 Ibid: 175–180.
79 Ibid: 182.
80 Ibid: 184–186, 189–191.
81 DOD AG (POW) 1527 Vol 2. *Present information on prisoners-of-war in Italy*. 31 July 1943. This list gives information on camp locations, strengths, nationalities, how many POWs were liberated and how many 'probably' transferred to Germany, how many POWs in Switzerland as at 31 July 1943. No information about Camp 38 appears on this list. DOD AG (POW) 1527 Vol 2. *Summary of present information concerning prisoners-of-war in Italy*. This document was compiled after the armistice and provides information on the number of POWs who were liberated, escaped, recaptured and transferred to Germany. The list does not mention specific camps but only regions in Italy.
82 Chambers, *For You the War is Over*: 277.
83 Linsenmeyer, WS. 1981. 'Italian peace feelers before the fall of Mussolini.' *Journal of Contemporary History*, 16(4): 651.
84 Shearing, T & D (eds), *From Jo'burg to Dresden*: 90.
85 Chambers, *For You the War is Over*: 58.
86 Shearing, T & D (eds), *From Jo'burg to Dresden*: 93.
87 Ibid: 95.
88 Ibid.
89 Linsenmeyer, 'Italian peace feelers before the fall of Mussolini': 649, 650, 659.
90 Wiskemann, E. 1946. 'The breaking of the Axis.' *International Affairs (Royal Institute of International Affairs 1944–)*, 22(2): 234.
91 Chambers, *For You the War is Over*: 63.
92 Lamb, *War in Italy 1943–1945: A Brutal Story*: 160; Gilbert, *POW*: 282.
93 Gilbert, *POW*: 283.
94 IS9 Historical Report. *Enclosure No 1 to attachment A to DDMI's memo. Historical Record of IS9*. Available at http://www.arcre.com/archive/mi9/is9. Accessed 18 September 2014.
95 Brighton, T. 2008. *Masters of Battle: Monty, Patton and Rommel at War*: 223–238.
96 Mervis, J. 1989. *South Africa in World War II*: 68–69.
97 Bourhill, J. 2011. *Come Back to Portofino: Through Italy with the 6th South African Armoured Division*: 31, 51.
98 Holland, J. 2009. *Italy's Sorrow. A Year of War 1944–45*: 178, 527.

NOTES

99   Rosmarin, *Inside Story*: 39.
100 Lamb, *War in Italy 1943–1945*: 161–163.
101 Ibid: 163.
102 Ibid: 166.
103 DOD CE 8/1/3. Prisoners of War. Released or Escaped POWs. Broadcasts by released POWs. Broadcast by Major-General Klopper. 18 October 1943. It is interesting to note that the broadcast was edited and all references to 'fascism' and 'the fall of Mussolini' were replaced by 'armistice'.
104 Krige, U. 1955. *The Way Out*: 1–5.
105 Hindshaw, *An Account of my Experience as a Prisoner-of-war*: 27.
106 Cremer, *Oorlogsherinneringe*: 28. 'Een oggend was al die wagte om die kamp skoonveld. Hulle het hul gewere weggegooi en laat spaander. Die kommandant het toe sy verskyning gemaak en ons vertel dat Italië oorgegee het en dat ons kan doen wat ons wil…'
107 Hindshaw, *An Account of my Experience as a Prisoner-of-war*: 28–63.
108 Saks, D. 2009. 'Long journey to Anzio: A Springbok escapee story.' *Krygshistoriese Tydskrif* 14(5): 190–193.
109 Stanley Smollan: private letters, 1944–1946.
110 Luyt, C, Barclay, J & R Andrews. nd. *'Escape' to Monte Gennaro: Survival in the Mountains during WWII*. While on the run in Italy, Luyt kept a diary which he and Barclay edited after the war to serve as their memoirs of their time as escaped POWs.
111 Geldenhuis, *A Soldier's Scrap Book*: 115–163.
112 Schamberger, *Interlude in Switzerland*: 1 & 11.
113 Mugglestone, *Destination Unknown*: 32.
114 Shearing, T & D (eds), *From Jo'burg to Dresden*: 97.
115 Ibid: 93.
116 Mugglestone, *Destination Unknown*: 32.
117 Ogilvie & Robinson, *In the Bag*: 78–79.
118 IS9 Historical Report. *Enclosure No 1 to attachment A to DDMI's memo. Historical Record of IS9*. Available at http://www.arcre.com/archive/mi9/is9. Accessed 18 September 2014.
119 Geldenhuis, *A Soldier's Scrap Book*: 1

CHAPTER FIVE

1 Evans, RJ. 2008. *The Third Reich at War*: 11.
2 Fritz, SG. 1995. *Frontsoldaten: The German Soldier in World War II*: 163, 199.
3 Evans, *The Third Reich at War*: 124, 133, 175.
4 Mineau, A. 2004. *Operation Barbarossa: Ideology and Ethics Against Human Dignity*: 1, 134.
5 MacKenzie, SP. 1994. 'The treatment of prisoners in World War II.' *The Journal of Modern History*, 66(3): 510–511.
6 Evans, *The Third Reich at War*: 418, 467–469.
7 Trevor-Roper, H. 1953. *Hitler's Table Talk 1941–1944: His Private Conversations*: 236.
8 Moore, B & K Fedorowich. 1996. 'Prisoners of war in the Second World War: An overview.' *Prisoners of War and Their Captors in World War II*: 1.
9 Schwikkard, BE. 1999. *My Life Briefly Told*: 38.

10　Chambers, J. 1967. *For You the War is Over*: 64.
11　Ibid: 65.
12　De Lisle, M. nd. *Over the Hills and Far Away*: 53–54.
13　Rosmarin, I. 1999. *Inside Story*: 39.
14　Although it is possible that SS troops were used in the takeover of POW camps, the supervision of all POW matters were transferred to the SS in September 1944 following an order by Hitler. As from 1 October 1944 SS Lieutenant General Gottlob Berger took control of all POW matters, while the OKW remained responsible for German POWs in Allied hands. AG (POW) 1527 Vol III. National Socialist German Workers' Party Circular Letter 288/44. 30 September 1944.
15　Rosmarin, *Inside Story*: 41.
16　Mugglestone, DIH. nd. *Destination Unknown*: 32.
17　Shearing, T & D (eds). 2010. *From Jo'burg to Dresden. A World War II Diary by E.B. Dickinson*: 96.
18　Brokensha, D. 2007. *Brokie's Way*: 94.
19　Rose-Innes, H. 1976. *The Po Valley Break*: 8.
20　Ibid: 19, 202–203. Harry spent the rest of the war in a POW camp in Germany but unfortunately he did not include these experiences in his memoirs.
21　Geldenhuis, FJW. nd. *A Soldier's Scrap Book*: 167.
22　DOD Div Docs. PW Interrogation Documents Vol. 1. Bombing of train carrying Allied PW. 21 June 1944.
23　Ibid.
24　Wolhuter, SG. nd. *The Melancholy State*: 59.
25　Ibid: 59–63.
26　Wood, HL. nd. *Memoirs of a Prisoner of War*: 16.
27　Cremer, AJ. nd. *Oorlogsherinneringe*: 28.
28　Geldenhuis, *Soldier's Scrap Book*: 167.
29　Kochavi, AJ. 2005. *Confronting Captivity: Britain and the United States and their POWs in Nazi Germany*: 10; Gilbert, 2006. *POW*: 44.
30　In November 1943, the ICRC inspector reported that Stalag IVB had a total of 7 092 prisoners. DOD AG (POW) 1527/IVB. UDF POW in Germany. ICRC Report on Stalag IVB by Drs O Lehner and P Ruggli on 13 November 1943.
31　Wolhuter, *The Melancholy State*: 64.
32　Brokensha, *Brokie's Way*: 96–97.
33　Chambers, *For You the War is Over*: 74–75.
34　Shearing, T & D (eds), *From Jo'burg to Dresden*: 102.
35　Wolhuter, *The Melancholy State*: 66.
36　Chambers, *For You the War is Over*: 77–78.
37　Ogilvie, P & N Robinson. 1975. *In the Bag*: 84–86.
38　Stalag IVA is in fact near Hohnstein and it is very possible that either Rosmarin or Robinson made an error regarding the camp number. Stalag VIIA is in fact near Moosburg and this is where, according to Ogilvie and Robinson, the Russian POW joined them.
39　Rosmarin, *Inside Story*: 41–43.
40　Chutter, JB. *Captivity Captive*: 109–110.
41　Kochavi, *Confronting Captivity*: 53–54.
42　Initially Germany had 31 POW camps, but by the end of the war there were 248 camps; Gilbert, *POW*: 65–66.
43　Wolhuter, *The Melancholy State*: 64; Brokensha, *Brokie's Way*: 97.
44　Vourkoutiotis, V. 2005. 'What the angels saw: Red Cross and protecting power visits to Anglo-American POWs, 1939–45.' *Journal of Contemporary History*, 40(4): 690–691.
45　Ibid: 691.
46　Gilbert points out that due to the influx of POWs and changes in policy, the exact number

of camps is difficult to determine. Gilbert, *POW*: 66.
47 DOD AG (POW) 1527/IVB. UDF POW in Germany. ICRC Report on Stalag IVB by Drs O Lehner and P Ruggli on 13 November 1943.
48 DOD CE4/15. Office of Censorship United States of America. Record no 98/5. From South African POWs in Stalag IVB, Germany, to Residents in South Africa. February 1944.
49 DOD AG (POW) 1527/XVIIIA. UDF (POW). Stalag XVIIIA Wolfsberg. 26 November 1943.
50 DOD AG (POW) 1527/XVIII. UDF (POW). Despatch 9309, 5 January 1944: DOD AG (POW) 1527/XVIII. UDF (POW). Military High Command to Swiss Legation in Germany; Foreign Interests Division; List No 126. 13 April 1944.
51 DOD AG (POW) 1527/VIIIA. UDF PW. Report by Gabriel Naville of the Protecting Power on 28 October 1943.
52 The total number of POWs in the camp was 3 486 on 28 October 1943. DOD AG (POW) 1527/VIIIA Report 277 on Stalag VIII A on 28 October 1944.
53 DOD AG (POW) 1527 Vol 2. General correspondence Political Secretary to Secretary of External Affairs, Pretoria. *Interrogation of Repatriates ex SS Gripsholm*. 5 July 1944.
54 DOD AG (POW) 1527/VIIIA Report 541 on Stalag VIII A on 27 July 1944.
55 DOD AG (POW) 1527/VIIIA. DCS (DMI) No 3144 WOI JJ Rossouw (PW No 82360): Stalag VIIIA.
56 Chambers, *For You the War is Over*: 76.
57 Ike Rosmarin's first transit camp was Stalag IVA (indicated in his memoirs as being near Moosburg, but actually near Hohnstein. Stalag VIIA is near Moosburg. It is possible that Rosmarin either made a mistake on the camp number or on the name of the nearest town.) Rosmarin was sent to Stalag VIIIB Lamsdorf a week after his arrival at Stalag VIIA or IVA. Rosmarin, *Inside Story*: 43–44.
58 Gilbert, *POW*: 83.
59 DOD AG (POW) 1527/VIIIB. UDF PW Vol I. Union of South Africa Censorship: Correspondence suspected to require special attention. Hendrik Erasmus, No. 25698; 23 May 1943.
60 DOD AG (POW) 1527/VIIIB. UDF PW Vol I. R Jones to Adjutant General 10 November 1943.
61 DOD AG (POW) 1527/VIIIB. UDF PW Vol I. Randall to Urquhart; 10 November 1943
62 DOD AG (POW) 1527/VIIIB. UDF PW Vol I. 0103/3969(PW2a) 22. 11. 1943. Departmental No1. 15 November 1943.
63 ICRC International Humanitarian Law, Treaties and Documents. Convention relative to the treatment of Prisoners-of-War, Geneva, 27 July 1929. Available at http: //www.icrc.org. Accessed 30 May 2011.
64 DOD AG (POW) 1527/VIIIB. UDF PW Vol I. TB Clapham to Urquhart; 15 November 1943.
65 Rosmarin, *Inside Story*: 44.
66 Bird, T. 1992. *American POWs of World War II: Forgotten Men Tell Their Stories*: 119–122.
67 The Geneva Convention states the following: 'Art. 27. Belligerents may employ as workmen prisoners of war who are physically fit, other than officers and persons of equivalent statue, according to their rank and their ability. Nevertheless, if officers or persons of equivalent status ask for suitable work, this shall be found for them as far as possible.' International Humanitarian Law – Treaties and Documents. Convention relative to the Treatment of Prisoners of War. Geneva, 27 July 1929. Available at http: //www.icrc.org. Accessed 30 May 2011.
68 Beaumont, J. 'Protecting Prisoners of War 1939–95', in Fedorowich, K & B Moore. 1996. *Prisoners of War and their Captors in World War Two*: 281 & 293.
69 DOD AG (POW) 1527/VIIIB/344. Vol 1. UDF PW. Report of inspection on 7–8 February 1944.

70 Rosmarin, *Inside Story*: 58.
71 Mugglestone, *Destination Unknown*: 35.
72 Wood, *Memoirs of a Prisoner of War*: 16–17.
73 Geldenhuis, *A Soldier's Scrap Book*: 174.
74 Cremer, *Oorlogsherinneringe*: 29–32.
75 Fritz, *Frontsoldaten*: 116.
76 Gilbert, *POW*: 98.
77 Shearing, T & D (eds), *From Jo'burg to Dresden*: 115.
78 Wolhuter, *The Melancholy State*: 65.
79 ICRC International Humanitarian Law, Treaties and Documents. Convention relative to the treatment of Prisoners-of-War, Geneva, 27 July 1929. Available at http://www.icrc.org. Accessed 30 May 2011.
80 Crompton & Johnson, *Luck's Favours*: 66.
81 Chambers, *For You the War is Over*: 77 & 87.
82 Ibid: 100–101.
83 Schwikkard, *My Life Briefly Told*: Epilogue.
84 Brokensha, *Brokie's Way*: 105.
85 Mortlock, J. 1956. *The Endless Years: Reminiscences of the 2nd World War*: 68.
86 Ibid.
87 Shearing, T & D (eds), *From Jo'burg to Dresden*: 104.
88 DOD AG (POW) 1533 A. UDF POW Medical. Report on the Conference of British Medical Officers in Captivity held at Schwanenwerder: Berlin. 18–22 March 1945.
89 Chambers, *For You the War is Over*: 172.
90 Spencer, J. nd. *No 1 Squadron SAAF*: 5; Chutter, *Captivity Captive*: 128.
91 Jack Spencer was a pilot in No 1 Squadron SAAF, captured on 27 June 1944. As an officer, he was sent to Stalag Luft III where he stayed until the end of the war. His experiences in an officers' camp highlight the different treatment that the other ranks received in ordinary Stalags in German-occupied territories. Spencer, *No 1 Squadron SAAF*.
92 Rosmarin, *Inside Story*: 76.
93 Shearing, T & D (eds), *From Jo'burg to Dresden*: 102.
94 Chutter, *Captivity Captive*: 115 – 116.
95 Ibid: 118.
96 IS9 Historical Report. *Enclosure No 1 to attachment A to DDMI's memo. Historical Record of IS9*. Available at http://www.arcre.com/archive/mi9/is9. Accessed 18 September 2014.
97 Pearson, S. 2013. *The Great Escaper: The Life and Death of Roger Bushell – Love, Betrayal, Big X and the Great Escape*: 8–9, 330–342.
98 IS9 Historical Report. *Enclosure No 1 to attachment A to DDMI's memo. Historical Record of IS9*. Available at http://www.arcre.com/archive/mi9/is9. Accessed 18 September 2014.

CHAPTER SIX

1 Roger Coward, a British POW at Blechhammer quoted in Gilbert, A. 2006. *POW: Allied Prisoners in Europe, 1939–1945*: 169.
2 Gilbert, *POW*: 161 & 167.

NOTES

3   Lamsdorf: *Stalag* VIIIB 344 Prisoner of War Camp 1940–1945. Available at http://www.lamsdorf.com/history.html. Accessed 10 October 2011.
4   Rosmarin, I. 1999. *Inside Story:* 47.
5   Gilbert, *POW*: 66 & 83.
6   Ibid: 167.
7   Harding, GM. 1943. 'Idle ambitions'. *The Clarion* 6. Stalag VIIIB, Germany: 3.
8   Gilbert, *POW*: 171; Ogilvie, P & N Robinson. 1975. *In the Bag*: 88.
9   Rosmarin. *Inside Story:* 67.
10 Ogilvie & Robinson, *In the Bag*: 89.
11 Ibid: 88.
12 Rosmarin, *Inside Story:* 65.
13 Wolhuter, SG. nd. *The Melancholy State*: 49 & 89.
14 World War II Escape and Evasion Information Exchange. Available at http://www.conscript-heroes.com/escapelines/EEIE-Articles/Art-16-Escapers-from-Germany.htm. Accessed 3 October 2014.
15 Rosmarin, *Inside Story:* 64 & 67.
16 Wolhuter, *The Melancholy State*: 88–89.
17 Schwikkard, BE. 1999. *My Life Briefly Told*: 43.
18 Part III: Captivity # Section V: Relations between prisoners of war and the authorities #Chapter 3: Penal sanctions with regard to prisoners of war #1. General provisions – Art. 52. Available at https://www.icrc.org/applic/ihl/ihl.nsf/ART/305-430052?OpenDocument. Accessed 30 September 2014.
19 Gilbert, *POW*: 161.
20 Rosmarin, *Inside Story:* 55.
21 Mugglestone, DIH. nd. *Destination Unknown:* 41.
22 Rosmarin, *Inside Story:* 47, 49, 52, 53, 57 & 61.
23 Wolhuter, *The Melancholy State*: 76.
24 Rosmarin, *Inside Story:* 58–59.
25 Shearing, T & D (eds). 2010. *From Jo'burg to Dresden*: 102.
26 Ibid: 115.
27 Chutter, JB. *Captivity Captive:* 107–108.
28 Gilbert, *POW*: 123.
29 Chambers, J. 1967. *For You the War is Over: The Story of Herbert Rhodes (Aussie) Hammond*: 74 & 79.
30 Mugglestone, *Destination Unknown:* 35.
31 Mortlock, J. 1956. *The Endless Years: Reminiscences of the 2nd World War*: 67.
32 Hynes, S. 1997. *The Soldiers' Tale: Bearing Witness to Modern War*: 58.
33 Ibid: 323–326.
34 Hynes, S. [date?] *Flights of Passage: Recollections of a World War II Aviator*: 259.
35 Shearing, T & D (eds), *From Jo'burg to Dresden*: 76. Dick Dickinson interview: 4 December 2010, Mossel Bay.
36 Brokensha, D. 2007. *Brokie's Way*: 57.
37 Edward Ward quoted in Gilbert, *POW*: 204.
38 Geldenhuis, FJW. nd. *A Soldier's Scrap Book*: 173.
39 Ibid: 171–172.
40 DOD AG (POW) 1527/IVB. UDF POW in Germany. ICRC Report on *Stalag* IVB by Drs O Lehner and P Ruggli on 13 November 1943.
41 Shearing, T & D (eds), *From Jo'burg to Dresden*: 102–103.
42 DOD AG (POW) 1527/IVB. UDF POW in Germany. ICRC Report on *Stalag* IVB by Dr Rossel on 3 July 1944.
43 DOD AG (POW) 1527/IVB. UDF POW in Germany. From Berne to Foreign Office. 0103/5777. (PW2) 8 March 1945.

44 Shearing, T & D (eds), *From Jo'burg to Dresden*: 108.
45 DOD AG (POW) 1527/IVB. UDF POW in Germany. ICRC Report on *Stalag* IVB by Drs O Lehner and P Ruggli on 13 November 1943.
46 ICRC International Humanitarian Law, Treaties and Documents. Convention relative to the treatment of Prisoners-of-War, Geneva, 27 July 1929. Available at http: //www.icrc.org. Accessed 30 May 2011.
47 Shearing, T & D, *From Jo'burg to Dresden*: 108.
48 Ibid: 102–103.
49 Brokensha, *Brokie's Way*: 98.
50 Mortlock, *The Endless Years*: 65.
51 Brokensha, *Brokie's Way*: 100–101.
52 Mugglestone, *Destination Unknown:* 35.
53 Mortlock, *The Endless Years*: 72.
54 Chambers, *For You the War is Over*: 85.
55 Ibid.
56 Ibid: 101.
57 Ibid: 92.
58 Rosmarin, *Inside Story:* 58–59.
59 Mugglestone, *Destination Unknown:* 35–41.
60 Mortlock, *The Endless Years*: 68.
61 Ibid: 69.
62 Brokensha, *Brokie's Way*: 107–108.
63 Cremer, AJ. nd. *Oorlogsherinneringe:* 31. 'Dit was die begin van 'n mooi vriendskap tussen twee oorlogsvyande. Hy kon nie Engels of Afrikaans praat nie, net so effens verstaan. My kennis van Duits was nie beter nie. En tog het daar 'n goeie verstandhouding tussen ons bestaan.'
64 Crompton & Johnson, *Luck's Favours*: 68.
65 Chambers, *For You the War is Over*: 122–123.
66 Wolhuter, *The Melancholy State*: 76.
67 Rosmarin, *Inside Story*: 69.
68 Gilbert, *POW*: 247.
69 Weale, A. 2010. *The SS. A New History*: 281; Gilbert, *POW*: 247.
70 Mason, WW. 1954. *Prisoners of War: New Zealand in the Second World War 1939–45*: 393.
71 Leigh, M. 1992. *Captives Courageous. South African Prisoners of War World War II*: 162–164.
72 Brokensha, *Brokie's Way*: 104.
73 Rosmarin, *Inside Story*: 63.
74 Cremer, *Oorlogsherinneringe:* 17.
75 Leigh, *Captives Courageous*: 164.
76 Weale, *The SS:* 283.
77 The High Command of the German Forces describing Churchill's interpretation of the Geneva Convention on reprisals between belligerent countries with regard to the treatment of prisoners-of-war. NASA BTS 9/55/1. Public announcement by the High Command of the German Armed Forces dated 16 October 1942.
78 ICRC International Humanitarian Law, Treaties and Documents. Convention relative to the treatment of Prisoners-of-War, Geneva, 27 July 1929. Available at http: //www.icrc.org. Accessed 30 May 2011.
79 MacKenzie, SP. 1995. 'The shackling crisis: A case-study in the dynamics of prisoner-of-war diplomacy in the Second World War.' *The International History Review,* 17(1): 83.
80 NASA BTS 9/55/1. Public announcement by the High Command of the German Armed Forces dated 16 October 1942.
81 Ibid.

NOTES

82 MacKenzie, 'The shackling crisis': 85.
83 NASA BTS 9/55/1. Copy of telegram from Secretary of State for Dominion Affairs, London, to High Commissioner for the United Kingdom, Pretoria. 2 November 1942. No 2000 Most Secret and Personal. Message from Prime Minister date 28/10.
84 DOD AG (POW) 1527/344 Vol I. Correspondence from Clara Urquhart, South African Red Cross Society to Colonel Clapham, Prisoner of War Directorate, Pretoria. 7 December 1943.
85 NASA BTS 9/55/1. Telegram from Secretary of State for Dominion Affairs, London, to Minister of External Affairs, Cape Town. Circular D No 166. Secret. 20 March 1943.
86 Other affected camps were Oflag 7B, *Stalag* 9C and Marlag Milag Nord. NASA BTS 9/55/1. Telegram from Secretary of State for Dominion Affairs, London, to Minister of External Affairs, Pretoria. Circular D No 670. Secret. 18 September 1943.
87 NASA BTS 9/55/1. Telegram from Secretary of State for Dominion Affairs, London, to Minister of External Affairs, Pretoria. Circular D No 670. Secret. 18 September 1943.
88 NASA BTS 9/55/1. Correspondence from Secretary for External Affairs to Director of Information. 20 December 1943.
89 NASA BTS 9/55/1. Telegram from Secretary of State for Dominion Affairs, London, to Minister of External Affairs, Pretoria. Circular D No 670. Secret. 18 September 1943.
90 DOD CE 15/8/155. Correspondence from DCS (DMI) Defence Headquarters, Pretoria, to DAG (POW), Commander Military Mission, Senior Army Education Officer. 10 December 1943.
91 Vourkoutiotis, V. 2000. 'The German Armed Forces Supreme Command and British and American Prisoners-of-War, 1939–1945: Policy and practice.' PhD Thesis: 192.
92 Rosmarin, *Inside Story*: 62.
93 Gilbert, *POW*: 244–245.
94 DOD AG (POW) 1527/344 Vol I. Report No 204 *Stalag* VIIIB. Date of visit: 29 June 1943.
95 NASA BTS 9/55/1. Telegram from Secretary of State for Dominion Affairs, London, to Minister of External Affairs, Cape Town. Circular D No 166. Secret. 20 March 1943.
96 Chambers, *For You the War is Over*: 80–81.
97 Gilbert, *POW*: 120.
98 Dickinson does not reveal his sources for this information and it is not known who was responsible for the woman's punishment.
99 Gilbert, *POW*: 120.
100 Vourkoutiotis, 'The German Armed Forces Supreme Command and British and American Prisoners-of-War': 194.
101 Bates, HJ. 1992. *Lest We Forget*: 121.
102 Crompton & Johnson, *Luck's Favours*: 71.
103 Borodziej, W. 2006. *The Warsaw Uprising of 1944*: 140.
104 Wolhuter, *The Melancholy State*: 103–104.
105 Borodziej, *The Warsaw Uprising of 1944*: 140.
106 Shearing, T & D (eds), *From Jo'burg to Dresden*: 124.
107 Ibid: 126.
108 Chambers, *For You the War is Over*: 105.
109 Ibid: 134–136.
110 Ibid: 144.
111 Childers, T. 2005. '"Facilis descensus averni est": The Allied Bombing of Germany and the Issue of German Suffering.' *Central European History* 38(1): 85–92.
112 Evans, RJ. 2008. *The Third Reich at War*: 462.
113 Kriwin, G. 1985. 'Allied bombing and Nazi domestic propaganda.' *European History Quarterly* 15(3): 341.
114 Werrel, KP. 1986. 'The strategic bombing of Germany in World War II: Costs and accomplishments.' *The Journal of American History* 73(3): 709.

115 Jacobsen, H-A. 1999. 'The structure of Nazi foreign policy 1933–1945' in Leitz, C & H James (eds), *The Third Reich: The Essential Readings:* 86–87. Evans, *The Third Reich at War:* 511.
116 Shearing, T & D (eds), *From Jo'burg to Dresden:* 119.
117 German Generals who were replaced included Kurt Zeitler, Chief of the Army General Staff, Field Marshal von Rundstedt and the Air Force Commander Hugo Sperrle. Evans, *The Third Reich at War:* 623–624.
118 Bessel, R. 2009. *Germany 1945: From War to Peace:* 16.
119 DOD AG (POW) 1504B/7 Vol I. UDF PW Camp Locations by Area (Germany) including strengths. Document 3. 28 September 1943.
120 DOD AG (POW) 1527/VIIIB Vol I. Sherrif [camp leader] to Protecting Power. 14 August 1944.
121 Wessel Oosthuizen interview: '*Party van die bomme het nie ontplof nie, dis tyd bomme jy weet, jy werk nog so en daar vlie die wêreld die lug op, dit was verskriklik.*'
122 DOD AG (POW) 1527/VIIIB Vol I. From Berne to Foreign Office. 15 December 1944.
123 DOD AG (POW) 1527/VIIIB Vol I. Reply to telegram 434. November 1944.
124 Friedrich, J. 2006. *The Fire: The Bombing of Germany 1940–1945:* 164.
125 Shearing, T & D (eds), *From Jo'burg to Dresden:* 124.
126 Mugglestone, *Destination Unknown:* 42.
127 Evans, *The Third Reich at War:* 441 & 460–463.
128 Ibid: 652.
129 Shearing, T & D (eds), *From Jo'burg to Dresden:* 126.
130 Friedrich, *The Fire:* 399–400.
131 Fritz, SG. 1995. *Frontsoldaten: The German Soldier in World War II:* 183.
132 Mortlock, *The Endless Years:* 68.
133 Chutter, *Captivity Captive:* 109.
134 Gilbert, *POW:* 157.
135 Evans, *The Third Reich at War:* 462.
136 Childers, '"Facilis descensus averni est": 100.
137 David Brokensha and two others were also sent to work for the same builder. Shearing, T & D (eds), *From Jo'burg to Dresden:* 132.
138 Chambers, *For You the War is Over:* 117–119, 131.
139 Mugglestone, *Destination Unknown:* 43.
140 Mortlock, *The Endless Years:* 71.
141 Shearing, T & D (eds), *From Jo'burg to Dresden:* 133.
142 Mortlock, *The Endless Years:* 76.
143 Miller, DL. 2006. *Masters of the Air: America's Bomber Boys who Fought the Air War against Nazi Germany:* 440–434.
144 Mortlock, *The Endless Years:* 77.
145 Schwikkard, *My Life Briefly Told:* 45.
146 Crompton & Johnson, *Luck's Favours:* 71.
147 Taylor, F. *Dresden Tuesday 13 February 1945:* np.
148 Crompton & Johnson, *Luck's Favours:* 77.
149 Bessel, *Germany 1945:* 38–39.
150 Schwikkard, *My Life Briefly Told:* 43.
151 Greeff, IB. 1991. 'South African prisoners-of-war on the long marches 1944–1945.' *Military History Journal*, 8(6). Available at http://samilitaryhistory.org/vol086ig.html. Accessed 22 September 2011.
152 Crompton & Johnson, *Luck's Favours:* 77.
153 Schwikkard, *My Life Briefly Told:* 44.
154 Bates, *Lest We Forget:* 135.
155 Ibid: 138.

NOTES

156 Ibid: 135–153.
157 Greeff, 'South African prisoners-of-war on the long marches'.
158 Ogilvie & Robinson, *In the Bag*: 94–95.
159 Rosmarin, *Inside Story*: 89.
160 Ibid: 93–95.
161 Chambers, *For You the War is Over*: 153.
162 Ibid: 172 – 173, 175, 195.
163 Gilbert, *POW*: 300.
164 Ibid: 300.
165 Crompton & Johnson, *Luck's Favours*: 85.
166 DOD AG (POW) 1527. Vol III. POW 40 File A2. Concerning the bombardments and air attacks on POW Camps, Hospitals and columns of prisoners of war on roads on the interior of the Reich. Red Cross 30 April 1945.
167 Crompton & Johnson, *Luck's Favours*: 86–88.
168 MacKenzie, SP. 1994. 'The treatment of prisoners in World War II.' *The Journal of Modern History*, 66(3): 494–495.
169 Brokensha, *Brokie's Way*: 115.
170 Mugglestone, *Destination Unknown*: 47.
171 DOD AG (POW) 1527 Vol III. Report. Concerning visits to the Camps *Stalag* VII A Moosburg, *Stalag* VII B Memingen, Ilag Biberach and Ilag Wurmach, from 27 April until 3 May, 1945.
172 Chambers, *For You the War is Over*: 198–199.
173 Shearing, T & D (eds), *From Jo'burg to Dresden*: 142.

CHAPTER SEVEN

1 Hately-Broad, B. 2002. '"Nobody would tell you anything": the War and Foreign Offices and British prisoner of war families during World War II.' *Journal of Family History*, 27(4): 461.
2 Ibid: 465.
3 NASA BTS 9/55/1A Vol 1. Directorate of Prisoners of War. Imperial Prisoners of War Committee; Sub Committee A. Channels of communication between prisoners of war information bureaux and enemy governments. 2 April 1943.
4 NASA BTS 9/55/1A Vol 1. Correspondence from High Commissioner, London, to Secretary for External Affairs, Cape Town. 22 April 1943.
5 NASA BTS 9/55/1A Vol 1. Correspondence from Postmaster, Johannesburg to the General Secretary, SA Red Cross Society, Johannesburg. 1 March 1943. NASA BTS 9/55/1A Vol 1. Correspondence from Clara Urquhart, South African Red Cross Society to Secretary for External Affairs. 3 March 1943.
6 NASA BTS 9/55/1A Vol 1. Directorate of Prisoners of War. Imperial Prisoner of War Committee. Sub Committee A. Channels of Communication between Prisoners of War Information Bureaux and Enemy Governments. 2 April 1943.
7 NASA BTS 9/55/1A. Clara Urquhart for the General Secretary, South African Red Cross Society to the Secretary for External Affairs. 13 October 1942.
8 DOD AG (POW) 1507E. UDF POW Vatican Messages. Correspondence between S Sweet, Secretary to the Central Committee and the Most Reverend Archbishop BJ

Gijlswijk. August 1941.
9 Geldenhuis, FJW. nd. *A Soldier's Scrapbook:* 94.
10 Fred van Alphen Stahl interview: '*Mevrou, liewerste dood as 'n gevangenis van die Duitsers.*'
11 Hately-Broad, '"Nobody would tell you anything"': 461.
12 DOD CE 8/1/3. Prisoners of War. Released or Escaped POWs. Broadcasts by released POWs. Correspondence suspected to require special attention. Mail from South African Prisoners of War in Germany. 23 February 1944.
13 Saks, D. 2009. 'Long journey to Anzio. A Springbok escapee story.' *Krygshistoriese Tydskrif,* 14(5): 193.
14 AG (POW) 1582A Vol 1. Minutes of meeting called for the purpose of considering the formation of a South African Association of Relatives and Friends of Prisoners of War. 21 July 1942.
15 AG (POW) 1582A Vol 1. Lewis J Grant, General Secretary of the South African Red Cross to the Secretary for External Affairs. 22 September 1942. AG (POW) 1582A Vol 1. AW Eaton, Acting Chairman of the Prisoners-of-War Relatives Association to Mr Forsyth, President, State Committee for the Prisoners of War, Department of External Affairs. 9 October 1942.
16 The South African Association of Relatives and Friends of Prisoners-of-War. *Our Prisoners of War in Germany.* Stewart: 12/43-368. Howard J Bates personal document collection.
17 Hately-Broad, '"Nobody would tell you anything": 472.
18 Leigh, M. 1992. *Captives Courageous. South African prisoners of war World War II:* 320–321. *Rand Daily Mail; War Prisoners Relatives Association to Form National Council.* 8 August 1944.
19 Cremer, AJ. nd. *Oorlogsherinneringe:* 38.
20 DOD AG (POW) 1582A. Vol I. Prisoner of War Relatives Association. Copy of letter from Gunner M Edwards, 'Personal Opinion'. 18 January 1946.
21 Wessel Oosthuizen interview: '*Ons [het] 'n koninklike lewe gehad.*'
22 Mason, WW. 1954. *Prisoners of War: New Zealand in the Second World War 1939–45:* 497.
23 *The Star,* 9 May 1945. Ogilvie's husband was also a POW held in Oflag VA.
24 Brokensha, D. 2007. *Brokie's Way:* 117.
25 Allport, A. 2010. *Demobbed: Coming Home After the Second World War:* 110–111, 197–202.
26 *Star,* 30 April 1945.
27 *Star,* 26 April 1945.
28 David W Bone CBE & Arthur HC Hope. Welcome note to troops aboard HMT 'Circassia', Howard J Bates personal document collection.
29 International Red Cross. Note to former POWs. Howard J Bates personal document collection.
30 Isie K Smuts. Letter to returning prisoners-of-war. Howard J Bates personal document collection.
31 Smuts, JC. 1945. Correspondence to demobilised soldiers. Howard J Bates personal document collection.
32 *Sunday Times,* 7 January 1945.
33 Graaff, De Villiers. 1993. *Div Looks Back: The Memoirs of Sir De Villiers Graaff:* 86–87 & 118–119.
34 Allport, *Demobbed:* 203.
35 Grey, J. 2000. '"Standing humbly in the ante-chambers of Clio": the rise and fall of the Union War Histories.' *Scientia Militaria* 30(2): 253–266.
36 DOD CE4/15. Report No 2012. CD 033348. Fortnightly summary covering British and Allied forces and P/W's in enemy hands (2.12.42–15.12.42). Received by Defence

NOTES

Headquarters, Pretoria on 15 May 1943.
37 Roos, N. 2009. 'The Springbok and the Skunk: War Veterans and the Politics of Whiteness in South Africa during the 1940s and 1950s.' *Journal of Southern African Studies* 35(3): 651.
38 Ibid: 651–652.
39 Ibid: 651–653.
40 Mohlamme, JS. 1995. 'Soldiers without reward. Africans in South Africa's wars.' *Military History Journal* 10(1). Available online at http: //samilitaryhistory.org/vol101jm.html.
41 *Rand Daily Mail,* 7 March 1945.
42 Brokensha, *Brokie's Way*: 119.
43 Rosmarin, I. 1999. *Inside Story*: 102–103.
44 Shearing, T & D (eds), 2010. *From Jo'burg to Dresden. A World War II Diary by EB Dickinson*: 145.
45 Ibid: 146–147.
46 Fred van Alphen Stahl interview: *'Oom is seker die oudste flippen lieutenant in hierdie weermag.'*
47 De Lisle, M. nd. *Over the Hills and Far Away*: 112–113.
48 Church of the Good Shepherd – Protea. Tribute to Michael de Lisle. Available http: //www.goodshepherd-protea.org.za/2012/11/michael-de-lisle/. Accessed 14 October 2014.
49 Geldenhuis, *A Soldier's Scrapbook*: 206.
50 Ibid: 211.
51 Wessel Oosthuizen interview: *'Nou sien ek my ma se Sondae braaiboud met die bruin sous en die ertjies daar, ag die heerlikste kos, jy dink nie aan die mense nie, jy sien die kos daar. En daai kos wil jy hê.'*
52 Mathys Beukes interview: *'Toe stuur hy my Kaap toe, toe lag ek lekker want ek het toe alreeds die army verneuk.'*
53 Tothill, FD. 1989. 'The soldiers' vote and its effects on the outcome of the General Election of 1943.' *South African Historical Journal,* 21(1): 85 & 93. Soldiers cast their votes between 15 June and 3 July, but at this time the POWs were more concerned with rumours concerning the Italian Armistice. None of those interviewed mentioned the 1943 election, nor was it highlighted in any of the memoirs.
54 Roos, 'The Springbok and the Skunk: 653–659.
55 *Rand Daily Mail,* 1 April 1945.
56 Marks, S. *Oxford Dictionary of National Biography*; Smuts, Jan Christiaan (1870–1950). Available at http: //www.oxforddnb.com/view/article/36171?docPos=1. Accessed 1 November 2011.

GLOSSARY

amn	ammunition
arme blanke	poor whites
arrivederci dedesci (tedeschi)	goodbye Germans
arty	artillery
bangbroeke	cowards
Bittereinder	'bitter-ender'
dass ist Scheisse	that's shit
domani	tomorrow
donnering	thumping, beating-up
'*Ek praat net Afrikaans*'	I only speak Afrikaans
Feldwebel	sergeant
handen hoch	hands up
handlangers	henchmen
hardegat	hard-arsed
Hensoppers	'hands-uppers'
herstigters	'purified' nationalists
'*hou umfundisi*'	greetings pastor
Ites, Ities, Itys	(slang) Italians
Jerries	Germans
ketang	chain
krank	ill
Kriegies	POW slang, based on the German
Kriegsgefangenen	prisoner of war

GLOSSARY

Lebensraum — living space
nee, ek is 'n Suid-Afrikaner — no, I'm a South African
Oberkommando der Wehrmacht — upper command of the German Army
onder die kombers — under the blankets
Ossewabrandwag — ox-wagon sentinel
rooi lussies — red shoulder tabs worn by UDF volunteers

Stormjaers — assault troops
Tiermenschen — animal people
Uitlanders — foreigners
Untermensch — sub-human
verboten — forbidden
verdammte Englander — damned Englishman
verkramptes — hard-line conservatives
verraaier — traitor
vorlager — temporary camp

SELECTED SOURCES

ARCHIVES

Department of Defence Archives (DOD), Pretoria
AG (POW): Adjutant-General; prisoner-of-war collection
CGS: Head of the General Staff
DC: Secretary of Defence
Div Docs: Divisional Documents
Narep: Narratives and Reports
UWH: Union War Histories

National archives (NASA), Pretoria
ARB: Department of Labour (1917–1967)
BLO: Ambassador, London (1910–1968)
BNS: Secretary of Home Affairs (1899–1973)
BTS: Secretary of Foreign Affairs (1919–1944)
BVE: Custodian of Enemy Property (1822–1975) & (1915–1930)
DGD: Director General of demobilisation (1940–1951)
GG: Governor-General (1905–1974)
JUS: Secretary of Justice (1899–1966)
KOG: Controller and Auditor-General (1910–1968)
PWD: Secretary of Public Works (1895–1966)
SAP: South African Police (1901–1975)
TES: Secretary of the Treasury (1904–1974)
UOD: Secretary of Union Education (1911–1968)
URU: Decisions of the Executive Council (1910–1985)

SELECTED SOURCES

Ditsong National Museum of Military History
B. 472.
PAM 472.

Interviews
Beukes, Matthys. Bloemfontein. 2 February 2011.
Brokensha, David. Fish Hoek. 10 September 2010.
De Lisle, Michael. Cape Town. 4 June 2010 and 15 June 2010.
Dickinson, EB (Dick). Mossel Bay. 4 December 2010.
Geldenhuis, Fred. Pretoria. 9 July 2010.
Hindshaw, William (Bill). Johannesburg. 19 March 2010.
Luyt, Clive. Cape Town. 19 May 2010 and 27 August 2010.
Oosthuizen, Wessel. Hartenbos. 4 December 2010.
Schwikkard, Bernard Egner. Johannesburg. 17 March 2010.
Smollan, Stanley. Johannesburg. 15 March 2010 and 19 February 2011.
Tewkesbury, George. Cape Town. 5 March 2010 and 28 May 2010.
Van Alphen Stahl, Fred. Cape Town. 25 May 2010 and 15 June 2010.

Unpublished memoirs, diaries and private documents
Bates, HJ. 1992. *Lest We Forget World War II 1939–1945*.
Bates, HJ. Personal document collection.
Cremer, AJ. nd. *Oorlogsherinneringe*.
De Lisle, M. nd. *Over the Hills and Far Away: My Twenties in the Forties*.
Geldenhuis, FJW. nd. *A Soldier's Scrapbook. The Memoirs of Frederik Jacobus Wagenaar Geldenhuis*.
Hindshaw, W. nd. *An Account of my Experience as a Prisoner-of-War and Escapee in the Italian Alps during the Second World War*.
Luyt, C, Barclay, J & R Andrews. nd. *'Escape' to Monte Gennaro: Survival in the Mountains during WWII. September 1943 to June 1944*.
Mortlock, J, 1956. *The Endless Years: Reminiscences of the 2nd World War*.
Mugglestone, DIH, nd. *Destination Unknown*.
Schwikkard, BE. 1999. *My Life Briefly Told*.
Smollan, S. Private letters: 1944–1946.
Spencer, J. nd. *No 1 Squadron SAAF*.
Tewkesbury, G. *Notes and observations in Red Cross Journal collected from fellow prisoners of war 1944–1945*.
Tewkesbury, G. *War diary*.

Wood, HL. nd. *Memoirs of a Prisoner of War.*

Published memoirs and diaries
Brokensha, D. 2007. *Brokie's Way: An Anthropologist's Story.* Fish Hoek.
Chambers, J. 1967. *For You the War is Over. The Story of HR (Aussie) Hammond.* Cape Town.
Chutter, JB. 1954. *Captivity Captive.* London.
Crompton, C & P Johnson. 2010. *Luck's Favours: Two South African Second World War Memoirs.* Fish Hoek.
Du Preez, L. 1973. *Inside the Cage.* Cape Town.
Friedman, G. 2003. *The Piano War: A True Story of Love and Survival in World War II.* Claremont.
Graaff, De Villiers. 1993. *Div Looks Back: The Memoirs of Sir De Villiers Graaff.* Cape Town.
Krige, U. 1980. *The Way Out.* Cape Town.
Ogilvie, P & N Robinson. 1975. *In the bag.* Johannesburg.
Rose-Innes, H. 1976. *The Po Valley Break.* Sandton.
Rosmarin. I. 1999. *Inside Story.* Cape Town.
Shearing, T & D (eds). 2010. *From Jo'burg to Dresden. A World War II Diary by EB Dickinson.* Mossel Bay.
Wolhuter, SG. nd. *The Melancholy State: The Story of a South African Prisoner-of-War.* Cape Town.

Books
Agar-Hamilton, JAI & LCF Turner. 1957. *The Sidi Rezegh Battles 1941.* Cape Town.
Allport, A. 2010. *Demobbed: Coming Home After the Second World War.* New Haven.
Battistelli, PP. 2010. *Erwin Rommel: The Background, Strategies, Tactics and Battlefield Experiences of the Greatest Commanders of History.* Oxford.
Bennet, A. 2005. *The Geneva Convention: The Hidden Origins of the Red Cross.* Gloucestershire.
Bessel, R. 2009. *Germany 1945: From War to Peace.* London.
Billig, M. 2005. *Laughter and Ridicule: Towards a Social Critique of Humour.* London.
Borodziej, W. 2006. *The Warsaw Uprising of 1944.* Madison.
Bosworth, RJB. 2005. *Mussolini's Italy: Life under the Dictatorship*

1915–1945. London.
Brown, JA. 1990. *The War of a Hundred Days: Springboks in Somalia and Abyssinia*. Johannesburg.
Brown, JA. 1991. *Retreat to Victory A Springbok's Diary in North Africa: Gazala to El Alamein 1942*. Johannesburg.
Churchill, WS. 1973. *The Collected Works of Sir Winston Churchill, Volume 1. My Early Life. My African Journey*. London.
Corjava, S. 2008. *Hitler and Mussolini: The Secret Meetings*. New York.
Crwys-Williams, J. 1992. *A Country at War 1939–1945: The Mood of a Nation*. Rivonia.
Deakin, FW. 1966. *The Brutal Friendship: Mussolini, Hitler, and the Fall of Italian Fascism*. London.
Evans, RJ. 2008. *The Third Reich at War*. New York.
Fennell, J. 2011. *Combat and Morale in the North African Campaign: The 8th Army and the Path to El Alamein*. Cambridge.
Frankl, VE. 1962. *Man's Search for Meaning: An Introduction to Logotherapy from Death-camp to Existentialism*. Boston.
Friedrich, J. 2006. *The Fire: The Bombing of Germany 1940–1945*. New York.
Fritz, SG. 1995. *Frontsoldaten: The German Soldier in World War II*. Lexington.
Gilbert, A. 2007. *POW Allied Prisoners in Europe 1939–1945*. London.
Gilbert, M. 1986. *Road to Victory: Winston S. Churchill 1941–1945*. London.
Giliomee, H. 2003. *The Afrikaners. Biography of a People*. Cape Town.
Grundy, KW. 1983. *Soldiers Without Politics. Blacks in the South African Armed Forces*. Berkeley.
Holland, J. 2006. *Together We Stand North Africa 1942–1943: Turning the Tide in the West*. London.
Holland, J. 2009. *Italy's Sorrow: A Year of War 1944–45*. London.
Hynes, S. 2005. *Flights of Passage: Recollections of a World War II Aviator*. London.
Hynes, S. 1997. *The Soldiers' Tale: Bearing Witness to Modern War*. London.
Klein, H (ed). 1946. *Springbok Record*. Johannesburg.
Klein, H. 1965. *Springboks in Armour. The South African Armoured Cars in World War II*. Michigan.
Kochavi, AJ. 2005. *Confronting Captivity: Britain and the United States and their POWs in Nazi Germany*. Chapel Hill.

Krige, U. 1960. *Sout van die Aarde*. Cape Town.

Lamb, R. 1993. *War in Italy 1943–1945: A Brutal Story*. London.

Leigh, M. 1992. *Captives Courageous: South African Prisoners of War World War II*. Johannesburg.

Leitz, C & H James (eds). 1999. *The Third Reich: The Essential Readings*. Hoboken.

Lowry, D. 2000. *The South African War Reappraised*. Manchester.

Mackenzie, SP. 2004. *The Colditz Myth: British and Commonwealth Prisoners of War in Nazi Germany*. Oxford.

Matin, HJ & N Orpen. 1979. *South Africa at War. Preparations and Operations on the Home Front*. Cape Town.

Mason, WW. 1954. *Prisoners of War: Official History. Prisoners of War: New Zealand in the Second World War 1939–45*. Wellington.

Mervis, J. 1989. *South Africa in World War II: 50 Years*. Johannesburg.

Miller, DL. 2006. *Masters of the Air: America's Bomber Boys who Fought the Air War against Nazi Germany*. New York.

Moore, B & K Fedorowich (eds). 1996. *Prisoners of War and their Captors in World War II*. Oxford.

Nasson, B. 2012. *South Africa at War 1939–1945*. Johannesburg.

Norton, C & U Krige. 1941. *Vanguard of Victory. A Short Review of the South African Victories in East Africa. 1940–1941*. Pretoria.

Orpen, N. 1971. *War in the Desert. South African Forces World War II, Volume II*. Cape Town.

Orpen, N. 1971. *War in the Desert. South African Forces World War II, Volume III*. Cape Town.

Pakenham, T. 1982. *The Boer War*. London.

Pimlott, J (ed). 1994. *Rommel in his Own Words*. London.

Pretorius, F. 2000. *Life on Commando During the Anglo-Boer War 1899–1902*. Cape Town.

Roos, N. 2005. *Ordinary Springboks: White Servicemen and Social Justice in South Africa, 1939–1961*. Hants.

Schamberger, P. 2001. *Interlude in Switzerland. The Story of the South African Refugee-Soldiers in the Alps during the Second World War*. Johannesburg.

Smuts, JC. 1942. *Plans for a Better World: Speeches of Field-Marshal the Right Honourable JC Smuts, PC, CH, KC, DTD. The Challenge to Freedom: Speech at St Andrews University on 17 October 1934*. London.

Somerville, C. 1998. *Our War: How The British Commonwealth Fought The Second World War.* London.
Spencer, J. nd. *No 1 Squadron SAAF.*
Trevor-Roper, H. 1953. *Hitler's Table Talk 1941–1944: His Private Conversations.* London.
Tungay, WR. 1948. *The Fighting Third.* Cape Town.
Van Heyningen, C. 1966. *Uys Krige.* New York.
Weale, A. 2010. *The SS: A New History.* London.
Whatley, CA. *Scottish Society, 1707–1830: Beyond Jacobitism, Towards Industrialisation.* Manchester.

Journal articles

Absalom, R. 1995. 'Hiding history: The Allies, the Resistance and the others in occupied Italy 1943–1945.' *The Historical Journal,* 38(1):111–131.
Beaumont, J. 1983. 'Rank, privilege and prisoners of war.' *War & Society,* 1:67–94.
Brewster, PG. 1944. 'Some African variants of Bucca Bucca.' *The Classical Journal,* 39(5):293–296.
Childers, T. 2005. '"Facilis descensus averni est": The Allied bombing of Germany and the issue of German suffering.' *Central European History* 38(1):75 – 105.
Dean, C & M. 2009. 'Games and pastimes helped POWs escape.' *Military History Journal,* 14(5):194–195.
Du Toit, BM. 1991. 'The far right in current South African politics.' *The Journal of Modern African Studies,* 29(4):627–667.
Furlong, P. 2005. 'Allies at war? Britain and the "Southern African Front" in the Second World War.' *South African Historical Journal,* 54(1):16–29.
Fedorowich, K. 2005. 'German espionage and British counter-intelligence in South Africa and Mozambique, 1939–1944.' *The Historical Journal,* 48(1):211–230.
Fennell, J. 2013. 'Courage and cowardice in the North African campaign: The Eighth Army and defeat in the summer of 1942'. *War in History,* 20/1:99–122.
Grey, J. 2000. '"Standing humbly in the ante-chambers of Clio": the rise and fall of the Union War Histories.' *Scientia Militaria* 30(2): 253–266.
Grundlingh, AM. 1999. '"The King's Afrikaners": enlistment and ethnic

identity in the Union of South Africa's Defence Force during the Second World War, 1939–45.' *Journal of African History*, 40:351–365.

Hately-Broad, B. 2002. '"Nobody would tell you anything": The War and Foreign Offices and British prisoner of war families during World War II.' *Journal of Family History*, 27(4):459–477.

Kienzle, K. 1979. 'German-South African trade relations in the Nazi era.' *African Affairs*, 78(310):81–90.

Kirwin, G. 1985. 'Allied bombing and Nazi domestic propaganda.' *European History Quarterly* 15(3):341–362.

Lambert, J. 2008. '"Their finest hour?" English-speaking South Africans and World War II.' *South African Historical Journal* 60:60–84.

Linsenmeyer, WS. 1981. 'Italian peace feelers before the fall of Mussolini.' *Journal of Contemporary History*, 16(4):649–662.

MacKenzie, SP. 1994. 'The treatment of prisoners of war in World War II.' *Journal of Modern History*, 66(3):487–520.

MacKenzie, SP. 1995. 'The shackling crisis: A case-study in the dynamics of prisoner-of-war diplomacy in the Second World War.' *The International History Review*, 17(1):78–98.

McCormack, RL. 1979. 'Man with a mission: Oswald Pirow and South African Airways, 1933–1939.' *Journal of African History* 20(4):543–557.

Nasson, B. 1995. 'War opinion in South Africa, 1914.' *The Journal of Imperial and Commonwealth History* 23(2):248–276.

Roos, N. 2010. 'The springbok and the skunk: War veterans and the politics of whiteness in South Africa during the 1940s and 1950s.' *Journal of Southern African Studies* 35(3):643–661.

Saks, D. 2009. 'Long journey to Anzio: A Springbok escapee story.' *Military History Journal*, 14(5):190–194.

Spitz, HH. 1978. 'The universal nature of human intelligence: Evidence from games.' *Intelligence* 2(4):371–379.

Stewart, A. 2006. '"The Klopper affair": Anglo-South African relations and the surrender of the Tobruk garrison.' *Twentieth Century British History*, 17(4):516–544.

Stewart, A. 2008. 'The "atomic" despatch: Field Marshal Auchinleck, the fall of Tobruk garrison and post-war Anglo-South African relations.' *Scientia Militaria: South African Journal of Military History*, 36(1):78–94.

Stewart, A. 2008. 'The British government and the South African neutrality crisis, 1938–39.' *English Historical Review* CXXIII(503):947–972.

Surridge, K. 2012. 'An example to be followed or a warning to be avoided? The British, Boers, and guerrilla warfare, 1900–1902.' *Small Wars & Insurgencies*, 23(4–5):608–626.

Ursano, RJ. 2003. 'Prisoners of war: long-term health outcomes.' *The Lancet Extreme Medicine* 362:22–23.

Van der Waag, IJ. 2010. '"The thin edge of the wedge": Anglo-South African relations, Dominion nationalism and the formation of the Seaward Defence Force in 1939–1940.' *Contemporary British History* 24(4): 427–449.

Van Heyningen, E. 2008. 'Costly mythologies: The concentration camps of the South African War in Afrikaner historiography.' *Journal of Southern African Studies* 34(3):495–513.

Vourkoutiotis, V. 2005. 'What the angels saw: Red Cross and Protecting Power visits to Anglo-American POWs, 1939–45.' *Journal of Contemporary History*, 40(4):689–706.

Werrell, KP. 1986. 'The strategic bombing of Germany in World War II: Costs and accomplishments.' *The Journal of American History* 73(3):702–713.

Wessels, A. 2011. 'Boer guerrilla and British counter-guerrilla operations in South Africa, 1899–1902.' *Scientia Militaria, South African Journal of Military Studies*, 39(2):1–24.

Wiskemann, E. 'The breaking of the Axis.' *International Affairs (Royal Institute of International Affairs)*, 22(2):227–239.

Theses and dissertations

Vourkoutiotis, V. 2000. 'The German armed forces supreme command and British and American prisoners-of-war, 1939–1945: Policy and practice.' PhD thesis, Department of History, McGill University, Montreal.

Zaloga, SJ & H Gerrard. 2002. *Poland 1939: The Birth of Blitzkrieg*. Oxford.

Online sources

ANCAZ POW Freemen in Europe. nd. http://www.anzacpow.com.

Archive Research and Document Copying. Available at http://www.arcre.com.

Greeff, IB. 1991. 'South African prisoners-of-war on the long marches 1944–1945.' *Military History Journal*, 8(6). Available at http://samilitary-history.org/vol086ig.html.

Howell, PA. Australian Dictionary of Biography; Sir Charles Willoughby Moke Norrie (1893–1977). Available at http://adb.anu.edu.au/biography/norrie-sir-charles-willoughby-moke-11254.

International Humanitarian Law, Treaties and Documents. Convention relative to the Treatment of Prisoners of War. Geneva, 27 July 1929. Available at http://www.icrc.org/ihl.nsf/FULL/305?OpenDocument.

Lamsdorf: Stalag VIIIB 344 Prisoner of War Camp 1940–1945. Available at http://www.lamsdorf.com/history.html.

Liddle, P & I Whitehead. 'Not the image but reality: British POW experiences in Italian and German Camps.' The Second World War Experience Centre. Available at http://www.war-experience.org/history/keyaspects/captivity/default.asp.

Marks, S. *Oxford Dictionary of National Biography*; Smuts, Jan Christiaan (1870–1950). Available at http://www.oxforddnb.com/view/article/36171?docPos=1.

Marx, C. 1994. 'The Ossewabrandwag as a mass movement, 1939–1941.' *Journal of Southern African Studies* 20(2): online at EBSCO Host Academic Search Premier.

Mohlamme, JS. 1995. 'Soldiers without reward. Africans in South Africa's wars.' Military History Journal 10(1). Available online at http://samilitaryhistory.org/vol101jm.html.

Marx, C. 1994. 'The Ossewabrandwag as a mass movement, 1939–1941.' *Journal of Southern African Studies* 20(2): online at EBSCO Host Academic Search Premier.

Mohlamme, JS. 1995. 'Soldiers without reward. Africans in South Africa's wars.' *Military History Journal* 10(1). Available online at http://samilitaryhistory.org/vol101jm.html.

National Ex-Prisoner of War Association POW Camp Listings. Available at http://www.prisonerofwar.org.uk/camp_list.htm.

Wessels, A. 2000. 'The first two years of war: The development of the Union Defence Forces (UDF) September 1939 to September 1941.' *Military History Journal* 11(5): online at http://samilitaryhistory.org/vol115aw.html.

INDEX

Note: Page numbers in italics refer to figures and illustrations.

Abyssinia, Italian colony 21, 22, 47
Active Citizen Force 9, 17
African and coloured
  POWS 57-8
  troops 60
African National Congress 29
Afrikaans-speaking POWs 110, 120
Afrika Korps 10, 23, 27, 30, 35, 42, 47, 49, 61
Afrikaner Broederbond 15
Afrikaner groups
  Bittereinders 11-12, 13, 14
  Hensoppers 12
  Joiners 12
  Uitlanders 13
Afrikaner Nationalists 29, 208, 255
  '*herstigters*' and '*verkramptes*' 7
  trade agreement with Germany 16
  volunteers as 'rooi luisies'/red lice 4
Afrikaners 4, 15-16, 49, 121
  Anglicisation 14
  patriotism 16
  resentment towards British 11
Agar-Hamilton, Captain JAI 245
aircraft supply 17
air death raids 219
Air Force 6
Akhaia camp, named 'Dysentery Acre' 79
Alexander, General 141
Alexander, Lieutenant Colonel JS 106-7
Allied and Axis governments 210
Allied forces 67, 68, 142, 151, 219, 227, 229
  aircraft dropping pamphlets 139
  air raids 157
  bombing Benghazi harbour 69
  bombs on Germany 219

  in North Africa 70
  and soldiers 1, 45
  strategic bombing campaign 218
Allied Normandy landings 219
Allied POWs 125, 166, 211, 221
  housed with Russians 153
Allies and Italy peace talks 134
America 120, 201, 218, 230
  POWs 118-19
Amery, John 207
Amery, Leo 207
ammunition 36-7, 67
anti-Semitic
  ideology of Nazis 21
  pamphlets 208-9
anti-South African attitudes 122
'Anxious Annies' support group 240
Armistice 105-6, 140, 142, 143, 144, 158
  negotiations 137
  repatriation to South Africa after 1943 241
arts activities 186
Auchinleck, Sir Claude ('The Auk') 25, 30-1, 34, 44
Auschwitz concentration camp 192
Australians 10, 217
  POWs 118
  at Tobruk 25, 36
Austria 21
Axis forces 43, 69, 104, 140-1, 210
  non-Axis countries 86
  propaganda 45, 60, 122

Badoglio, Pietra 136
Bailie, Lieutenant LH 66
Baird, John 68
'barbed-wire disease' 242-3
Barclay, John 147

adopted name Giovanni 147
Bardia
  fighting in 48
  guns at 46
Bates, Howard 8, 24, 41–2, 109, 110, 121, 126, 214, 224–5, 231–2
  first communication after capture 234
  registered letter confirming captivity 233
  telegram from Red Cross to parents 232
Battle of Benghazi 32
  known as Benghazi Handicap, Gazala Gallop 32–3
BBC World Service propaganda 141
'Beetle-Brows', American POW 118–19
Belgian(s)
  girls 229
  POWs 176
  prisoners 169–70
Benghazi Forum, The, newspaper 65, 67, 99
  'Rogues Gallery', illustrations 65
Benghazi POW camp 54, 55, 65–8, 125–6, 232
Berdia dug-out 47
Berlin conference report 180
Beukes, Mathys 8, 95–6, 108, 120, 127, 128–9, 140, 148, 149, 151, 253
Bird, Allan 42
black communities 15
black POWs 57, 70–1
black servicemen 59
black soldiers 57, 124–5
  discriminatory treatment of 59–60
black South African men 17
Black Watch Regiment, Scottish 120, 185, 258
black workers, competitive threat of 246
Bloemfontein Race Club 249
Boer
  cause 12
  Republics 11, 12, 13, 14
  War 14
Bofors gun ready near Bardia 26
Bolshevism 209
bombing and relationships between POWs and civilians 222
Bonnant, George 105
books 98, 101
Border War of South West Africa/Namibia 248
Botha, General Louis 14
Breslau
  capital of Silesia 224

sugar factory 177
Brink, Major General 29
Britain 4, 8, 11, 213, 235
  colonial interests in Africa 21–2
  communication with POW families 236
  declaration of war on Germany 16
  Dominions separate camp for demobilisation 241
  Fleet Air Arm 5
British
  bombing on Germany's transport infrastructure 218
  concentration camps 4
  NCOs 200
  POWs 114, 119, 120, 123, 169, 201, 221, 245
  prisoners 185
  soldiers 10
British Empire 13
British Free Corps (BFC) 207, 208, 209
  pro-BFC propaganda 209
British Imperial Airways 16
British Military Intelligence (MI9) 101, 141–2, 150, 154, 181–3
  secret code 207–8
British Red Cross Society 89, 96
British Seventh Armoured Division, Desert Rats 62
Brokensha brothers 85–6, 122, 168, 178, 201, 227–8, 239, 242
  David 5, 31–2, 33, 40, 46, 47, 49, 56, 62–3, 73, 97, 99–100, 102, 116, 119, 132, 134, 149, 157, 164, *165*, 167, 177–8, *178*, *179*, 191, *194*, 198, 205, 208, 223, 228–9, 247, 250–1
  Guy 5, 135
  Paul 5, 31, 40, 63, 73, 116, 134, 149, 177–8, *178*, *179*, *194*, *195*, 195–6, 201–2, 208, 209, 217, 229, 251
Brokensha, Rae (father of brothers) 239, 241–2
Brown, John 207–8
Bushell, Squadron Leader Roger 114–15, 182

Camp E276 170
Camp 5, near Gavi 134
Camp 12, near Florence 132
Camp 38, near Poppi 138
Camp 49 near Reggio Fontanelllo 143
Camp 52, near Chiavari 95, 118, 119, 121, 132, 155–6

INDEX

access to hidden radio and news 139
Camp Amateur Dramatic Society (CADS) 100
  performing arts and productions 100
  productions 100
Camp 54, near Fara Sabina 83, 84, 94, 97, 129, 134–5, 139
  cricket and soccer 100
  mass escapes 145
Camp 60, near Lucca 133
  described as 'Hell Camp' by Rose-Innes 158
Camp 65, near Gravina 90–1, 125, 127, 139
  'escape season' 134
Camp 75, near Bari 101, 103, 133
Camp 78 143
Camp 82, near Laterina 83, 86, 94, 117, 122, 123–4, 137, 154, 155
Camp 85, near Tuturano 84, 85, 99, 103, 121, 125
Camp 122, near Rome 100–2
Canada 213
Cape Corps 241
  coloured servicemen 57
  POWs 126
Cape Field Artillery 8
Cape Methoni 77–8
Cape Town Highlanders 38–9
captivity 10, 116
  mental phases during 113–14
captors and captives, links between 199
Caserta hospital, shipwrecked prisoners at 105
Chaka, Private Hermanus 59, 60
  Military Medal 60
Charters, Major DL 244
Chinese labour 14
chocolates as propaganda tool 214
Churchill, Winston 11, 13, 21, 44, 136, 138, 211
  My Early Life 11
Chutter, Reverend James 181, 193, 220
cigarettes
  as camp commodity 96–7, 122
  rations 162
civilian deaths 222
Civil Resettlement Units 245
Clarke, Keith 109
clothing 66, 128, 188
Cockcroft, Regimental Sergeant BR 117–18, 122
  known as Snakebite among POWs 117

MI9 'stay put' order 141, 154
Collet, GH 52, 62
Commonwealth
  policies 254
  POWs 114, 119, 120, 123
communication
  censor's stamp on letters 240
  costs 235
  letters with codes 110
  POW deaths and serious injuries 235
  POWs and friends and families 109, 231–42
  request for Church liaison assistance 236
  telegram and registered letter 232, 233
  Vatican radio and Catholic channel 236, 237
'Communist' tendencies among returning soldiers 245–6
concentration camps 114, 208, 215
Connelly, Private 56
cooperation, supportive 205–6
correspondence between POWs and families 237, 239
  censor's stamp on letters 240
Cremer, AJ 34–5, 37, 49, 53, 55, 59, 83, 84, 91, 120, 144, 168–9, 205, 209, 241
Crockatt, Brigadier Richard 141
Croft, Lord 243
Crofts, Captain 127
Crompton, Cyril 20, 22, 24, 26, 71–2, 74, 75, 76, 135, 176, 205–6, 223, 224, 227
  friendships with Danish women 215
Cypriot POWs 91
Czechoslovakia 228

Daily Dispatch, newspaper 66
Davidson, John 42
D-Day invasions 120
  secret camp radio broadcasts 220
death
  information on camp deaths 235–6
  penalty threats by German authorities 214
'death zones', warning to prisoners 187–8
De Jager, Captain 39
De la Rey, Koos 14
De Lellis family 145
  son Tammaso 145, 146, 250
De Lisle, Michael 6–7, 20, 22, 34, 41, 51, 52, 57, 60, 63, 65, 70, 73, 84, 85, 92, 94, 98, 99, 103, 104, 107, 117, 132, 138, 141, 155, 159–60, 231, 236, 247, 249

ordained as Anglican priest 250
demobilising experiences 241
depression 115–16, 197
    and homesickness 193, 197
De Villiers, Major-General IP 31, 35
De Villiers Graaff, Sir 44, 64, 244
Dickinson, Dick 6, 30, 33–4, 43, 50, 62, 64, 71, 83, 92, 96, 107–8, 109, 115–16, 121, 128, 134, 135, 139–40, 149, 157, 166, 168, 175, 193, 197–8, 199–200, 200–1, 214, 215–16, 219, 221, 227–8, 230 247–8
    diary record 179–80, 199, 218–19, 222
    friend Frank 92, 159
    German woman friend Brigitta 216
    postal work at camp 1169 193
Directorate of Demobilisation 246
Directorate of Prisoners of War 105, 125, 234
Dlamini, Private Andrews 126
Dresden mass bombing 216, 222–3
dug-outs 47, 69
Duke of Edinburgh's Own Rifles 23
Dunkirk casualties 45
Du Plessis, Colonel 39
Durban Club 5
Dutch POWs 199
dysentery 68, 69–70, 71–2, 82, 88, 91, 163, 193–4, 241

East Africa 23, *23*
    Italian forces in 22
economic depression 5
education 99, 184, 186, 191
Edwards, Gunner Maurice 241
Egypt 35, 69
Egyptians 24
Eichstätt, Bavaria 212
Eighth Army 25, 30–1, 45, 49, 60, 66, 69, 70, 141
El Alamein 67, 69, 70
English POWs 199
English-speaking South African POWs 49, 121
entertainment for POWs 184
Eritrea, Italian colony 21
escapes 133, 182–3
    attempts 135
    committees 187–8
    in pre-Armistice Italy 132–3
escaping as big business 188–9
Evans, Dog Dead 119

1st Battalion Transvaal Scottish 23
1st Brigade Signal Corps 27
1st South African Anti-Aircraft Regiment, 3rd Battery 21
1st South African Infantry Division 23
1st South African Irish 74–5
1st South African Police Battalion 35–6
5th South African Infantry Brigade 27, 29
15th Field Ambulance, Tobruk 66–7
Fannin, Captain DG 35–7
farm and agricultural work 103, 121, 171–2
fascist ideology 126
Featherstone, Lieutenant CR 42–3
food 86–7, 92, 241
    bread and potatoes for POWs *175*
    in Germany 175
    last in the line 95
    poor quality 170
    shortage 62–3, 196
    supplies 69
    see also under Red Cross
Foreign Office 240
Forsyth, DD 212
Fouché, JJ (Jim) 248–9
France 8, 144
    yielded to German offensive 152
Francis, Robert 212
Frankl, Viktor 113–14
Freeman, Vincent 148
French
    girls 229
    POWs 198–9
Friedlander, Bernie 76
    recommended for George Medal 76
Fry, Gordon 38–9

Geldenhuis, Fred 2, *3*, 36, 79–80, 84–5, 89, 134, 149, 160–1, 163, 198–9, 236–7, 251–2
    broadcast from Berlin confirming capture 237, *237*
    cared for by Italian girl Lina and her mother 148
    escape in Greece 135
    letter from father *3*
    letter to father about capture 238
Geneva Convention 57, 58, 81, 82, 85, 86, 93–4, 103, 105, 106, 124, 126, 127, 130, 176, 183, 190, 194, 200, 202, 210
    Allied POWs protected by 153
    British contraventions 210
    Italy and Britain signatories 125
    Detaining power, Article 14 105

INDEX

separation of the Jews, Article 9 171
Genshagen camp 207–9
German Army, surrendered in Stalingrad 153
German *Oberkommando der Wehrmacht* (OKW) 163–4
  Italian and Allied POWs accommodated 167
German POWs
  resided with Italian and Allied POWs 154, 167
  tying up of by Britains 210
German Reich 21
Germans 45, 155, 162, 202
  armaments 35
  camps 120, 184
  captors 151
  contact with civilians 214
  forces 152, 223–4
  guards 52, 217
  history of escaping in 183
  invasions and civilian panic 152
  POWs resided with Italian POWs 154
  prisoners 47
  South African guards 49
  South African trade agreement with 16
  women 217, 220, 230
German South-West Africa 14
Germany 16, 61, 137, 213
  evacuation of POW camps 224
  invasion of Belgium 8
  POW camps crowded with Allied soldiers 167
  public support towards Boer cause 11
  Union declaration of war on 5
  and white South Africans 50
Germany Security Service (*Sicherheitsdienst*) 221
Gestapo 206, 214
prison, Prague 181
Goebbels, Josef 228
Goldman, Lieutenant AN 40, 42
Gott, General 36
Great Escape, The, film 114–15
Great Trek centennial celebrations 16
Greece 71, 78–9, 80
grief, coping with 196
Griff, The, news sheet 110
  first edition on Italian soil 111
  statement on Camp 82 111–12
guerrilla fighting units 141

Halfaya Pass dug-out 47
Hammond, Herbert (Aussie) 27, 74, 77, 90, 97, 100, 108, 115, 118–19, 120–1, 129, 140, 155, 165–6, 166, 168–9, 176–7, 180–1, 195, 202, 206, 213, 214, 217, 221, 226–7, 230
Hansen, Oswald 212
Happy Harry 196–7
Harrison, Captain DS 161–2
Hermer, Ben 59, 65, 67–8, 69
  fiancée Olda Mehr 67, 68, 69
  Jewish religious services 67
Hertzog, JBM 10–11, 15, 16, 17–18
Het Volk, Afrikaner political party 14
Himmler, Heinrich 218
Hindshaw, Bill 9, 37, 82, 85, 86, 89, 98, 102, 109, 122, 133, 144, 149, 151, 251
Hitler, Adolf 6, 8, 17, 21, 43, 152 153, 182, 207, 211, 219, 228
  Lebensraum and *Untermensch* ideas 16
  storm troopers 16
Hitler Youth movement 152
HMS Formidable 135
Hogmanay Scheme 182
Home Army 215
hunger 118, 197
  and desperation 221
  and malnutrition 89–90
Hurst, Eric 65, 67, 116
Hutton, Christopher 101
Hynes, Samuel 197

1st Brigade Signal Corps 27
Imperial Prisoners of War Committee 'A' 93
  and South Africans 123–4
Imperial War Cabinet 254
imprisonment experience 64–5
  hunger, lice, dysentery 64
Indians 10
indoor games 98
Intelligence School 9 (IS9) 141
International Committee of the Red Cross (ICRC/IRCC) 84, 125, 168, 235–6
  Swiss-funded 81
International Red Cross 110–11, 232
Isle de France troopship 31
Italian Armistice 125, 132, 154
Italians 46, 51–2, 70
  guards 54–5, 77, 81, 93–4, 127–8
  hospital ship 77
  local Senussi guards 53, 68

peasants 149
POWs 47
quarters in Abyssinia 47
South Africans' view of 23
Italy 21, 71, 84, 99, 113–17, 162, 167
   camps 42, 151–2
   prison camps 113

Jacobson, Jake *178, 179, 194*
Jewish Club in Cairo, Stanley Smollan and friends 24
Jewish labour camps 171
Jewish POWs 171
   discrimination and maltreatment 171
   in Stalag VIIIB 170–1
Jewish refugees 225
Jews 153
   work in coalmines 177
Jodl, Colonel-General Alfred 228
Johnson, Brigadier 36
Johnson, Peter 135–8
Joint Air Training Scheme 17

Kaffrarian Rifles 53, 66
Keeling, Squadron Leader 89
'KGF' (*Kriegsgefangenen/ prisoner-of-war*) 150
Klein, Harry 59, 126
Klim Orpheans Band entertaining POWs *190*
Klopper, Major-General 34–6, 39, 42, 44, 45, 64, 143
Koza, Nelson 59, 126
Krige, Uys 29–30, 56–7, 108–9, 143
   Totensonntag prose work 29

labour
   camps 104, 164, 181, 188–9, 215
   detachments 102
   slave 153, 171
Lamsdorf camp 199, 206, 219
   carnival acts 206
   courses 191–2
   hobbies fair in aid of Red Cross 192
   hospital camp 196
   liberation of 226
   Zulu mimicry 206
Lancashire Penny Fund 182
leaders in camps, called Men of Confidence 117, 194
League of Nations 254
lectures on variety of topics 184

Leibbrandt, Robey 18, 50
Libya 80–1, 125
   North African Italian colony 21, 23
Libyan Desert 10, 24
lice plague/epidemics 79, 82
   and flies 24, 83
   and rats 185
literature 99
Lithuania, German-occupied territory 224
Llangibby Castle, arrival in Kenya 20
London War Offfice 142, 235–6
Louw, Gunner 65
Lowe, Frederick 212
Luyt, Clive 8–9, 20, 22–3, 39, 88, 94, 97, 108, 133–4, 141, 146–7, 149, 151, 250
   adopted name Carlo 147
   Italian friend Mariano 147

MI9 101, 141, 142, 150, 181–2
   coded instruction 141, 207–8
   escape schemes 182
Maddocks, Pvte J (Jim) 107–8
Mainz, Horst 200–2, 217
malaria 107, 156
male friendship and homosexual attractions 197–8
Maloyi, Reuben 66–7
   friend Shaw 67
Mamitwa, Chief 126
marijuana seeds, sharing of 122
Marxism 21
Masamudi, Private Sprinkaan 59, 60
Maseko, Job 59–60
   Military Medal 60
Mauritania troopship 31
medical care and treatment 67, 105
   camp dentist 107
   German 180
   inoculation 164
   insufficient supplies 108, 170
   officers 108
   permanent disabilities 106
   to POWs 168
Mediterranean crossing 71–3
   called 'cruise' by David Brokensha 73
mental-health effects, psychiatric and unstable 115–16
Mersa Matruh 31, 67
   anti-aircraft protection 24–5
   dug-out 47, 69
   temporary camp 66–7
Middellandse Regiment 31, 42–3, 44, 52, 88

INDEX

Middle East Defence Committee, Cairo 142
military equipment supply 17
Military Hospital, Naples 77
Military Hospitals at Perugia 105
Military Service Bill 247
Milner, Lord Alfred 13, 14
minefields and mines 34–5
miners' strike, 1922 15
mines 14
Mixed Medical commission 131
Mombasa 21, 22
Monaremi, July 59
Montgomery 141–2
morale
　German fighting soldiers 220
　in POW camps 115
Moriji hospital camp, Piacenza 106–7
Mortlock, Harry 32, *178*, *195*
Mortlock, Jack 31, *32*, 37, 41, 47, 53, 70, 82, 83, 84, 94–5, 97–8, 129, 149, 168, *178*, 179, 195–6, 201, 202, 204–5, 220, 222–3, 227–8
　German acquaintance Annie 222
MOTHS (Memorable Order of Tin Hats) 246
Mugglestone, Dennis 37, *38*, 49, 58, 72, 82, 86, 89, 94, 117, 123–4, 149, 156–7, 168, 178, 195, 202, 203–4, 219, 221–2, 229, 255–6
music 99
　camp bands 99
　instruments 98
Mussolini, Benito (fascist *IL Duce*) 21–2, 57, 91, 134, 137, 138, 139, 140, 144, 153
coup d'état against 136
Myles, Private 56

'national games' 101
Nationalists, *see* Afrikaner Nationalists
National Party government 4, 16, 245, 248–9
　won 1948 election 249
National Socialism 216
naval and merchant marine POW camps 164
naval vessels 17
Nazi(s) 152, 228
　creation of the *Volkssturm*, civilian forces 219
　ideology 15–16, 50, 152
　indoctrination efforts 61
　intelligence 220–1

leadership 223
losing grip on Europe and Middle East 153
opposition to Nazi Party 218
propaganda 153, 221
radio broadcasts, Radio Zeesen 50
Wehrmacht and Volkssturm 223
Nazism 15
　anti-Semitic ideology 21
Neame, Lieutenant-General Sir Philip 186
newspapers at camps 186
　'Idle Ambitions' article 186
New Zealanders 169
Nicholls, Heaton 243
nicknames for commanders
　Fish-Eyes, Snapperguts 202–3, 217
　Glass-eye, Scarface, Swine 203, 221
Nixon-Eckersol, Captain 80
Nolan, Reverend Major Patrick J 62
Non-European Army Services Corps 43, 57, 241
Norrie, Sir Charles Willoughby Moke 30
Norris, George 20
North Africa 23, 57, 61, 80, 113, 127
　camps 57
　desert 99
　temporary camps 231
Northern Silesia 223–4
Norton, Sergeant 'Toys' 66
Nova Amsterdam troopship 31

officer camps (*Offizierlager* or *Oflag*) 164, 181
　fantasy games 184
Oflags and Stalags, difference between 181
Oflag 7B 213
Oflag XIIB 198
Ogilvie, Mrs AS 242
Ogilvie, Peter 90–1, 92, 132, 150, 170, 173–4, 186, 187, 212–13, 226
OKW (*Oberkommando der Wehrmacht*) 163, 210–11, 214
O'Neill, Staff Sergeant 226
Oosthuizen, Wessel 4–5, 49, 71, 94, 95, 120, 168, 209–10, 217–18, 219, 252–3
Operation Barbarossa 152
Operation Crusader, Libya 23
Oram, George 208, 209
Orange Free State 13
Ossewabrandwag 4, 16, 18, 19, 50, 250, 252
　auxiliary Stormjaers 16, 18
overcrowding 199

Palestinian POWs 91, 171
Pallotta, Colonel 99
peace
   agreement between Italy and Allies 106
   treaty 13
People's Court 220
performing arts 184
permanent camps (*Stammlagers*, or *Stalags*) 164
Permanent Force 2, 17
Pieterse, Piet 5–6
Pirow, Oswald 16, 18, 50
pneumonia 107
Poland 17
   invaded by Germany 16, 152
   POWs in vicinity of Breslau 223
   refugees 226–7
Police College 4
post-war
   government aid schemes 246
   life and trauma 245
POW Directorate 211
POW Information Bureau
   British Foreign Office 234–5
   at South Africa's High Commission 242
POW News, news sheet 110
POWS (prisoners of war) 29–30, 44
   categories allowed to work 173
   codes of morality 63
   Czechoslovakian border with Germany *189*
   Germans used as slave labour 153
   handed over to Italian control 45–7
   hospital camps 105
   liberation 230
   sexual relations 216–17
   shackling of 210–12
   waiting for liberation 70
   war labour 103–4
   white 246
prison camps 85, 126, 151, 163–4
Prisoner of War Directorate, Pretoria 211
prisoners
   black POWs remained interned 143
   white POWs released 143
Prisoners-of-War Association 110
Prisoners of War Convention 88–9
Prisoners of War Parcels Department 110–11
pro-Nazi section of population, South Africa 18
prostitutes 47

Protecting Power 81–2, 85, 93, 98, 99, 125, 126–7, 168, 169, 170, 219, 229, 234
   camp inspectorate reports 121
   inspections 167
   reports on Italian camps 86–7
Pullen, Harold 100
punishment camps 215
Purchase, Lieutenant-Colonel BP 28, 53
pwibs (prisoner of war information bureaux) 236

race 125
   and nationality separation 193
radios, hidden 221
Randall, AC 170
Rand Daily Mail, newspaper 255
Rand Light Infantry 9
recreational activities 185
Red Army 153
Red Cross 57, 82–90, 98, 131, 184, 188, 220, 239, 240, 243
   battle dress uniforms 128
   destruction of equipment 101
   food parcels 85, 91–2, 124, 127, 133, 176, 221–2
   food parcels in South Africa 87–8
   inspectors 117, 167, 194, 199
   report on basic rations in Italy 87
Rees-Bevan, Private Vivian 74, 75–6, 78
relationships
   at camps 193–206
   with civilian women 214
Relatives Association 239–40
repatriated POW, interrogation report on 169
repatriation 106–7, 130
   agreements 131
   German matters 180
   medical as option to freedom 130–1
Repatriation agreements between Italy and Allies 130
Richards, Colonel 36–7
Ripley News, propaganda news sheet 110
Ritchie, Lieutenant-General Neil M 31, 34–5
Robinson, Newman 27–8, 50–1, 54–5, 74–9, 81, 91, 109, 122, 131–2, 133
Rome, bombing raid on 139, 140
Rommel, General Erwin 23, 43, 45, 47, 61, 69
   attack on Tobruk 33–5, 42
   forces defeated by Allies at El

INDEX

Alamein 153
known as the Desert Fox 47
Roosevelt 138
Rosalina Pilo trip, Benghazi to
    Tripoli 72–3, 82–3
    hold with POWs 72
Rose-Innes, Harry *158*, 158–9
    Taffy, friend and fellow POW 159
Rosmarin, Ike 38, 44–5, 49, 53, 64, 72, 123, 142, 155–6, 170, 171, 173, 185–6, 187–8, 191–2, 203, 207, 208, 209, 212–13, 226, 247
    escape committee at Stalag 344, Lamsdorf 192–3
    Jewish 156
Rossouw, Regimental Sergeant Major 169–70
Royal Air Force (RAF) 132, 138
    air raids 58–9
    officers 185
    pilots 189–90
Royal Army Medical Corps 244
Royal Durban Light Infantry (RDLI) 20, 40, 42
Royal Marines 80
Royal Natal Carbineers 23
Russia 122, 152
Russians 166, 224
    advance as imminent threat 224
    armies 223–4
    cannibalism in compound 166
    girl Doushka 217
    POWs 211
    prisoners 217
    soldiers 225

1st South African Infantry Division 23
2nd Anti-Aircraft Regiment, Cape Town 7–8, 41, 208
    known as Ack Ack regiment 240
    'rousing send-off' 7, 8
2nd SA Division 31, 34, 38
2nd South African Anti-Aircraft Brigade 20
2nd Transvaal Scottish Regiment 6, 117
6th Infantry Police Brigade 37
6th South Africa Armoured Division 142
    known as 'Tobruk Avengers' 142
17th Field Ambulance 59
Samuels, RSM 124
San Sebastian torpedoed by HMS *Porpoise* submarine 74
Scheidhauer, Bernard 182

Schwikkard, Bernard 2, 22, 23–7, 46–7, 74, 76–8, 88, 96, 97, 118, 121–3, 154, 177, 189, 224, 251, 252
    and brothers 20, 27, 77
Scotland and England united 15
    Act of Union, 1707 15
    James VI as James I of England 15
'Scramble for Africa' 21
Seaward Defence Force, South Africa 43
septicaemia 106
shackling of enemy prisoners and POWs 210–12
    reprisals to 212–13
'Shirt reading' *84*
Sicily
    Allied landings in 135
    fall of 140
    invaded by Allies 127
Sidi Barrani dug-out 47
Sidi Rezegh, Battle of 24–47, 50, 61, 71, 113, 122, 151, 184
    first anniversary 239
    Native Military Corps 59
    thirst marches of POWs 50
Simonds, Lieutenant-Colonel 142–3
Singapore surrender 45
Smith, AB 161
Smollan, Stanley 9, 40, 57, 63, 94, 96, 97, 145–6, 149, 151, 239. 250
    and fellow escapees in Italy 145
Smuts, Isie 243
Smuts, Jan (JC) 7, 8, 13, 14, 15, 17–19, 245, 253–6
    assassination attempt on 50
    and Fred Geldenhuis at parade 254
    post-war peace process 243
    South African Party 10–11
    supporters 29
Snyman, Sergeant-Major 129
sociability across hierarchies 193
Soldiers' Charter 246, 247
Soldiers Fund, good news letter *257*
Sollum dug-out 47, 69
Somaliland, Italian colony 21, 22
South African Airways' fleet of German-made Junkers 16
South African 5th Brigade 30
South African Gifts and Comforts Organisation 240
South African Naval Forces 43–4
South African Police (SAP) 2, 18
    Training Depot 4

South African police band 98–9
South African POWs 123, 184–5, 202, 241
  communication problems 235
  mining experience 189
South African Prisoner-of-War
  Relatives and Friends Association
  (POWRFA) 239–40, 241–2
South African Red Cross Society 103, 231
  London Committee of 110–11
South African Republic 13
South African War 4, 11, 13, 208
Soviet POWs 166
Soviet Union
  against German POWs 152–3
  casualties 152
  forces 223
  troops 224
Spain, civil war 21
Spear, Sergeant CH 42
Special Service Battalion 2
Spencer, Corporal Jock 121
Spencer, Jack 181
sports 99, 184, 190–1, 199
  between British Commonwealth
    nations 99–100
  equipment 98, 185
Springbok, daily paper 110
Springbok Legion 245
SS (*Schutzstaffeln*) troops 155–6, 207–8,
  218, 221
Stalag IVA 200
Stalag IVB transit camp, Mühlberg 164,
  166, 168, 188, 199, 200, 215
  Empire theatre 192
  escape committee 188
  Red Cross report 200
  women led into temporary camp 215–16
  Zulu war dance 207
Stalag VIIA 198, 229
  black market trade, POWs and
    civilians 220
  and POW registration procedure 165
  racial harmony 193–4
Stalag VIIB 229–30
Stalag VIIIA 168–9
  South Africans 169
Stalag VIIIB, near Lamsdorf 1, 164, 167,
  170, 173, 185, 203, 211
  hospital complex 185
  later known as Stalag 344 173
Stalag Luft camps
  for British and American airmen 164
  digging of tunnels 182
  Escape Committee 183
  MI9 account on Stalag Luft III
    escape 182–3
Stalag 344 185–7, 226
  escape committee 188
  Red Cross reports 213
Stalag 357, near Fallingbostel 185, 258
Stalag 383 211–12
  Senior British Medical Officers 211–12
Stalag XVIIIA, Wolfsberg 168, 219
Stalin's Red Army 220
Star, The, newpaper 243
starvation and illness 171
'stay put' order 149, 150
Steyn, Regiment President 8
suicides in camps 114
sugar factory 202–3
Sunday Times, newspaper 244
Swiss diplomacy 211–12
Switzerland 81–2
Sykes, Bill 65
Syrian guards 55–6

10th South Africa Field Ambulance 27–8
Tewkesbury, George 119–20, 185, 258–9
  friend Willy 258
Theunissen, Captain 127
Thring, Corporal Jack 127, 140
Tillard, Sergeant 74
Times, The, newspaper 35
Tobruk 30–50, 71, 113, 151, 239
  black South African POWs 58
  camp 56
  fall of 43, 45, 58, 122
  Gazala garrisons 34
  Point 209, known as Commonwealth
    Keep 41
  POWs 122, 184
  prisoners 122–3, 236
  siege of 30–8
toilet facilities 64, 70, 162, 206
  'latrinograms', rumours 70
Torch Commando 249, 250
trading 203
  cigarettes for thermometers 177
  illicit 203
  in sugar 177
  tea as currency 97
trains 162–3
  poor hygiene conditions 163
transit camps 55–6, 64

INDEX

converted to permanent camps 85
German 167
known as *Durchgangslager* or *Dulag* 164
Moosburg 166
Transvaal Scottish Regiment 2
treason cases against South Africans 61
Trippi, Captain L 106
tuberculosis 126
tunnels for escapes 187, 188
  Fara Sabina 134
Tupper, LG 53, 69, 70
Turkey 80
Tuturano Times, newspaper 68, 99, 116
  'In Memoriam' section 100
typhoid 68

Umvoti Mounted Rifles 39
  HQ Company 39
Union Day celebrations 207
Union Defence Force (UDF) 1-2, 4, 10, 11, 17, 18-19, 22, 27, 33, 246
  captives 230
  capture of Italian soldiers 47
  men at Sidi Rezegh 29, 31
  POWs 50, 86, 110-11, 125
  prisoners 229
  Prisoners-of-War Welfare Committee 240
  servicemen 201
  volunteers 2, 61, 132
Union POWs 123, 151, 152, 154, 198, 213, 254
  communication to families 236
Union's Non-European Army Services forces 121
Union War Histories 245
United Party 244-5, 254-5
Urquhart, Clara 103, 170, 211
US Air Force air raids 58-9

Van Alphen Stahl, Fred 1, 7, 20, 39-40, 41, 45, 47, 49, 51, 52, 63, 89-90, 92, 96-7, 104, 107, 119, 123, 152, 156, 164, 170, 171, 173-4, 186-7, 191, 196, 198-9, 206, 212-13, 237
  mother member of Anxious Annies 240
  post-war experience 248-9
Van der Burg, Rollo 43
Van der Merwe, Dawie 65
'Van der Walt, Jan', alias of Russian captive 166
Van der Westhuizen 88
Van Heerden, Carl 88

Van Heerden, Dr 108
Van Rensburg, Dr JFJ 50
Van Ryneveld, General Sir Pierre 18
Van Zyl, Gert 36, 42
Venetonni, Attilio 145, *146*
Venetonni, Berchina 145, *146*
Verwoerd, Dr Hendrik 245
veterans, female and black 246
Vichy Government, self-ruling 152
Voortrekker Monument 2, 15-16

Waffen-SS 208
War Cabinet 211
War Office 234, 240
Warsaw uprising 215
water shortages 206
Wessels, Major 37
Western Desert campaign 210
Westernland troopship 20
white war veterans in labour market 246
Whittaker, Private 74, 76
Wilson, John 110
'wire happy' state of mind 115-16
Wolfgang, guard and friend of David Brokensha 204, 205, 223
Wolhuter, SG (Wally) 44, 49, 62, 81, 110, 118, 119-20, 128, 162-3, 164, 166, 167, 175, 188
Women's Auxiliary 251
Wood, HL 39, 70, 163
Woodley, Sergeant 43
Work Camp, Breslau 215
Work Camp, Czech Republic 209
Work Camp E22 170
Work Camp E793, near Stalag 344 219
Work Camp, near Gorlitz 214
Work Camp, near Graz 219
  work amidst unexploded bombs 219
Work Camp 1169, near Dresden 200-1, 204-5, 208, 214, 217, 220, 221
  Brokensha refereeing in game *191*
  German guard 172
  Jock the barber 200
  layout of 172
  South Africans in 173
  workers 178
Work Camp 10001, near Dresden 214
Work Camp 4008, near Breslau 195, 214
work camps 85, 164, 175, 199
  known as *Arbeitskommandos* 164
  Laussig soccer teams 191
World War I 14-15

World War II 1, 11

YMCA 98, 136, 184

Zehlendorf camp for captive Allied
    officers 207
Zollinger, Monsieur 110–12
Zonderwater training camp 20

www.ingramcontent.com/pod-product-compliance
Lightning Source LLC
Chambersburg PA
CBHW070527090426
42735CB00013B/2893